Finding the Beat

Finding the Beat

Entrainment, Rhythmic Play, and Social Meaning in Rock Music

Nathan Hesselink

BLOOMSBURY ACADEMIC
NEW YORK • LONDON • OXFORD • NEW DELHI • SYDNEY

BLOOMSBURY ACADEMIC
Bloomsbury Publishing Inc
1385 Broadway, New York, NY 10018, USA
50 Bedford Square, London, WC1B 3DP, UK
29 Earlsfort Terrace, Dublin 2, Ireland

BLOOMSBURY, BLOOMSBURY ACADEMIC and the Diana logo are trademarks of
Bloomsbury Publishing Plc

First published in the United States of America 2023
This paperback edition published 2024

Copyright © Nathan Hesselink, 2023

For legal purposes the Acknowledgments on p. x constitute an extension of
this copyright page.

Cover design: Louise Dugdale
Cover image: hurricanehank / Shutterstock

All rights reserved. No part of this publication may be reproduced or transmitted in any form or by any means, electronic or mechanical, including photocopying, recording, or any information storage or retrieval system, without prior permission in writing from the publishers.

Bloomsbury Publishing Inc does not have any control over, or responsibility for, any third-party websites referred to or in this book. All internet addresses given in this book were correct at the time of going to press. The author and publisher regret any inconvenience caused if addresses have changed or sites have ceased to exist, but can accept no responsibility for any such changes.

Library of Congress Cataloguing-in-Publication Data

ISBN: HB: 978-1-5013-9297-9
PB: 978-1-5013-9301-3
ePDF: 978-1-5013-9299-3
eBook: 978-1-5013-9298-6

Typeset by Deanta Global Publishing Services, Chennai, India

To find out more about our authors and books visit www.bloomsbury.com and sign up for our newsletters.

For my mother, Etta Marie Hesselink

CONTENTS

List of Figures viii
Acknowledgments x

1 Preamble 1

2 Ambiguity, Rhythm, and Participation in Radiohead's "Pyramid Song" 7

3 Rhythmic Play, Compositional Intent, and Communication in Rock Music 40

4 The Backbeat as Expressive Device in Rock Music 69

5 Entrainment and the Human-Technology Interface, Historical and Technological Considerations 97

6 Entrainment and the Human-Technology Interface, Sociological and Aesthetic Considerations 121

7 Radiohead, Oxford, and a Rhythmic Holy Grail 147

Appendix: Los Angeles and Vancouver Crews 151
Bibliography 154
Index 172

FIGURES

2.1 Radiohead full-length studio album releases 13
2.2 Track listings for *Amnesiac* (2001) 16
2.3 First four iterations of piano cycle 20
2.4 Metrical realizations of first iteration of piano cycle 27
2.5 "Compound meter neutral" realization of entrance of drums 29
2.6 9/8, 9/8, 6/8 realization, first phrase of cycle 30
2.7 4/4 with swung eighth notes (12/8 realization), first phrase of cycle 32
2.8 4/4 realization, first phrase of cycle (8 beats over 2 bars) 33
2.9 4/4 realization, one complete cycle (8 beats over 2 bars) 36
3.1 Police full-length studio releases 44
3.2 "Bring On the Night" opening four bars (first phrase) 49
3.3 Entrance of bass drum (third phrase) with same metrical realization 49
3.4 "Edge of Seventeen," bars 5–8 50
3.5 Entrance of arpeggiated guitar, bass, and vocal 51
3.6 Correct metrical realization of opening four bars 52
3.7 "Sixteen Note One Drop" as played in "Tribulation" 52
3.8 Radiohead full-length studio releases 55
3.9 Fan-created YouTube content related to Radiohead's "Videotape" 57
3.10 Score version, (a) one cycle of piano part, core cell; (b) entrance of electric bass, one cycle 58
3.11 Score version, entrance of drum set, one cycle (1:20-) 59
3.12 Score version, (a) addition of hi-hat (3:05-); (b) addition of snare (3:37-) 60
3.13 Radiohead version, entrance of drum set, one cycle (1:20-) 64
3.14 Radiohead version, (a) addition of hi-hat (3:05-); (b) addition of snare (3:37-) 65
4.1 Introduction to "Darkest Light," implied rhythmic organization 79
4.2 Introduction to "Darkest Light" (after entrance of drum set), actual rhythmic organization 79
4.3 Return of verse 1, "Just What I Needed," first four bars (2:05-) 81
4.4 Return of verse 1, "Just What I Needed," second four bars (2:12-) 81

4.5	"Sunshine of Your Love" opening guitar riff and basic drum part	83
4.6	Introduction to "Northshore," potential rhythmic organization	85
4.7	"Northshore," entrance of drums	86
4.8	Pre-chorus to "Cult of Personality"	88
4.9	"Kashmir" opening	89
4.10	One possible grouping of opening bass riff, "Dazed and Confused"	90
4.11	Beginning of verse 2, "Dazed and Confused"	91
4.12	Beginning of verse 3, "Dazed and Confused"	91
4.13	Opening four bars of "Broken Toy"	94
4.14	"Three of a Perfect Pair," 7/4 (7/8)	95
4.15	First full bar of "St. Augustine in Hell," 7/4 realization	95
4.16	First two full bars of "St. Augustine in Hell," 7/8 realization	96
5.1	Streamers (left and middle) and punch (right) applied to *Mabel and Fatty*	101
5.2	Disney patent Figure 4	103
5.3	Disney patent Figures 5–7	104
5.4	Disney patent Figure 8	105
5.5	UREI 964 Digital Metronome	107
5.6	Russian Dragon	108
5.7	"Optical Metronome" (del Castillo 1976), left; and "Digital Pulsing Visual Metronome" (Duke 2008), right	113
5.8	"Visual Music Conducting Device"	114
5.9	Soundbrenner Pulse on guitarist	117
5.10	A tempo map using Logic Pro	119
6.1	LA's great independent recording studios of the 1950s	125
6.2	Albums released by Little Mountain Sound Studios from 1980 to 1995	127
6.3	Los Angeles and Vancouver crews	127

ACKNOWLEDGMENTS

This book signals a return journey to much of the music and artists that I grew up with and which enriched my youth in so many ways. It also reflects a kind of second life for me as an academic, having spent the first half of my career immersed in the world of South Korean drumming and dance. In the process, I received help from friends and scholars old and new, embarked on journeys to familiar and novel locations, and was introduced to scholarship and ways of analyzing, synthesizing, and sharing insights gleaned from such encounters. As with all acknowledgments, I will fall short in properly giving credit to everyone who contributed along the way; and as with my previous publications, I trust that my love of, dedication to, and overall enthusiasm for the music and ideas will compensate for glaring shortcomings.

My home institution, the University of British Columbia (UBC), graciously granted me a sabbatical to pursue interests that would eventually lead to the writing of this book. I spent a magical year in Oxford, England, as a guest of St John's College, where I met and interacted with a remarkable group of individuals, both at college and in the community. Gratitude is offered to Martin Stokes, Linda McDowell, Dai Griffiths, Carolyne Larrington, Noel Lobley, Nomi Dave, and Michael Wright. I also had the privilege of having coffee and conversation with John Lubbock (Orchestra of St John's), as well as engaging with unwitting participants Phil Selway and Thom Yorke of Radiohead.

After my return from England, I benefited from a network of music theorists who helped guide me with my new-found knowledge, both directly and from afar: Brad Osborn, Roger Mathew Grant, Yonatan Malin, Mark Abel, Mark Butler, Mark Spicer, John Covach, Kevin Holm-Hudson, Nicole Biamonte, and my colleagues at UBC, John Roeder and Ève Poudrier. Graduate seminars introduced me to a multitude of gifted students from various music fields, who all stretched me in challenging and fascinating ways; for their shared enthusiasm of and expertise in pop music, I highlight Deirdre Morgan, Leslie Tilley, Robin Attas, Juan Diego Diaz, Iljung Kim, Jonathan Adams, Kirk King, Curtis Andrews, Eshantha Peiris, Gina Choi, Michael Ducharme, Kelsey Lussier, Blaire Ziegenhagel, Jason Winikoff, and Aram Bajakian. This expansion of consciousness took place against a nurturing background of fellow faculty members, of whom I would also like to thank: David Metzer, Patrick Raftery, Kofi Gbolonyo, Gloria Wong, Keith Hamel, Robert "Dr. Bob" Pritchard, and Sharman King. And I express my long-standing indebtedness to Elizabeth Branch Dyson—patron saint of drumming (now of rock music)—whose focus, knowledge, and friendship helped me once again at a crucial point in a project's direction.

A second generous sabbatical allowed me to split a year between Vancouver and Los Angeles to pursue the final research for this volume. While at home I drew on the industry expertise of Spencer Carson, Mike Fraser, Rolf Hennemann, Ron "Obvious" Vermeulen, Charlie Richmond, Randy Raine-Reusch, and Gord Lord. While in LA, I was adopted by a family at UCLA of previous fellow graduate students and mentees, now all turned faculty members: Tim Taylor, Tara Browner, Farzad Amoozegar, Anna Morcom, and Katherine In-Young Lee. This solid foundation allowed me to reach out to the infinite riches of the area, represented by a group of engineers, producers, and/or drummers who shared invaluable life experiences with me: Neal Avron, Gregg Bissonette, Bob Ezrin, Denny Fongheiser, Brian Foraker, Mike Frondelli, Ross Hogarth, David Leaf, Mark Linett, Stan Lynch, Keith Olsen, Jim Scott, and Mike Shapiro. I single out with distinction Mike Flicker, active in both Vancouver and LA, the only name and phone number I had in my pocket when arriving in Hollywood, who instigated a series of introductions that flowered into this community.

This manuscript with its multifaceted and interdisciplinary leanings was not an easy sell, with many eyes and opinions influencing its long gestation. It was Leah Babb-Rosenfeld at Bloomsbury, however, who saw its value and took the risk of working with me to create a better book than that which was first presented, for which I will always be grateful. The process was ushered through by fellow staff members Amy Martin, Carah Naseem, and Elizabeth Kellingley; cover designer Lou Dugdale; and project manager Nivethitha Tamilselvan. Assistant editor Rachel Moore became a trusted and greatly appreciated co-conspirator.

Lastly, this project was completed during a trying period in my life, and it wouldn't have been possible without the support and love of dear friends Michael Tenzer and Pam Hetrick; family members John, Ann, Paul, Jud, Greg, and Katie; and my wife Serra and our son Braque. It is dedicated to my mother—musician, missionary, world traveler, art lover, intellectual—who created a safe, supportive, and loving home that allowed me to thrive to my potential.

1

Preamble

This book is about humankind's ability, propensity, and enjoyment in finding the beat in live and recorded experiences of music-making with an emphasis on rock. It is an experiment in exploring the phenomenon from various disciplinary angles, drawing inspiration from many intellectual traditions but cleaving solely to none. My fascination with this topic began more than ten years ago when I—an ethnomusicologist and percussionist—found myself initially unable to find the beat to Radiohead's "Pyramid Song." A frustrating and exciting challenge had been born.

Why the interest in such a ubiquitous yet seemingly easy and trivial pursuit? Anyone who has attended a concert, gone to a club, or watched a sporting event has witnessed and/or participated in tapping, clapping, or dancing along with a piece, song, or chant. It doesn't matter who or where you are in the world—as humans we spend a lot of time taking pleasure in matching our bodily movements with a perceived beat, regardless of geography, cultural background, social class, or historical period. So again, what's the issue?

The simple answer is found in the concept known as *entrainment*. Also called "attunement" (London 2012: 12) and "beat perception and synchronization" (or, simply, "BPS"; Patel 2006: 100), entrainment, as understood within the cognitive neuroscience community, refers to the human capacity to perceive a beat and to synchronize to it.[1] What used to be considered a very simple activity—sensing where the beat is and tapping along with it—is now known to be a highly complex mental and physical

---

[1] This is in contrast to the broader application of entrainment theory, extended to two or more interacting and synchronizing human agents (live performance) as well as non-musical and nonhuman contexts (Clayton 2013: 17–39). See also Patel (2006) for its examination of similar kinds of interactions with several species of frogs and insects.

activity that might only be shared among a few nonhuman animals with the capacity for complex vocal learning (Patel et al. 2009; Cook et al. 2013).[2]

Research has demonstrated how there is much more to the ability to entrain than just coordinating with an external pulse. According to Aniruddh Patel, one of the leading researchers on music and the brain, there are six key features of human beat perception and synchronization (after Patel 2015: 81–4):

(1) It is predictive: humans anticipate the onset of a tone or stroke, predicting when the next event will happen; they do not react to it like other nonhuman animals capable of interacting with a pulse

(2) It is highly tempo flexible: we can accurately synchronize with a beat over a broad range of speeds

(3) It is modality biased: we tend to get a stronger sense of the beat, including our ability to synchronize with it, from rhythms we hear versus rhythms we see

(4) It is constructive: "the beat is a mental periodicity, constructed in the brain in response to a rhythmic pattern" (p. 83); the way Patel illustrates this point is that in syncopated patterns we can still feel a beat, even if nothing sounds on the beat[3]

(5) It is hierarchical: we perceive beats in a sequence as differing in strength, which contributes to our perception or formation of meter[4]

(6) It strongly engages the body's motor system: as Patel notes, "This happens in the absence of any overt movement or any intention to move" (p. 84)[5]

These key observations already explain so much about why music, especially rhythmically engaging music, moves us in the ways that it does. It's not just that we are able to perceive a beat and/or abstract out a meter or periodicity—studies have shown how we actively search out a beat and look

---

[2]Numerous traits are shared in particular between humans and parrots, who also have the ability to entrain; an even greater cross-species resonance is entertained in Ted Chiang's provocative short story "The Great Silence" (2019).
[3]Roughly analogous concepts include David Huron's schema (2006: 203–18) and Peter Vuust et al.'s predictive coding: "The predictive coding model entails that the brain constantly tries to extract structural regularities from the surroundings" (2009: 81). See also London (2012: 9–24) and Tal et al. (2017).
[4]Writings on non-isochronous pulse and subtactus levels by Kvifte (2007) and Polak et al. (2016) do not negate these basic findings on entrainment research, while they may call certain aspects of Western metric theory into question. Johansson (2017), however, would seem to be describing musical phenomena that fall outside of what we commonly understand as contributing to beat perception and synchronization, though he does speak about entrainment (and, crucially, his core research is only based on one musician's performance).
[5]Patel cites here as a key study Grahn and Rowe (2009).

for patterns even when they don't exist in the auditory stimuli (Temperley 2001: 25; Povel 1981). As listeners we feel a beat or groove more strongly when we can tap to it (Temperley 2018: 146); and as we know, such activity also confers considerable pleasure (Trost et al. 2014).

This capacity and predilection, however, also strongly suggests a long history of what Gary Tomlinson has referred to as biocultural coevolution, such that the development of our ability to entrain over time is believed to have directly contributed to our transition from early hominin to modern human society and the development of the modern brain.[6] The activity of entrainment engages both recent and ancient structures of the brain, spread widely across various motor networks, and it is further credited with giving early modern human populations distinct advantages in terms of prediction, behavioral flexibility, and the ability to work and play together as communities, to great economic and cultural success (Merker et al. 2008; Tomlinson 2015: 77; Sacks 2007: 268).

Entrainment makes rhythmic play possible in all of its structural and social dimensions. Recent and highly influential research on expectation relies heavily, if not primarily, on this ability, as music is the temporal art par excellence (Meyer 1956; Huron 2006; Trainor and Zatorre 2016). Composers and performers who tap into this cognitive need and desire for finding the beat and matching what one hears with pre-formed mental templates through rhythmic-metric play do so to great advantage and pleasure. From a rock music perspective, as I will demonstrate in the chapters that follow, it is often those songs that play with our rhythmic expectations, thwarting simple metrical understandings and/or conventional formal constructions, that grip listeners in deep and compelling ways. It's also what makes highly complex structural traditions such as Indian traditional percussion music, for those willing to spend the time, so intellectually and emotionally satisfying.

Socially, entrainment provides a powerful mechanism by which we can coordinate our activities with others, creating shared frameworks for meaning. In its mundane or mercenary capacities it helps human societies to hunt and march to war; in its more sublime moments, to create a safe arena for the exploration and confirmation of group sentiment and communal consciousness through shared musical performance. When combined with the propensity to physically move, entrainment also begins to explain why dance and music are almost always found together throughout the globe, and why many traditions don't have separate words for these interrelated realms. In the history of North American and British popular music, nearly every major new genre was, in fact, linked to a social dance (big-band jazz, country, blues, R&B, rock 'n' roll, funk, disco, hip-hop, and EDM).

---

[6]Tomlinson (2015: 13, 77, 81), Levitin (2009: 50), Brown et al. (2000: 12), Geissman (2000: 119).

A study of entrainment could be applied to almost any world music tradition; in this book, it happens to be mainstream "Western" (i.e., North American and British)[7] rock music. The decision was an easy one to make, as such music has been a part of my musical DNA since I was a child. As I began to expand outward from that initial song that challenged my capabilities at time-keeping, reflecting on other works that similarly captured my imagination when trying to find a beat, a rich world of processes and themes opened up in front of me (each of which would eventually become a chapter):

(1) Rhythmic ambiguity: when we can't determine where the beat is, or if more than one option presents itself
(2) Rhythmic deception: when we clap or tap our foot in the "wrong" place
(3) Expressivity in the time-keeping role of the backbeat: what happens to listeners when a snare backbeat lands in an unexpected place
(4) The technological mediation of time and the beat: what happens when machines become part of the process of producing and finding the beat

Entrainment, of course, doesn't say enough about all of these issues. Music theory helps standardize the language for describing the structural elements of the repertoire when establishing different kinds of rhythmic play; it also provides connections between psychology, expectation, and cognitive neuroscience. Curiosity in understanding what these phenomena mean socially and aesthetically to composers, producers, performers, and listeners leads to the field of popular music studies, especially the musicology of popular music, and its interest in history and social context. And as an ethnomusicologist, also deeply concerned with social and aesthetic meaning, this pursuit means engaging in fieldwork and maintaining an interculturally comparative perspective whenever possible.

⌘

The analysis proper in this book begins with Chapter 2, an examination of how the confluence of ambiguity and rhythm in a rock song creates a powerful force for audience participation. The central focus is Radiohead's "Pyramid Song" (2001), the work that challenged my abilities to find a beat and kicked off this whole study. I document in detail the myriad ways

---

[7]"Western" has always been a problematic designation; in the context of this book, I am simply referring to rock music primarily conceived and produced in North America and the UK, to distinguish such activity from rock music composed and performed in South America, East and Southeast Asia, sub-Saharan Africa, etc.

listening audiences have made sense of its meter and how this knowledge has informed their interpretations of compositional intent. This chapter relies primarily on internet fieldwork, providing one way forward for those interested in applying different methods to popular music studies. I conclude with further thoughts on the roles and possibilities of ambiguity and the directions it points toward mass participation and collaborative problem-solving in aesthetics and music theory. Radiohead holds a place of privilege in this volume because of this song's importance to the entire project, as well as my personal admiration of the band and its output, and they will appear again in the second half of Chapter 3 and the closing outro.

Chapter 3 looks at the use of rhythmic play in the form of deception in the compositional strategies of rock musicians, with case studies on the Police's "Bring On the Night" (1979) and Radiohead's "Videotape" (2007). Such formal play is seen as both embodying an attitude on the part of the performer-composer in which music as pure structure tests one's skill and imagination in sonic reality, and as an attempt at a special form of communication with his/her/their audience. In this latter capacity, the musical work becomes an unspoken or hidden challenge to the listener as a kind of in-group or insider knowledge. Listening thus becomes a window into the creative act, bands and their audiences forming an extended community based on trust, respect, and a sense of shared ownership.

In Chapter 4, I challenge conventional wisdom on the backbeat, one of the most common and distinctive rhythmic features of post-1950s popular music. Rather than relegating the backbeat to a purely time-keeping role, I offer four categories in which the backbeat is used as an expressive device: (1) to achieve clarification and resolution (the Lafayette Afro Rock Band's "Darkest Light," 1975); (2) to create a sense of play, fun, and/or deviance (the Cars' "Just What I Needed," 1978); (3) to create a sense of ambiguity and uncertainty (Tegan and Sara's "Northshore," 2009; Living Colour's "Cult of Personality," 1988); and (4) to simultaneously provide clarification and ambiguity (Led Zeppelin's "Dazed and Confused," 1969). Both as a rhythmic place keeper and as an expressive device, the backbeat is a central element in audiences' understanding of popular music, particularly groove- and/or dance-based genres. This chapter provides further evidence of the connections made by music theorists and cognitive scientists between metrical prediction, entrainment, embodiment, listener participation, and meaning.

The last of the four themes of this book, the technological mediation of time and the beat, is distributed across the next two chapters. In most world music traditions a metronome—essentially an externalized, mechanized entraining agent—was never developed, nor was metronomic playing adopted as a norm. And while the European classical music tradition seldom succumbed to performing to its beat, in the rock music world the device found its way into recordings and live concerts through the back door in the form of click tracks, sequencers, and electronic drum machines. Chapter 5 provides the historical and technological contexts for this transformation, drawing primarily on newspapers, print interviews, and patents as source material.

Chapter 6 then expands on this discussion, raising various sociological and aesthetic considerations of playing to a click track as understood through interviews—both live and as documented in trade magazines—with drummers, recording engineers, and producers. Drawing on recent cognitive studies, I attempt to reveal the technological and cultural motivations and meanings of "playing in time" and "playing with the beat" and what the impact of externalized entraining agents has been on our collective engagement with music as temporal art.

The closing chapter, envisioned as an intimate and personal outro, returns to the band and song that inspired this entire project.

Readers in the first instance should not look to this book for a genre study. I am not making claims about all rock bands and artists, though I have included analytical samples from alternative rock, reggae-rock, progressive rock, new wave, post-punk, classic rock, hard rock, and pop-rock. Black, female, and queer artists are also a part of this collection, but there is certainly much more room for diversity of identities and perspectives.[8] While this volume should, nevertheless, sit comfortably on a bookshelf dedicated to rock music studies, representatives of various disciplinary traditions will want more. Musicologists studying rock will desire greater attention paid to history and critical theory and a more comprehensive engagement with genre. Music theorists will appreciate more disciplined and focused analytical rigor, as well as expanded discussions on meter. Cognitive neuroscientists will have further questions about evolutionary roots and connections, in addition to wanting to see a more lab-based, scientific approach. And ethnomusicologists will take issue with the relative lack of anthropological theory, as well as the applicability of such claims in non-North American/British contexts. These are, of course, broad (and slightly unfair) generalizations, yet it is my desire that audiences of this text will allow such sacrifices or shortcomings to serve the greater good of having access to other ways of viewing and understanding processes and themes of considerable interest and significance to (rock) musical scholarship.

What I offer in this book are windows onto worlds of creative, aesthetic, and participatory pleasure and wonder afforded by our collective ability to find the beat. It is nothing less than a celebration of human music-making and a shared joy in experiencing time together.

---

[8]I also recognize here the bias of mainstream North American and British listening audiences toward songs in the English language.

2

Ambiguity, Rhythm, and Participation in Radiohead's "Pyramid Song"

Is communication something made clear?
What is communication?
Music, what does it communicate?
Is what's clear to me clear to you?

(CAGE 1973: 41)

Ambiguity begets participation.

(LEVITIN 2009: 26)

I first heard Radiohead perform live on August 19, 2008, at UBC's Thunderbird Arena. I hadn't purchased a ticket; unfamiliar with their music at the time (minus the ubiquitous "Creep" due to heavy radio play) but encouraged to attend by numerous friends, students, and professional colleagues, I wandered out into the rain from my university apartment only three blocks away and stood, umbrella in hand, for the full duration of the show just outside of the northern wing of the arena. I was in good company—a large group of students, families with children, and tourists had similarly amassed for the free musical strains—and in spite of the bad weather and bass-heavy sound making its way over the stands, I was intrigued enough to purchase their entire oeuvre on CD and begin to work through their songs, one at a time.[1]

I made the decision early on to tackle their albums in chronological order, listening to each one a minimum of three times and at different times of the day, without any reference to guides or record reviews, before moving on to the next. And so it took me a while to make it to their fifth full-length studio release, *Amnesiac* (2001). I had already noticed up to that point that Radiohead was fond of metrical shifts and other interesting rhythmic constructions, but when I came to the second track on the CD, titled "Pyramid Song," I was completely baffled as to not only what the song's underlying meter could be but also where even to tap my foot. With an opening that featured just a series of sustained piano chords with no drum beat or discernable regular pulse, it would take repeated listenings to begin to come up with my own rhythmic understanding.

Feeling energized by such activity, and full of curiosity as to how others might interpret the meter, I went to the web to search out potential fellow lovers of rhythmic ambiguity, albeit with only modest expectations for what I would find. What I stumbled upon was simply astonishing: a large and rich body of material directly addressing rhythm in "Pyramid Song" that spanned dozens of websites and hundreds of individual entries over roughly a five-year period. As an ethnomusicologist and reader of the cultural studies and sociology literature, it didn't surprise me to find a fan base that was actively engaged in listening and constructing musical-social meaning—including online criticism and the sharing of playlists, photographs, and videos—rather than a body of passive consumers (Crafts et al. 1993; DeNora 2000; Hubbs 2008; Kot 2009). What I wasn't quite prepared for, however, was the role that creative listening with attention paid specifically to metrical complexity played in the formation of such meaning, even among listeners with little formal music training.

The central task of this chapter will be to demonstrate how the confluence of ambiguity and rhythm in a rock song creates a powerful force for audience participation. As hinted at by John Cage in the first epigraph, music is predicated on ambiguity in its lack of one-to-one correspondence to language, emotions, and tangible objects of human experience. Numerous writers have shown how ambiguity—understood in its full sense of encompassing uncertainty/opacity, two or more possible meanings and/or

---

[1] Research for this chapter was completed during a sabbatical year spent at the University of Oxford. Gratitude is firstly offered to Martin Stokes, Noel Lobley, and the graduate students in ethnomusicology at St John's College for providing such a warm and stimulating environment. While in Oxford I also benefited from the institutional support of St John's Research Centre and its director, Linda McDowell, as well as numerous conversations with Dai Griffiths at Oxford Brookes University. The chapter is based on an article first published in *Music Theory Online* 19/1 (2013), https://mtosmt.org/issues/mto.13.19.1/mto.13.19.1.hesselink.html

interpretations, and the blurring of boundaries—feeds our imaginative and interpretive engagement (Bernstein 1976; Copland 1980: 7; Thomson 1983; Cook 1990: 14; Cross and Morley 2009: 69).[2] Rock and pop music have often played upon vagueness and/or multiple possibilities to great critical and commercial success; it is easy to recall examples of such ambiguity with regard to race and vocal timbre (Elvis, Chuck Berry), gender (Michael Jackson, Boy George, Prince, kd lang), and even species (David Bowie/Ziggy Stardust, Lady Gaga/various human-alien hybrids). In all cases, such a lack of concrete references—visual, lyrical, musical—allows a fertile space for active listeners to personalize the experience in ways that are deeply and complexly emotional, intellectual, and spiritual.[3]

Rhythm, as has been amply documented across numerous disciplinary fields, is a fundamental aspect of music and its appreciation.[4] Meter, in particular, plays an essential role in our ongoing and real-time perceptual organization of music, with research demonstrating how the average listener attempts to impose a meter on whatever he/she/they hears (Povel and Essens 1985; Temperley 2001: 24, 205–6). Knowledge of this foundational structure—including what the beat[5] of a song is and how to predict its recurrence—is a key ingredient in creating (positive) musical emotions, with our human concern or preoccupation with seeking out a regular pulse in musical sound most likely based on an evolutionary adaptation (Levitin 2006: 168–9, 171–80; Patel 2006; Sacks 2007: 240). In the context of the typical rock song, it is the beginning or intro that creates that pregnant moment when listeners attempt to engage in the groove, to be rewarded by the "promise of entrainment" (London n.d. (a): 10). Through an understood meter, glimpses of forthcoming timbres, textures, chord progressions, and melodic fragments unfold, with the more "successful" (i.e., innovative or creative) intros "conceal[ing] enough to stimulate the appetite without blunting it" (Hennion 1983: 165). As this chapter will show, in the case of

---

[2]For an overview and synthesis of the ways ambiguity have been discussed in the music theory literature, see Agawu (1994) and Stein (2004). Other realms of ambiguity that combine with music in the creation of the commodified pop/rock CD (a product that relies on liner notes, packaging, and advertising) include photography, especially of men and women (Sontag 2001), stage lighting (Scoates 2011: 34–5), language (Pinker 2008: 175–85), and symbolic imagery (Jung 1997: 203–84).
[3]David Huron in a work on anticipation makes it clear that such engagement requires the listener "to be *challenged*, not simply *pampered*" (2006: ix; emphasis in original); in a similar vein, a large part of the Beatles' success has been credited to the "vagueness" of their lyrics (MacDonald 2005: xii).
[4]These perspectives include human evolution (Brown et al. 2000: 12), Western rock music analysis (Moore 2001: 37), cross-cultural or "world music" studies (Tenzer 2006: 22–5), early childhood development (Mazokopaki and Kugiumutzakis 2009: 189), and human biology (Osborne 2009).
[5]Throughout this book I understand the beat as "a perceived periodic pulse that listeners use to guide their movements and performers use to coordinate their actions" (Patel 2015: 80).

"Pyramid Song" where the meter itself is withheld, many listeners went the extra mile to search it out, adding additional layers of meaning and personal investment.

Rhythmic ambiguity draws its power from connections between emotions and expectations buried deep in human evolutionary history. As David Huron observes:

> Emotions are motivational amplifiers. Emotions encourage organisms to pursue behaviors that are normally adaptive, and to avoid behaviors that are normally maladaptive. In this regard, the emotions evoked by expectation do not differ in function from other emotions. As we will see, the emotions accompanying expectations are intended to reinforce accurate prediction, promote appropriate event-readiness, and increase the likelihood of future positive outcomes. We will discover that music-making taps into these primordial functions to produce a wealth of compelling emotional experiences. (2006: 4)

Huron goes on to note that our capacity and desire to predict confers very specific biological advantages, including our preparedness for advantageous opportunities and the avoidance of potentially dangerous situations; accurate expectations also optimize our expenditure of energy and help focus our attention in economical ways (2006: 3, 176). We see such factors at play in the writings of music theorists who have long noted that musically ambiguous or even suspenseful events are often pleasant for a listener, depending on how long it takes for clarification or resolution to occur (e.g., Meyer 1956: 26–8). Similarly, Daniel Levitin has made the analogy between such resolutions and joke-telling, since in both cases the listener enjoys being led (temporarily) astray and realizing that there is more than one way to proceed through a piece/passage/story (2009: 110).

The analysis and insights in this chapter complement and develop ideas from Mark Butler's *Unlocking the Groove* (2006), particularly in his focus on metrical ambiguity, audience participation, and the specific role that underdetermination (metrical vagueness)—the form of ambiguity featured in "Pyramid Song"—plays in fostering interpretive multiplicity.[6] Butler

---

[6]Two passages from Butler's work that clearly illustrate this viewpoint are as follows: (1) "Much of the significance of ambiguous structuring in electronic dance music, however, lies in its potential for drawing the listener in. Rather than demanding a particular way of hearing for the listener, passages such as the one heard in example 3.2 encourage each of us to seek out our own preferred interpretation—to actively participate in the construal of our musical experience" (2006: 127); and (2) "[M]etrically ambiguous sections encourage the listener to *construe the meter actively* rather than absorb metrical information passively" (2006: 137; emphasis in original). While not directly acknowledged in this work, Butler's theory is bolstered by Justin London's idea of "meter as a kind of attentional behavior" (2012: 9–24). The idea of

engaged in ethnographic fieldwork, an approach he openly credits to his studies in ethnomusicology (2006: 26–9); this chapter similarly draws upon such a strategy, as well as fan reception studies, and its application to music theory and analysis. My research diverges from Butler's, however, in the following ways: (1) the responses of my studied subjects are drawn almost exclusively from the internet; (2) these responses form the central text in my analysis, whereas in Butler's work such remarks serve more as occasional commentary; and (3) my focus is on active *listeners*, who may or may not be dancing as they experience the music. Our research parameters nevertheless encompass the same domains, as stated in the opening of Butler's second chapter: "I will be concerned with rhythm and meter in a broad sense: with the ways that those who listen to the music have described and categorized its rhythmic and metrical attributes, and with music-theoretical concepts that can clarify these phenomena as they occur in this repertory" (2006: 77).

Ethnographic research focused on internet communities has particular value for the expansion of existing music-theoretical and cognitive science models. As the responses in my sample will clearly illustrate, audiences are no longer homogenous—if they ever were—due to the eclectic nature of modern listening, continued travel and immigration, and exposure to and knowledge of non-Western musical genres and rhythmic constructions. Categories such as "Western listener" or "youth audience" are thus problematic on a number of fronts, calling into question many assumptions and protocols in (Western) analyses of expectation and entrainment. Internet research engages audiences on their own terms—where they provide their own analytical-interpretive language, instead of having to choose from pre-established categories (a norm in academic research questionnaires)—and in their natural places of experiencing the music (often within the home from their computer, stereo, or mp3 player, rather than in a university lab). Re-presenting these views in their entirety, preserving the "grain" of the individual voice, reflects as well a long-held ethical imperative within ethnomusicology and anthropology not to speak for others.[7]

As Butler also notes, the use and integration of field research can serve as an alternative to music theory's tendency to emphasize individual analytical engagements (2006: 27). Including audiences' views from dedicated websites thus signals the move away from typical author/lone-analyst-centered music analysis toward a more interactive and collaborative research model. The

---

meter as embodied experience has also been explored in connection with other forms of dance/popular music (Attas 2011; this research is openly indebted to Hasty 1997).
[7]My internet research methodology most closely resembles what Abigail Wood has called "e-fieldwork," by which she means "Internet activity primarily based around human interaction" (2008: 172). Other overlapping but not always completely analogous terms include "virtual ethnography" (Hine 2000), "digital ethnography" (Underberg and Zorn 2013), and "netnography" (Kozinets 2015). I thank Gina Choi for pointing me to these authors' writings.

potential benefits of such dialogic encounters are at least twofold: (1) concrete examples of audience responses expose the richness and complexity of fans' listening experiences; and (2) broader theoretical perspectives or possibilities are allowed and encouraged through a decentralized approach to analysis and interpretation. In the context of the present research, a music-theoretical sophistication or savvy on the part of audiences emerges that has as yet gone unacknowledged in the literature on fan cultures and the media,[8] at the same time calling out for the tools of music theory to standardize and thus compare these views.

I begin by providing a general context for understanding the place of "Pyramid Song" within the broader Radiohead repertoire—historically, textually, visually, and musically. The main body of the chapter then outlines in some detail the myriad ways listening audiences have made sense of its meter—or lack thereof—in the absence of reliable published scores and expressed intent by the band.[9] The primary goal is to document the activities of a community that coalesced around a riddle of metrical ambiguity; I will also draw attention to the fans' expressions of their interpretation of meter as a key to unlocking semantic content, as well as the sources of authority on which they drew. I conclude with thoughts about additional research on musical ambiguity and further possibilities for mass participation and collaborative problem-solving in music theory and aesthetics.

Radiohead/*Amnesiac* Background

Radiohead is Thom Yorke (lead vocals, guitars, and piano), Ed O'Brien (guitars, backing vocals), Phil Selway (drums/percussion), and brothers Jonny Greenwood (guitars, keyboards) and Colin Greenwood (bass). Formed in Abingdon, Oxfordshire, in 1985, the band has remarkably kept the same personnel over its roughly thirty-five years of existence, though members' roles have changed over the decades, as has their arsenal of musical instruments, including electronics. As of 2022, Radiohead has released nine full-length studio albums, six under contract with Parlophone/EMI and the last three independently via the tbd and XL record labels (see Figure 2.1).[10] Generally classified as "alternative rock" (a designation now

---

[8]For representative examples of this work, see Lewis (1992, 1994), Hills (2002), and Pickering (2010).
[9]With degree of accuracy dependent on the artist, publisher, and transcriber, Allan Moore has noted (at least in the past) that published scores are "notoriously inaccurate as a coded version of the sounds heard" (2001: 61). In the case of the "official" notation of "Pyramid Song" sanctioned by Radiohead's record label, the work was carried out by an editorial team, not by members of the group.
[10]Radiohead also released *I Might Be Wrong: Live Recordings* (2001), a collection of live tracks recorded during a European and North American tour taken primarily from *Kid A* and

1. *Pablo Honey* (Parlophone/EMI) 1993. Produced and engineered by Sean Slade, Paul Q. Kolderie, and Chris Hufford; art by Lisa Bunny Jones, Icon, and Tom Sheehan.

2. *The Bends* (Parlophone/EMI) 1995. Produced by John Leckie, engineered by John Leckie, Nigel Godrich, Chris Brown, and Jim Warren; art by Stanley Donwood and The White Chocolate Farm.

3. *OK Computer* (Parlophone/EMI) 1997. Produced and engineered by Nigel Godrich with Radiohead; art by Stanley Donwood and The White Chocolate Farm.*

4. *Kid A* (Parlophone/EMI) 2000. Produced and engineered by Nigel Godrich with Radiohead; art by Stanley [Donwood] and Tchock.

5. *Amnesiac* (Parlophone/EMI) 2001. Produced and engineered by Nigel Godrich with Radiohead; art by Stanley Donwood and Tchocky.

6. *Hail to the Thief* (Parlophone/EMI) 2003. Produced by Nigel Godrich, engineered by Darrell Thorp; art by Stanley Donwood.

***

7. *In Rainbows* (tbd records) 2007. Produced by Nigel Godrich, engineered by Nigel Godrich, Richard Woodcraft, Hugo Nicolson, and Dan Grech-Marguerat; art by Stanley Donwood and Dr Tchock.

8. *The King of Limbs* (tbd records) 2011. Produced and engineered by Nigel Godrich; art by Zachariah Wildwood [Yorke] and Donald Twain [Donwood].

9. *A Moon Shaped Pool* (XL recordings) 2016. Produced by and mixed by Nigel Godrich, engineered by Nigel Godrich and Maxime Legull; art by Stanley Donwood and Dr Tchock.

*A reissue of *OK Computer* was released June 2017 to celebrate the twentieth anniversary of the original recording. Titled *OK Computer OKNOTOK 1997 2017*, it featured a second disc with B-sides and three unreleased songs.

FIGURE 2.1 *Radiohead full-length studio album releases (*** indicates end of contract with Parlophone/EMI).*

almost meaningless), they are acknowledged and admired for their eclectic influences ranging from classic and progressive rock, post-punk, classical music, jazz, Dixieland, and the avant-garde to electronic music (including techno and post-serialist studio work). Radiohead is regularly featured on fans' and critics' top choice lists, and they have won numerous prizes on both sides of the Atlantic, including three Grammys for Best Alternative Music Album.[11]

As is apparent from Figure 2.1, a number of consistencies appear across the albums when viewed as a composite whole. For many critics, fans, and even the band members themselves, the "true" Radiohead sound and approach began to emerge with their second release in 1995, *The Bends* (though see

---

Amnesiac, and a collaborative remix album of *The King of Limbs* titled *Radiohead TKOL RMX 1234567* (2011).

[11]Further biographical information is readily available on the web (various fan and Wikipedia sites) and in print sources (see, as examples, Hale 1999; Paytress 2005; Clarke 2010; and Randall 2011).

Osborn 2017: vii). Sonically it introduced the work of Nigel Godrich as a recording engineer, brought on under the producer John Leckie. Godrich's ear and work habits were such that Radiohead would ask him to be their producer on the subsequent *OK Computer* (released in 1997), a position he has held for the remainder of their recorded work (Godrich has further collaborated with Thom Yorke on his tours with Atoms for Peace and the solo project Tomorrow's Modern Boxes, as well as his spin-off band The Smile).

The Bends also introduced to the world the artistic vision of Yorke's personal friend Stanley Donwood (b. Dan Rickwood), a fellow art student from their University of Exeter days, who has been responsible for all of Radiohead's cover and liner art since (see Donwood and Tchok 2007).[12] Unacknowledged in Figure 2.1 but equally important to the visual impact and meaning of Radiohead's performances is the work of lighting and stage designer Andi Watson, who joined Radiohead around this same period and is often considered a sixth member of the band while on tour. And while it is clearly reductionist to subsume the band's entire lyrical content under a single emotional rubric, one researcher has noted the prevalence of anxiety spanning the output from *The Bends* through to *Hail to the Thief* (2003), a catchall that includes the recurring themes of broken relationships, paranoia, powerlessness, fear of technology, mistrust of government, physical and emotional brutality, suicide, death, hell, and alien abduction (Letts 2005: 85–7).[13]

The Bends also critically marks a tacit agreement between Radiohead and its serious fans that ambiguity would form a central pillar on which they would build their collective and ongoing working relationship. Intentional vagueness and/or multiplicity of meanings in the artwork, lyrics, musical references, websites, concerts, and videos created a fan culture (and significant academic base) that routinely pores over the imagery, sounds, and words looking for clues and hidden meanings: "such deliberate ambiguity has become a hallmark of Radiohead's presentation and has created a community of fans joined by their shared interpretations of the band's projects" (Letts 2005: vi; see also Forbes and Reisch 2009). The academic and popular press now routinely speak of Radiohead's reliance on ambiguity (Tate 2005a: 1–4), obscurity (Paytress 2005: 4; Clarke 2010: 65, 95–6), and the enigmatic (Fricke 2001a: 44), with "the band's reflexive esthetic effectively disrupt[ing] naïve consumption, confronting the listener with music and art that adheres to opacity versus authenticity as a guiding principle" (Tate 2005b: 115). In an interview with the music critic Alex Ross,

---

[12]Thom Yorke has also collaborated on the artwork, disguising his input under the pseudonyms The White Chocolate Farm, Tchock, Tchocky, and Dr. Tchock.
[13]A complete (unofficial) list of Radiohead lyrics can be found at: http://www.greenplastic.com/radiohead-lyrics/

Radiohead—in an uncharacteristically straightforward manner—likened their work to the solving of musical puzzles:

> What fans seem to like, even more than the content of the songs, is the sense that the band members have labored over every aspect of the product. They are skilled, first of all, at inventing the kinds of riddles that people enjoy unraveling. The records, the videos, the official website, even the T-shirts all cry out for interpretation. Why are the words spelled funny? What are all these charts and diagrams? . . . "We liked worrying over that kind of thing when we were kids, and we're still in the same mind-set a lot of the time," Selway said. "But it's a bit incidental. We're dead set on the music. That's the thread running through this whole thing. We met at school playing music together, and we still get together over music now. We like solving musical puzzles. That's what Thom gives us." (2010: 89)

It is also a culture built on respect and trust. As has now been amply documented, in late 2007 with perhaps their greatest gesture of invitation to the fans, Radiohead released *In Rainbows* digitally such that fans could choose what to pay for the download (including nothing at all), could create and donate music videos, were given access to some of the music files to create their own unique pieces, and were allowed to write their own reviews before large outlets and the press were sent the standard media packet (see Lawson 2009: 61–79 and Randall 2011: 235–40, 254–6; see further Chapter 3).

Ambiguity was a special hallmark of the pair of albums *Kid A* and *Amnesiac*, recorded during the same sessions but released eight months apart as separate projects. In both cases, the musical roles of the band members became newly obscured or obliterated, with Radiohead choosing to leave their guitar-based sound behind in favor of electronic experimentation and non-traditional lineups such that it was often impossible to match a particular sound with a specific individual (band members also switched instruments, or were absent on some tracks). Even Thom Yorke's distinctive voice was manipulated or masked by studio techniques so that the comprehension of words and, at times, entire phrases was made extremely problematic (Hainge 2005: 63). Such opacity was enhanced by Radiohead's choice not to include lyrics with *Kid A* (a first for the group), and to provide only snippets of text—some of it from sung lyrics, others not, but all out of order—on *Amnesiac*; Yorke admitted in an interview with *The Wire* that it was his desire that listeners did not focus too carefully on the words with this pair of releases (Reynolds 2001: 26). As former *Guardian* music critic Garry Mulholland acknowledged, "No one else on Radiohead's creative and commercial level makes music like *Amnesiac* and *Kid A* that felt so open to individual interpretation [and] gave so much credit to their fans for an

> 1. "Packt Like Sardines in a Crushd Tin Box"
> 2. **"Pyramid Song"**
> 3. "Pulk/Pull Revolving Doors"
> 4. "You and Whose Army?"
> 5. "I Might Be Wrong"
> 6. "Knives Out"
> 7. "Morning Bell/Amnesiac"
> 8. "Dollars and Cents"
> 9. "Hunting Bears"
> 10. "Like Spinning Plates"
> 11. "Life in a Glasshouse"

FIGURE 2.2 *Track listings for* Amnesiac *(2001).*

adventurous ear" (2006: 348; see Collins 2004 and Letts 2010b for further discussion of similarities and differences between these two albums [Collins also compares their relationship to the album that followed]).

Amnesiac was initially released in three formats: a standard CD, a deluxe box set (standard CD, CD with B-sides, DVD, and three postcards), and a special edition book (CD with bound book, winner of the 2001 Grammy Award for Best Album Package). Where *Kid A* was essentially sprung on the world without the usual fanfare of singles, videos, or concerts to promote the album (it nevertheless shot to number one on the charts, and won the Grammy for Best Alternative Music Album), with *Amnesiac* Radiohead decided to return to more conventional practices by releasing three singles with B-sides ("Pyramid Song," "I Might Be Wrong," and "Knives Out"; refer to Figure 2.2), producing a number of videos, and embarking on a world tour.[14]

Before even taking the standard CD out of the case, audiences are confronted with—and ultimately challenged by, if so choosing—the packaging of *Amnesiac*. On the cover of the booklet is the picture of an orange/red-colored book with a damaged spine; the only design is a cartoon figure with its hands over its eyes, crying, superimposed on what appear to be star charts.[15] Once the booklet is opened, the viewer is presented with twenty-six separate artistic works that include drawings, sketches, cartoons, photographs, computer-generated art, x-rays, and hand-written and typed excerpts of texts, with no apparent connection or identification provided. The cartoon character from the cover does reappear on some

---

[14]*Kid A* and *Amnesiac* were reunited twenty years later (2021) as a single project, *Kid A Mnesia*. In addition to including a third disc with B-sides and unreleased material (*Kid Amnesiae*), the re-release was further celebrated by a collection of Stanley Donwood's art, new music videos, and an interactive art exhibit playable on the Epic Games platform.

[15]Like many others, I have attempted to identify these charts but have found no constellations that match any seen from earth.

of the pages (one only discovers that this is a "weeping Minotaur" if one goes to Radiohead websites or reads print interviews),[16] but overall its presence seems only loosely related as a kind of general commentary on a collective ethos of sadness, confusion, destruction, and despair reflected in images of gravestones, skeletal faces, fires, otherworldly figures, and nuclear explosions.

Such mysteries are compounded for the fan who also buys the box set and special edition book. Apparently, some of the artwork matches specific songs (the postcards in the box set make connections to "Pyramid Song" and "Knives Out"), and the standard CD booklet is missing six of the special edition book's prints, raising the obvious question, Why?[17] And then there are those text excerpts, requiring the enthusiast with additional energy to first seek out the lyrics on an unofficial website, then try to match them against what is found.[18]

While a later analyst argued against thinking of *Amnesiac* in terms of a concept album, because of "material that requires effort on the part of the listener to make sense of, yet offering little to no plot, characters, or dramatic action to clarify the concept" (Letts 2005: 167), both Yorke and artist Donwood offered enticing, if not characteristically ambiguous, commentary on their project:

> *Amnesiac* is about seeing really awful things that you try to forget and can't quite. Whereas *Kid A* is deliberately trying to keep everything at a safe distance. (Yorke in Watson 2001: 46; see also Letts 2010a)

> *Kid A* was kind of like an electric shock. *Amnesiac* is more about being in the woods (laughs), in the countryside. I think the artwork is the best way of explaining it. The artwork to *Kid A* was all in the distance. The

---

[16] The context for the genesis and use of the "weeping Minotaur," as well as its accompanying cartoon character the "toothy Bear" and various interpretations as to their meaning, is found in Hainge (2005: 78–84), Leblanc (2005: 93–6), and Donwood and Tchok (2007) (second essay).

[17] For the truly curious reader, I have correlated the artwork of the special edition book and the standard CD as follows. The first number in each pair is the special edition book pagination, followed by the standard CD booklet page number (an empty space represents a "missing" page in the booklet): 1/1, 2/2, 3/3, 4/4, 5/5, 6/6, 7/7, 8/8, 9/9, 10/10, 11/11 (both pages modified so that subtle differences exist), 12/12 (both pages modified with subtle differences), 13/, 14/13 (crying Minotaur added in special edition), 15/14, 16/15, 17/16, 18/17, 19/18, 20/19, 21/20, 22/21, 23/22 (booklet image altered), 24/23, 25/24, 26/25, 27/26 (instruction sheet added to booklet), 28/, 29/, 30/, 31/, 32/.

[18] Here I have also done the legwork for those who might be interested. The following pairings identify the page of the standard CD booklet and the track from which a text excerpt is provided (remembering that no titles are given anywhere in the booklet): 10/ "Morning Bell/ Amnesiac," 12/ "Packt Like Sardines in a Crushd Tin Box" and "Like Spinning Plates," 16/ "I Might Be Wrong" and "Like Spinning Plates," 18/ "Packt Like Sardines in a Crushd Tin Box," 21/ "Life in a Glasshouse," 22/ "Knives Out."

fires were all going on on the other side of the hill. With *Amnesiac*, you're actually in the forest while the fire's happening. (Yorke in Kent 2001: 63)

Something traumatic is happening in *Kid A* . . . is looking back at it, trying to piece together what has happened. (Yorke in Linder 2009)

[*Amnesiac*] has a very different identity. . . . There's a lot of violence in soft sounds and language, staring at something very frightening square in the face. . . . There's also some of the most reassuring stuff we've ever done. (Yorke in Anonymous 2001: 79–80)

With *Amnesiac* it was going in very close. Too close. So close you can only see a wall—graffitied, scratched, clawed at—in front of you. This is the home of the Minotaur. . . . They were sections of wall in some horrible labyrinth under the burning cities. . . . The *Amnesiac* book is designed to be left for decades in a drawer, in an old cupboard, in a dusty attic, in an abandoned house, and found after I am dead. (Donwood in Leblanc 2005: 100)

It is against this backdrop of richly and complexly textured imagery, themes, and texts that I now turn to the track "Pyramid Song," and to the myriad detailed audience responses elicited by its metrical challenges.

"Pyramid Song"

Known alternatively as "Egyptian Song" and "Nothing to Fear" during its gestation period, what came to be called "Pyramid Song"—debuted in Amsterdam at the 1999 Tibetan Freedom Concert—is now considered by the band and its audiences to be one of their finest works (Paytress 2005: 59). The choice of the final title has been scrutinized by fans and critics alike— nothing new for Radiohead—as there are no direct references to Egypt or pyramids in the lyrics (there is, however, a sizable community that believes it has found pyramid-like dimensions in the metrical structure of the song, to be addressed below). Many theories abound: (1) Yorke immersed himself in Tibetan and Egyptian books of the dead in preparation for the Amsterdam concert, which could account for lyrical references to rivers, boats, angels, and the heavens (Hale 1999: 116–17); (2) musically the song was inspired by Charles Mingus's song "Freedom" and its subject matter relating to the flight of Moses and the Israelites, hence the earlier reference to Egypt and rivers (Letts 2005: 136); (3) the last line of the verse is nearly identical to content found in Tom Waits's 1985 song "Clap Hands," which itself is lifted from "The Clapping Song" by Shirley Ellis (1965), which refers back to the handclaps in

Mingus's "Freedom" of 1963[19]; and (4) the lyrics suggest an Egyptian funeral (Pareles 2001: 74; Dimery 2006: 883).[20] Yorke's own musings on the album title are also suggestive: "I read that the Gnostics believe when we are born we are forced to forget where we have come from in order to deal with the trauma of arriving in this life. I thought this was really fascinating. It's like the river of forgetfulness" (quoted in Fricke 2001b: 25).

"Pyramid Song" is composed of a single verse with refrain ("there was nothing to fear and nothing to doubt") played twice.[21] For the first statement of the verse, there is only Yorke singing, accompanying himself on an acoustic piano. An orchestral string section enters with the intro to the second verse,[22] then drums followed by upright bass provide a context for interpreting the song's meter (the overall texture later enhanced by the sounds of the ondes Martenot).[23]

What first attracted me and many others to this track, however, was the opening of the song where little is provided for the listener in terms of rhythmic orientation. There is no "beat" or regular pulse, no percussion or text, just a series of piano chords played at an even dynamic level with (slight) pauses occurring after the third and eighth chords (the pauses are repeated structurally at the same points throughout the remainder of the song; refer to Figure 2.3). Most listeners identify this series as a kind of cycle divided into two phrases of five chords each because of the upward and downward movement of the bass line and inner voices and the parallel placement of pauses after the third chord in each group of five. And most focus on the third or fourth iteration of the cycle as a kind of model to base their analyses, most likely because these versions are played more than any other.[24] It should also be noted that many respondents commented on

---

[19]http://www.greenplastic.com/radiohead-lyrics/amnesiac/pyramid-song/
[20]While not meaning to take away any of the mystery or interpretive challenge that the lyrics present, Radiohead's bass player Colin Greenwood provided a clear and succinct account of the genesis of the words in a 2001 interview for the Sundance Film Festival: "The inception of the song was when we were in Copenhagen and Thom went 'round the museum of culture and there was an exhibition of Egyptian underworld and tomb art of people being ferried across the river of death—I don't know what it's called in Egyptian mythology—and he was very affected by it and he went back and sat at the piano and wrote it" (recorded in Douridas 2001).
[21]The refrain is one of two "slogans" printed on the back cover of the CD booklet (the other being "spine damaged," a reference to the condition of the book printed on the front cover of the booklet).
[22]Isolated string tracks from this session are found on track #9, "Pyramid Strings," of the 2021 disc *Kid Amnesiae*.
[23]The ondes Martenot, an early electronic instrument named after its inventor Maurice Martenot in 1928, was first made popular by the composer Olivier Messiaen in his 1937 composition "Fête des belles eaux" (Celebration of the Beautiful Waters). The instrument was added to Radiohead's sonic palette by Jonny Greenwood.
[24]Two other variants of the model cycle are occasionally played, but without changing the feeling of the cycle length or the harmonic rhythm.

FIGURE 2.3 *First four iterations of piano cycle (pause indicated by *).*

the cycle's "gypsy" feel due to its adherence to a standard I-bII-bIII chord progression found in Andalusian Phrygian tonality (see Manuel 2006: 97).

The opening of "Pyramid Song" is a clear example of the ambiguity of metrical type featuring underdetermination, as defined by Butler: "Underdetermination usually occurs when one or more layers of motion needed to make a decisive metrical interpretation are absent; in such a case, the meter is 'not clearly defined' as in the first sense of ambiguity described by the *OED*" (2006: 129–30).[25] The Radiohead introduction also fits especially well within Justin London's category of "vague metric context" under his taxonomy of metric ambiguity: "[I]n metrically vague situations there is a discernable sense of regularity, but the listener is stymied when he or she tries to construe any particular metrical organization" (2012: 106). It is this lack of metrical clarity, taken in conjunction with its relationship

---

[25]This kind of rhythmic ambiguity has been similarly described by the psychoacoustician Ernst Terhardt in terms of "insufficiency of structural information included in the stimulus" (1991: 229); see also Attas (2015).

to the later entrance of the drum set, that has provided the impetus behind the outpouring of listeners' interpretations, not only of the meter but also of Radiohead's underlying semantic intent. What is important for me here is the wide range and inventiveness of perspectives and meanings generated by these audiences as a potent indicator of ambiguity inviting participation. Looking to maintain a decentralized approach to analysis and interpretation, it is not in my present interests to advocate for any particular viewpoint. What is central to this process (for reasons outlined in the Introduction) is to let respondents speak in their own voices so that the original feeling and texture of the analytical and emotional content remains intact.

To this end, I have provided below the unedited responses of participants drawn from a pool of six print publications, thirteen websites, and 261 individual web entries logged between 2007 and 2011 related to rhythm and meter in "Pyramid Song" (this number runs to well over a thousand if all threads addressing this song and/or *Amnesiac* are included).[26] These responses—chosen as representative examples of a much larger base—are organized into nine categories of metrical interpretation to facilitate comparison: first by the existence/absence of a meter, and secondly by the quality of the meter. To further cut down on redundancy, I have used the following method for marking web entries: "FB Stephen" identifies an entry by "Stephen" (in some cases these are real names, in others an assumed one) from the Facebook (FB) page titled "Time Signature in Pyramid Song???" (refer to the websites section in the Bibliography for the full list of abbreviations and corresponding page titles).[27] And while "participation" for many of the respondents represented "just" listening and commenting, there were also a number of instances of fans attempting to play the music themselves, demonstrating various instrumental lines on YouTube, producing original-content video, or running the song through sound-analysis software.[28]

Opening Philosophical Musings

The stakes, at least for one philosophically minded listener, are high, extending beyond this individual song to the sources of individual temporal experience. In his contribution to the tome *Radiohead and Philosophy*,

---

[26]Spelling and grammar has been cleaned up in some cases, but without affecting the meaning or tone of the response.
[27]While it would be of considerable interest to know who these audiences and/or fans might be in terms of gender, age, place of residence, occupation, and socio-economic class, there is unfortunately not enough information revealed in the entries to warrant such speculation (and personal contact information is not as a rule provided).
[28]In the original article on which this chapter is based, I also included listening challenges for readers; see Hesselink (2013), very end of the document.

Michael Thompson begins with an observation that perfectly encapsulates my own initial encounter with the song:

> After hearing "Pyramid Song" from *Amnesiac*, most people say, "Something's not quite right with that song." ... Yet neither the vocals nor Yorke's delivery seems to account for the arresting qualities of "Pyramid Song." It is, rather, the mood of the song that seems to grab and keep your attention. And that mood has everything to do with the song's rhythm. (2009: 221)

From here Thompson goes on to provide a more ambitious explanation for the song's ability to challenge a listener's sense of self, time, the world, and even the afterlife:

> The rhythm of the song seems skewed. As it plays, you might ask, "why does it sound like the notes are played a split-second too late?" It's because the song has a complex time signature that leads to rhythms that are out of joint with those of our ordinary experience. This is what is so compelling about "Pyramid Song." Its timing, rhythm, and beat are literally out of sync with the way we ordinarily experience the world. (2009: 221–2)

> This makes sense of the effects the song has and suggests that different listeners may in fact hear the song differently—that the debate about time signature rests on the subjectivity of perception Yorke points to [the time is just "felt"]. If you tend to see life as a sequence of small cluster of events with strange emphases [reference to syncopation in the opening of the song], a simpler time signature [4/4] is what you will recognize in the song. If you see life as a larger sequence with regular patterns and rhythms, you will hear a more complicated time signature. If you see life as a constantly shifting series of events, some smaller, some larger, and recognize the cyclicality of these events, you will hear shifting time signatures. (2009: 223)

> The rhythmic oddness of "Pyramid Song" is then an opportunity to become aware of temporality itself. By breaking from the regular rhythms we expect to hear in popular music, Radiohead nudges us to adopt phenomenological perspectives on time—something one must do with caution. Remembrance and recognition of our lives in the past can be painful, as it seems to be for Chopin. For others it can lead to a difficult realization about death and finitude. (2009: 228)

Two Separate Songs

Most listeners made attempts at exacting a rhythmic structure and/or meter—either right from the beginning or based on the interaction of drums and piano in the second iteration of the verse—and then assumed that this structure was applicable to the song in its entirety. While this was my own strategy and, generally, the way I listen to this song, the following respondents were happy to think of the two verses as inhabiting different realms, almost as if they were two separate songs linked together by a common text (without going any further to establish a unifying, underlying rhythm):

> YT CallMeVann: "Beautiful, I love how the drum beat completely changes the song at 2:05."
> YT magikmalick: "Astounding song. The first time I heard it, when the drums started I remember thinking there was no way to expect this particular rhythm. (If that ever makes sense to someone . . .)"

After having spent numerous listenings perfecting my tapping abilities to an underlying but hidden pulse (see below), I now also enjoy hearing the first time through the verse as a kind of rhythmic dream state without a beat, allowing myself to be surprised by the entrance of the drums the second time through.

A Regular Meter

As mentioned earlier, the majority of respondents felt that there was some kind of regular meter that applied to "Pyramid Song" from beginning to end. Radiohead, on the whole, has been silent on this issue,[29] though a quote attributed to Thom Yorke suggests a circular orientation that could be construed as a reference to a regular meter:

> SF: "This was written by Thom Yorke after a visit to an exhibition of Egyptian art, during a two-week sojourn in Copenhagen in 1999. He told MTV: 'That song literally took five minutes to write, but yet it came from all these mad places. [It's] something I never thought I could actually get across in a song and lyrically. [But I] managed it and that was really, really tough. [Physicist] Stephen Hawking talks about the theory that time is another force. It's [a] fourth dimension and [he talks about] the idea that time is completely cyclical, it's always doing this [spins finger]. It's a factor, like gravity. It's something that I found in Buddhism as well. That's what 'Pyramid Song' is about, the fact that everything is going in circles.'"

---

[29]In an interview with Alex Ross, Radiohead's drummer Phil Selway was quoted as saying "there is no time signature [in "Pyramid Song"]," though Ross (and many others) recognize Selway's shuffling rhythm implying a compound meter standard in jazz (2010: 95 [to be discussed in more detail later]). It is also difficult to imagine how Radiohead could perform a piece with such intricacy and required coordination without any metrical organization.

What is more significant about a unifying metrical structure in the context of this song is that it requires the listener to abstract out a silent or "hidden" beat, at least at the beginning, which is not provided by the piano chords or singing—a very difficult task, even for professional musicians. Parallels here with African drumming and its rhythmic orientation are striking: John Blacking speaks of "the rhythm of an invisible conductor" (1973: 30), Simha Arom conceives of a "mold" into which surface structures would fit (2004: 18), and Richard Waterman describes an additional (unheard) rhythm against which an obvious surface structure pulled (1952: 211–12; see also Chernoff 1979: 49–50). Justin London further identifies this phenomenon in "Pyramid Song" as a kind of "metric fakeout" which "starts with [a] complex beat pattern that then becomes [the] rhythmic figure against [a] 'correct' meter" (n.d.(b)). This explanation is similar to David Huron's application of the "garden path" phenomenon to music in which someone might feel he/she/they understands an utterance but must then reanalyze it in light of a later happening (in this case, the entrance of the drums; 2006: 279–81).

No Specific Meter Identified, or Respondents Unsure

One of the first responses I encountered on the web essentially matched my bare-bones description of the piano chords at the beginning of this chapter, a view that seemed to assume that all the chords were the same length (no syncopation) with a kind of artistic loosening of the tempo (rubato?) applied to every third and eighth chord:[30]

> GPT: "Now the timing of the song is really tricky. Thom hits all the chords at an even pace throughout the chord sequence, but at certain points he stops for a split second longer. So after each chord I will put a * so as to let you know to hold the time signature a little longer before moving on to the next chord." [no time signature is provided, just a series of isolated chords][31]

A number of listeners, however, were content to just "feel" the piece, regardless of what the meter might be:

---

[30] I thank Dai Griffiths for suggesting the idea of rubato in this context (personal communication, 2011).
[31] This analysis matches a listening experience described by Longuet-Higgins and Lee: "In choosing a rhythmic interpretation for a given note sequence the listener seems to be guided by a strong assumption: if the sequence can be interpreted as the realization of an unsyncopated passage, then that is how he will interpret it" (1984: 424).

> YT interpolluter29: "The way you do it at first is forget about rhythm and play the song like a classical piece. Or rather just feel the music, and the rest will fall into place."
>
> YT thedonedude: "All you guys are getting it wrong! It doesn't matter if it's 4/4 or and 8/8 etc. You'll never figure it if you use your head. Music is all about feel and if you can't feel it you will never get that magic spark that will make you play anything."
>
> YT 5T41KER: "I don't think Radiohead wrote this gem of a song to spark up in depth debate on its time signature to be honest. Just enjoy it, and play/believe/write it out in whatever time signature works for you."
>
> MG Check My French: "You can't count that song, you just gotta feel it. I tried to play it while counting for weeks. Then I stopped and just listened."
>
> MG castlebuilding: "Yorke, like most members of Radiohead, has never learned how to read music. He said, 'If someone lays the notes on a page in front of me, it's meaningless ... because to me you can't express the rhythms properly like that. It's a very ineffective way of doing it, so I've never really bothered picking it up.'"

Numerical ratios also captured the imagination of a number of individuals; while certain meters are implied by such discussions, I have included the following ruminations more for their relationship to the title and deeper meaning of the song (these ratios will appear again, and will be fully explicated, in categories that follow):

> YT PrincessPunzee: "If you go back a few comments or comment pages, someone explained it. It's like a 3-3-4-3-3 timing. Very interesting stuff. I'm almost sure I've never known any song to do that ... apparently it's supposed to do with the shape of a pyramid, you know: 3 sides for each triangle and four sides for the bottom."
>
> Paytress (2005: 60) "Given the near triangular rhythm at its heart, 'Pyramid Song' seems an appropriate title."
>
> FB Sam: "The Ancient Egyptian Pyramids were all built in a 3:4:5 ratio. Some people see elements of the golden ratio in this construction, something which is used frequently in architecture and music (e.g., Bartok). It was argued that it was somehow 'pleasing' to the ear and eye. Since there's no other reference to pyramids in the song, I assume Radiohead were going after this golden ratio in the rhythms of this song. Sorry, I'm not a massive fan of Radiohead so I'm not going to slave away working out HOW they went about this, but it seems like the sort of thing they'd be into."

Other listeners had more philosophical and/or creative ways of accounting for the feeling and structure of the song:

> YT DKsmiles: "This isn't 4:4, the emphasis is completely wrong. I'd say your best bet is to say that it either doesn't have a time signature, or it's a complicated mix of 2 or 3 different ones. The point is, however, that Thom Yorke is a genius to such an extent that he can write a song in a completely random time signature and make it sound pretty normal."
>
> Letts (2005: 124, 134): "Pyramid Song"'s meter as "out of time" and representing the "nonsense" side of a binary that includes "sense"; "Pyramid Song"'s rhythm is "dreamy" and creates "a sense of timelessness."
>
> FB Danni: "I just put the file into a program called sonic Visualiser. So far I have looked at the piano Intro. . . . There are two note sizes (one exactly half the size of the other)—the whole pattern is exactly 22 times the size of the smallest note. When broken up into phrases it works out to 7, 6, 5, 4 of what I assume are 8ths. I haven't yet looked at how the piano fits in with the other instruments so the overall key [time] signature may be different. But I am pretty sure that this is the conceptual pattern behind the piano."

And my sympathy goes out to the following individual:

> FB Shannon: "I have just spent the last half hour listening to it repeatedly with a pen and paper trying to work it out . . . neighbours would be going crazy if it wasn't such a great song;-) I couldn't work it out btw . . . !"

Non-Isochronous Meters: Alone and in Combination with Simple Meters

Before moving on to more common simple and compound meter constructions, I begin with examples of non-isochronous meter interpretations, both alone and in combination with simple meter interpretations. A non-isochronous meter, as defined by London (2012: 121–5), refers to a collection of asymmetrical pulse lengths where the integrity of the subtactus is maintained (such as in the example $\frac{2+3+3+2}{8}$). My assumption with the responses that follow, therefore, is that each number in a non-isochronous grouping refers to a single piano chord placed metrically (i.e., aligned with a pulse, *not* syncopated against some other underlying meter).

Non-isochronous meter discussions centered on the possibility of 11/8. In each case the 11/8 interpretation remained consistent, each phrase of the piano cycle (five chords) envisioned as composed of five pulses with the first, second, fourth, and fifth chords being equal in length ($\frac{2+2+3+2+2}{8}$):

> YT butler: "Quarter note, quarter note, dotted quarter note, quarter note, quarter note ostinato over and over, making it (5.5)/4 or 11/8."
> FB Patrick: "It's in 11/8 guys. Eighth notes are grouped 2-2-3-2-2 (counted: 12-12-123-12-12). Every measure. For the entire song."
> FB Noele: "Um, it's definitely 11/8.
> 2+2+3+2+2. It's a palindrome. Or pyramid."

On the surface the core interpretation of combined non-isochronous and simple meters created by listeners—7/8, 3/4, 5/8, 2/4—bears little resemblance to the 11/8 examples. However, if one doubles the 11/8 phrase to cover an entire piano cycle (22 eighth notes in length)—maintaining the same pulse length relationships—then what one discovers is an astounding yet logical way of dividing the cycle that breaks across the symmetrical model of two bars of 11/8 but is still composed of ten pulses arranged in a way that mirrors the harmonic rhythm of the first iteration of the piano cycle (especially the changes at A^{add6}, Gmaj7, and finally Gmaj). Written in eighth note groupings, the full cycle is represented by 2+2+3, 2+2+2, 2+3, 2+2; written using time signatures, we are presented with $\frac{2+2+3}{8}$, 3/4, $\frac{2+3}{8}$, 2/4 (see Figure 2.4):

FIGURE 2.4 *Metrical realizations of first iteration of piano cycle: (a) 11/8; (b) 7/8, 3/4, 5/8, 2/4.*

FB Quang: "Hey . . . from what I feel it's a loop of 4 different bars: 7/8—3/4—5/8—2/4. And the pattern repeats over and over. I played the piano groove with this counting, and I find it matched. Try it!"

SF Stacy: "Are there any 'classically' trained musicians out there? If you listen carefully, you'll find that the song is in a repeating pattern of 7/8, 3/4, 5/8, and 2/4. It completely makes sense, because it makes the [piano] phrasing so that it ends up equal every time."

Compound Meters

For the majority of respondents "Pyramid Song" was in a more common compound or simple meter. Within the compound meter camp, many individuals cited a "jazz" or "swing" feel to the entrance of the drums at the second verse to support their interpretation of metrical intent (and many websites and blogs made references to Yorke's inspiration in Charles Mingus's jazz classic "Freedom"):[32]

WP: "The song builds to a climax with the introduction of Phil Selway's jazz-influenced compound rhythm."

Figure 2.5 provides a "compound meter" realization of the entrance of the drums without any grouping (or "measure") indications within each set of five chords. Two important features distinguish all compound meter interpretations structurally from those of the non-isochronous type: (1) the first two piano chords (as well as a number of subsequent chords) are viewed as unequal in duration; and (2) a number of chords are felt as syncopated against a stream of symmetrical pulses.

A number of individuals were happy with a straight 9/8 or 12/8 organization:

FB Will: "Yea, it's definitely 9/8. I've asked 2 of my old music teachers, 3 professional guitarists, 2 drum teachers, a jazz percussionist and a jazz singer/keyboardist and they all agree. This has been bugging me for months but I'm fairly sure that's right."

SF Rob: "Well . . . technically . . . the way it is recorded the song is in 12/8 (similar to 4/4 but it is a triple meter feel). This is very clear when the drums enter. You could feel it as 9/8, 6/8, 9/8 (similar to 3/4, 2/4, 3/4 in duple meter). A time signature is just used to break up the music in a logical way for the performer to interpret, similar to 'The Rite of Spring' being written out in 4/4. It is the same music but has a different feel and is in turn interpreted differently."

---

[32] In Butler's terms, the entrance of the drums would signal a "reinterpretation of metrical type" (2006: 130).

FIGURE 2.5 *"Compound meter neutral"* realization of entrance of drums (beginning of second verse).

A larger group, however, had fun employing a cycle with alternating compound meters:

> 8N: notated in bars of 9/8, 9/8, 6/8.
> YT thatboneguy: "It sounds to me like 9/8, 9/8, 6/8 repeating throughout. I guess you could say 8/4 with a swing. Or you could say 24/8. I think. But I love how you think it's just a piano hesitating randomly at the beginning, but you then hear the beat come in. Simply genius."
> YT gypsyljg: "Jibblegit you're correct in saying it's in a shuffle-influenced style. The 4:4 that you're referring to is simply an illusion—the beats you are counting are slightly unequal lengths. The piece goes 9:8 for two bars then one bar 6:8 and repeats! The chord lengths are either 4, 5, or 6 quavers long :-) Hope this helps."
> YT gypsyljg [again]: "I've never understood this debate. The song is clearly in compound time—a mixture of 6/8 and 9/8 in this case. It frequently switches between the two—but since the chords are syncopated and never fall on a strong beat, the time signature is irrelevant. When the drums enter the rhythm is revealed as being compound (when before the chords, without the rhythmic reinforcement of the drums, sounded almost un-notatable.)"
> FB Graham: "It works either way. It just depends how you want to write it. A 9/8 9/8 6/8 time signature is easier to write, but in the end it ends up the same number of beats and same phrase length as two bars of 12/8. That does make a little more sense though."
> SF Caroline: "Yep, I hear 3-2-3 3-2-3 (or 9/8|6/8|9/8|9/8|6/8|9/8). The sheet music I have says 9/8|9/8|6/8."[33]

---

[33]Dai Griffiths also chose the rhythmic grouping of 3-2-3, 3-2-3, but unfortunately didn't specify the meter (2005: 164).

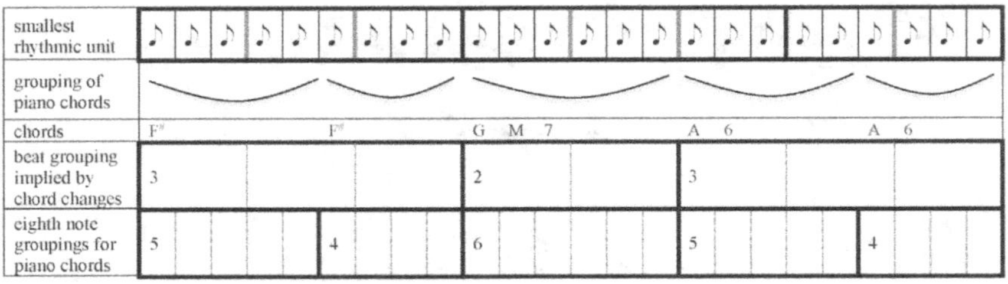

smallest rhythmic unit	♪	♪	♪	♪	♪	♪	♪	♪	♪	♪	♪	♪	♪	♪	♪	♪	♪	♪	♪	♪	♪	♪	♪	♪
grouping of piano chords	⌣					⌣				⌣						⌣					⌣			
chords	F♯					F♯				G M 7						A 6					A 6			
beat grouping implied by chord changes	3									2						3								
eighth note groupings for piano chords	5					4				6						5					4			

FIGURE 2.6 *9/8, 9/8, 6/8 realization, first phrase of cycle.*

Because of the recurrence of certain numeric ratios in the previous discussion (3-2-3, 3-3-2, 4-5-6), but also to be able to compare these ratios with time signatures that follow, I have provided in Figure 2.6 a 9/8, 9/8, 6/8 realization of the first phrase (opening five piano chords) of the third iteration of the cycle. The top row of boxes represents the smallest rhythmic unit implied by this meter (the eighth note), bracketed off into groups of 9, 9, and 6 (9/8, 9/8, 6/8); immediately below this, I have added slurs to indicate possible groupings of the piano chords. I say "possible" in that only one of the responses provides specific piano chord lengths (4, 5, or 6 eighth notes), and that this only makes sense when corroborated with another entry that dictates that one should "syncopate" the chords (even with this knowledge, I had to exercise some interpretive license). Below this, I then provide the chord qualities, with the remaining two rows of boxes showing groupings by beat (according to chord changes) and eighth note lengths of the piano chords. Two items of note: (1) beat groupings by chord change (3-2-3) do not coincide with the bar lengths (3-3-2), unless one chooses a 9/8, 6/8, 9/8 cycle; and (2) 4-5-6 only makes sense when looking at the eighth note groupings for the piano chords but written in the order 5-4-6-5-4.

4/4 with Swung Eighth Notes

In keeping with common practice in jazz notation (and, to a certain extent, pop), a number of respondents chose to describe the meter in "Pyramid Song" as 4/4 with the instructions to "swing" the eighth notes. While a number of writers and theorists refer to "swing" in such a context to describe expressive timing (including Butler 2006: 22),[34] most of the respondents below used such terminology to indicate what they felt was essentially a

---

[34] The relationship between swung, shuffle, and compound meters is more complex and beyond the discussion provided here; for those so interested, see de Clercq (2017).

12/8 compound meter (and, in fact, a number of scores referenced gave direct instructions to play each eighth note pair as a quarter-eighth triplet[35]):

> FB Jane: "4-beat with shuffle. That's what I'd call it anyway. Others might say swung 4/4 or whatever but it all means the same thing at the end of the day. Ever since I realised that after hearing it 3 or 4 times, I have to deliberately try to make myself not realise it, in order for it to sound as good as it used to, which is difficult but possible. I preferred back when I thought it was some kind of weird alien time signature, lol."
>
> YT cashdollar: "Close, it's just 4/4—4 bar phrases even. You are right about the swing feel. Just beat out 4/4 right from the beginning and follow along. It's hypnotic and beautiful. I thought it was alternating time signatures too ever since the first time I heard this. I just figured this issue out a few days ago :)"
>
> FB Graham: "Sorry, swung 4/4. I'm an idiot. '12/8' if you want to be old fashioned. The phrases clash with a 6/8 time signature and although 3/4 5/4 does work, there is no point in making a time signature any more complicated than it needs to be, and the eighth notes are definitely swung. The drum pattern makes that really clear. It's especially hard to tell the time signature in 'Pyramid Song' before the drums come in."
>
> FB Kristian: "Pyramid Song is simply 4/4 all the way through without any changes to the signature whatsoever. Points to remember are: It's swung . . . it's a 'compound' rhythm . . . so basically you count triplets on every crochet (or quarter note for the Americans). The syncopation literally happens on the second piano chord . . . most people screw up counting this at that stage. . . . You have to allow the second chord (from the very start of the track) to happen before the beat—it in fact falls on the 'a' after '2&a'. This rhythmic form would have originated from Africa and over the centuries found its way to Rio, Cuba and pretty much the whole South America. It is communicated as and named the 'Bossa nova clave' and the score explaining its pattern can be found here."

This last response identifies clearly what I set out previously as distinguishing features of the compound meter interpretations: (1) the first two piano chords are unequal in duration (the first is longer than the second), and (2) the chords are felt as syncopated against a stream of symmetrical pulses (see Figure 2.7, a rendition of the first phrase written out in 12/8 time

---

[35]This is the meter and instruction noted on the "official" score for "Pyramid Song" (Artemis Music Ltd 2008), though see comments below.

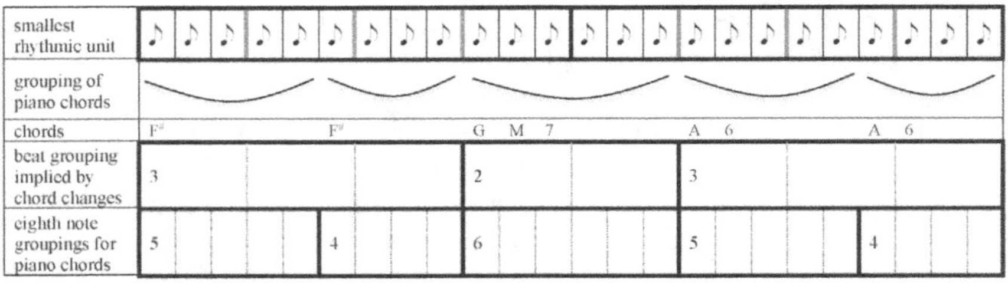

smallest rhythmic unit	♪	♪	♪	♪	♪	♪	♪	♪	♪	♪	♪	♪	♪	♪	♪	♪	♪	♪	♪	♪	♪	♪	♪	♪
grouping of piano chords	⌒				⌒				⌒					⌒					⌒					
chords	F♯				F♯				G	M	7			A		6			A		6			
beat grouping implied by chord changes	3								2					3										
eighth note groupings for piano chords	5				4				6					5					4					

FIGURE 2.7 *4/4 with swung eighth notes (12/8 realization), first phrase of cycle.*

to illustrate visually what happens when swinging the eighth notes). In such a "swung" (12/8) interpretation, there is further syncopation with the metrically consonant third and fourth chords landing on weak beats (beat 4 and beat 2, respectively), as well as beat groupings by chord change that do not coincide with the bar lengths (3-2-3 versus 4-4).

When comments begin to address specifics, however, the language and numerical ratios become more obscure. For the following entry, the note lengths of the piano chords are correct when writing out the swung eighths in full (here the sixteenth note is considered the smallest rhythmic unit but with the same numeric results):

> YT skotoseme: "You'll notice that if you subdivide all the eighths into sixteenth triplets to account for the swing, the chords have a rhythmic ratio of 5:4:6:5:4 [refer to bottom row, Figure 2.7] (=24 sixteenth triplets=a full measure of 4/4). No wonder it's so disorienting before the drums come in."

For the remaining entries and published scores, one must look at a strictly 4/4 rendition (no swung eighth notes) to understand the numbers, which I have provided in Figure 2.8. This then accounts for the sequence "33433" (refer to the row of boxes showing eighth note groupings for the piano chords), and its related "1.5 beats" (3 eighths) and "2 beats" (4 eighths), and/or dotted quarter note (3 eighths) and two tied quarter notes (4 eighths):

> Artemis Music Ltd (music score) 2008: 6–9: 1st bar: dotted quarter, eighth tied to quarter, quarter tied to [next bar] quarter, quarter tied to eighth, dotted quarter [this equals the first two bars or first phrase; this rhythmic figure then repeats].
>
> FH: 1st bar: dotted quarter, eighth tied to quarter, quarter tied to [next bar] quarter, quarter tied to eighth, dotted quarter [this equals the first two bars or first phrase; this rhythmic figure then repeats].

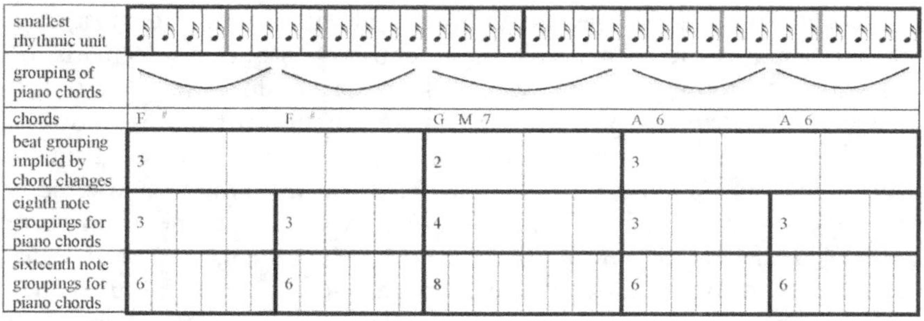

AMBIGUITY, RHYTHM, AND PARTICIPATION 33

smallest rhythmic unit	♫♫	♫♫	♫♫	♫♫	♫♫	♫♫	♫♫	♫♫	♫♫	♫♫	♫♫	♫♫	♫♫	♫♫	♫♫	♫♫
grouping of piano chords	⌒		⌒			⌒			⌒			⌒				
chords	F♯		F♯			G M 7			A 6			A 6				
beat grouping implied by chord changes	3					2			3							
eighth note groupings for piano chords	3			3		4				3			3			
sixteenth note groupings for piano chords	6			6		8				6			6			

FIGURE 2.8 *4/4 realization, first phrase of cycle (8 beats over 2 bars).*

    YT sqmuth: "That's what I thought at first. I think Geekman1118's take on it is the best. It's like the faces of a pyramid, arranged 3:3:4:3:3. (The 4 triangles are the 3's, and the 4 is the square base). Notate all those chords as dotted quarters (a beat and a half), except the ones with asterisks [the third piano chord of each group of five] are half notes (two beats). Finally, swing it. Voila, straight time."
    YT jwr24: "The song is in 4/4 with a swing feel. The pattern goes like this (over 2 bars): dotted quarter, dotted quarter, quarter tied to quarter, dotted quarter, dotted quarter. Then the pattern repeats itself. So the notes are held for 1.5 beats, 1.5 beats, 2 beats, 1.5 beats, 1.5 beats, repeated."

4/4, 1 Complete Cycle over 4 Bars (16 Beats)

If any conflict or rivalry exists within the "Pyramid Song" metrical world, it is felt most strongly by those aligning themselves with the "straight" (simple meter) 4/4 camp, versus those who adhere to some kind of compound meter. While I have no way of evaluating the view from the opening philosophical musings that those who "see life as a sequence of [a] small cluster of events with strange emphases" will recognize "a simpler time signature [4/4]" (Thompson 2009: 223), music theorists and cognitive scientists have documented how Western listeners carry with them a default binary expectation—because of a predominance of binary meters in Western music (especially popular genres)—which they will generally apply when confronted with an unknown rhythm (Brochard et al. 2003; Huron 2006: 194–5).[36] Precisely whether or not this applies to the listening perceptions

---

[36]While I should reiterate that I am not advocating for any particular single metric interpretation of "Pyramid Song," if one accepts the eighth note groupings of the piano chords in Figures 2.6 and 2.7 (5-4-6-5-4) we are presented with a series of note durations with highly complex

of the 4/4 contingent is beyond the scope of this chapter; in most cases, the stated reasons for the simple meter choice was one of pragmatism: it was easiest to think of it this way, and the beats added up most directly to bars of four beats. In order for this interpretation to work, however, one of two viewpoints must be held: (1) the first verse (without drums) is played in its own (simple) meter in a different way from the second verse (an acknowledgment of a change to compound meter); or (2) the drum part is heard as binary (ternary divisions of the beat are not recognized). Either way, significantly the opening two piano chords are seen as equal in duration.

A number of respondents identified a 4/4 meter, but without specifying the length of the entire cycle:

> MG Drunkk Machine: "It is in 4/4. Just because the hits on piano are on off beats and the pattern concludes in four bars doesn't make it not in 4/4. Count Phil's ride, it's pretty easy that way."
>
> FB Kristian: "I'm afraid it's in 4/4 . . . anyone struggling to count it just needs to learn to [think] simply. It's in 4/4—don't try to be clever with it. Radiohead had no intention of some stupid cumbersome set of measures."

Most web entries, however, described or notated the full cycle—ten piano chords, returning to the F# triad—as occurring over four bars, or sixteen full beats (refer again to Figure 2.8 for the numeric ratios of the first phrase):

> YT ingloriousbastard: "The song is in 4/4. To understand the drum pattern though, I find it easier to break the rhythm into quarter notes (16 beats, 16/4), which is what Phil's ride signature is. The pattern is then 123-123-12-123-123-12 (the last 1, 2 is a drum fill). That's a basic time of 3/4, 3/4, 2/4, 3/4, 3/4, 2/4." [similar to 9/8, 9/8, 6/8, but not swung]
>
> YT pennypthree: "Actually I think you'll find the time signature is even simpler than that, the whole thing is in 4/4 but strangely syncopated. The best way to count it I find is 1-2-3-4-5-6 1-2-3-4 1-2-3-4-5-6 [(3+3)-4-(3+3) = eighth note level] or half time 1-2-3 1-2 1-2-3 [quarter note level]."

---

ratios that are difficult to hear: "[W]e understand notes as being in one rhythmic category or another, rather than merely perceiving them as continually varying. This process of sorting or 'quantizing' notes has been demonstrated experimentally as well; when played patterns of alternating notes whose durations are related by complex ratios (such as 1.5:1 or 2.5:1) and asked to reproduce them, subjects tend to adjust the durations toward simple ratios (such as 2:1)" (Temperley 2001: 25; see also Povel 1981). The note durations 5-4-6-5-4 become 1.25:1, 1:1.5, 1.2:1, and 1.25:1; without any other outside stimuli, it could account for why many listeners hear the first two chords (and the fourth and fifth) as being even in length.

> YT PhishFluid714: "It actually is in 4/4 the whole time. It applies a bossa nova rhythm but really slower than you would normally get in bossa nova (about twice as slow). The duration of each chord is 3 3 4 3 3 in terms of eighth notes."[37]
>
> FB Scott: "Great discussion. I've found the easiest way to count it for me is to think of each loop of the piano chords as 3 2 3 3 2 3 (crotchet [quarter note] beats), which does—interestingly—add up to four bars of four."
>
> FB Aaron: "Exactly right. Subdivisions and polyrhythms can exist within simple time signatures in order to make things more interesting, but the time signature itself, in this case, is 4/4. I didn't believe it at first, either, but I sat down and analysed it, and anyone can count along and see that the phrasing resets every 16 beats. It's 4/4. I'm sure Thom and Johnny would be very amused by this conversation, however. =)"

The strongest argument for 4/4 was made by an unnamed listener who created a YouTube video with the first iteration of the piano cycle looped over a click track to "prove" his/her/their 4/4 explanation (refer to Hesselink (2013), Example 9).

It is also interesting to note that a number of individuals heard the cycle beginning on the third (longer) piano chord, such that the song then began on the last two beats of the previous cycle:

> FB James: "I love how the 5-chord phrases on the piano cover multiple measures. The third chord is always on the measure mark, which is why at the beginning and end of the song, there's only 3 chords. At the beginning, the 3rd, 4th, and 5th chords complete the first phrase, while the first 2 chords are omitted, since they would have fallen before the beginning of the song. At the end of the song, the 1st, 2nd, and 3rd chords complete the song. Throughout the song, those 5-chord phrases on the piano help you follow the simple 4/4 time signature, with the 3rd chord of each phrase being your measure marker."

4/4, 1 Complete Cycle over 2 Bars (8 Beats)

Identifying a pulse or beat to tap along with is of course a subjective enterprise, although there are some parameters by which most of us seem

---

[37] See further Taylor (2010).

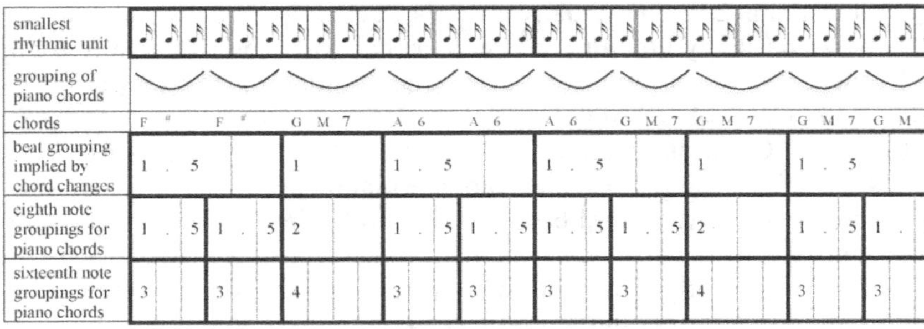

smallest rhythmic unit	♪ ♪										
grouping of piano chords	⌣ ⌣ ⌣ ⌣ ⌣ ⌣ ⌣ ⌣ ⌣ ⌣ ⌣										
chords	F#	F#	G M 7	A 6	A 6	A 6	G M 7	G M 7	G M 7	G M 7	
beat grouping implied by chord changes	1 . 5	1	1 . 5	1 . 5	1	1 . 5	1				
eighth note groupings for piano chords	1 . 5	1 . 5	2	1 . 5	1 . 5	1 . 5	1 . 5	2	1 . 5	1 . 5	
sixteenth note groupings for piano chords	3	3	4	3	3	3	3	4	3	3	

FIGURE 2.9 *4/4 realization, one complete cycle (8 beats over 2 bars).*

to adhere (see Huron 2006: 175–6; Martens 2011). While a minority view within the 4/4 group, a significant number of listeners nevertheless heard "Pyramid Song" at exactly half the speed of the above category, so that a complete cycle took only 2 bars to complete:

> PB: piano score notated as 4/4 (1 bar: 2 dotted eighths, then a quarter, then two dotted eighths) with the entire figure lasting 2 bars before repeating.
>
> FB Jacob: "Here is my own transcription of Pyramid Song . . . http://s53 .photobucket.com/albums/g54/dreddnott/music/ The piano part is exactly what's played, the guitar part is an arrangement of my own making. It's been performed as written with guitar and piano by The Thom Yorke Experience tribute band. It's the standard 123-123-123-123-1234 syncopation that you hear in jazz or progressive rock, 'shifted over' (for lack of a better term) by six [sixteenth] notes to 123-123-1234-123-123 [3-3-4-3-3]. It's a very slow 4/4, and that's all there is to it."
>
> FB Rodney: "Two dotted eighths, a quarter and two dotted eights [1.5-1.5-2-1.5-1.5]. That's the rhythm for the entire song. It adds up to four beats. The pulse isn't what your ears are going to tell you, I know it's ridiculous. The tempo is like 50 bpms. Also, since the pattern repeats you get four dotted eighths in a row which makes it harder to discern."

Mentally it is easy to just halve all of the values found in Figure 2.8; but for ease of comparison—and for a clear visual representation—I have provided a realization of the entire cycle in Figure 2.9.

Mixed Meter

In this final section, I have documented various mixed meter interpretations, "mixed meter" understood as a stream of perceptually isochronous beats with asymmetrical groupings by bar (such as in the example 3/4, 5/4, 2/4). Such responses often resulted in unusual and/or challenging breakdowns, though in every instance the larger integrity of the phrase (8 beats) or entire cycle (16 beats) was maintained, as was a feeling that the first two chords are equal in length (the second chord syncopated against the pulse stream).

The following respondents felt a significant break at the A^{add6} chord (sixth beat in 4/4 meter), similar to the non-isochronous grouping illustrated in Figure 2.4 (b):

> YT lampshade429: "It's in 16/4 but it's broken down like a measure of 5 and then a measure of 11. This song is amazing." [5/4, 11/4]
>
> YT xenotoxette: "1 bar of 5/4, 2 bars of 4/4, and one bar of 3/4."
>
> FB Pierre: "It could be interpreted in so many ways, depending on what you consider to be the downbeat. And it is hard to discern without the drums ... The phrase is 5/4 (or 3/4 -2/4 to make up the 5/4)—11/4 (or 8/4 and 3/4 to make up the 11/4)—8/4—8/4. So, to make it clear, the phrase is 5/4—11/4—8/4—8/4 for the entire song. It changes slightly when the strings come in at the very end. The phrase then simply becomes 5/4—11/4."
>
> FB Johan: "Personally, I can't [get] the feeling that it's a 5/4 + 11/4 out of my system. The fourth chord, the A, always brings me back to this, even if I set out trying to find the 4/4 feel. I know when the drums kick in he doesn't denote the A but the piano does, at least in my head."
>
> SF Dan: "First of all, this song is very hypnotic—I have listened to it like 5 times in a row now and can't seem to bring myself to stop and travel to my other school to teach Chorus like I am supposed to be doing! The meter issue is certainly divisive. Everyone that has posted something about the time/meter has a good point. I think John from Lenexa, KS got it the most right for me. I hear the 3/4 + 2/4 + 3/4 + 3/4 + 2/4 + 3/4 the best. If those divisions are too small for you, try 5/4 + 6/4 + 5/4, but even those numbers don't really show the tonal rhythm very well. Any song that garners this much discussion is a winner in my book!"

Others felt the first significant break to occur with the Gmaj7 chord (fourth beat in 4/4 meter):

> YT johng61: "‖: 3/4 + 2/4 + 3/4 :‖ repeated throughout." [directly matches harmonic rhythm of first phrase of piano cycle]
>
> MG Creep: "So, 3/4, 5/4, 2/4 completes the cycle of a single phrase."
>
> FB Ben: "This is a question that has been killing me for some time now. ... Maybe I'm the only one but I love trying to figure out the time signature in Radiohead and Tool songs. 'Pyramid Song' has had me

stumped for some time now. I've heard it was 12/8, 6/8, even 4/4. But I believe it's in 3/4 5/4. Any thoughts?"

And numerology and the pyramids also found their way back into the fray:

YT ManianHedgehog: "If you count the beat carefully, you will hear the period of 4 3/4-measures and 1 4/4-measure. It's just like a pyramid—4 faces with 3 sides, 1 face with 4 sides."
YT rawwqq: "Heard that this song's time signature forms a pyramid. 4/4 3/4 2/4 1 2/4 3/4 4/4 maybe? Or a really slow 4/4."

Conclusion

Taken as a whole, the community that coalesced around the rhythm/meter of "Pyramid Song" represents a diverse and energetic body that demonstrated considerable patience, sophistication, and interpretive insight. In looking to solve a musical riddle, their arsenal of tools drew on music theory, structural formulae, notation, intuition, numerology, mathematics, cosmology, history, philosophy, technology, classical training, help from friends and teachers, and perspectives from non-Western music. Their responses reflect a blend of curiosity, adventure, posturing, passion, deference, and humor. And while this chapter only focused on those who were self-consciously reflective and vocal about the metrical aspects of this song, there are of course many others who didn't or couldn't identify the rhythm but who nevertheless felt something special about this composition, a kind of deep affinity for something textually, visually, and (crucially) musically that in combination created a work that was deeply moving and otherworldly:

PS2 speedybill47: "This is the song you hear in an ambient dream/nightmare. This is what a trapped soul in purgatory listens to as a lost being wandering aimlessly through an endless desert. This is beauty at the maximum of beauty. I was walking one night when this song played on my iPod. A bright lightning storm was in the distance. And the moon shined bright on the ocean. It overwhelmed me to the point of tears of beauty and sadness. From then on my life changed with how I felt about the world in a better way."

Ambiguity in the form of underdetermination created a rich forum for participation as listeners grappled with the song's rhythmic organization and developed strategies for entrainment, satisfying biological and cognitive needs. Ethnographic research focused on internet communities brought these perspectives to light, though the tools of music theory were required to make sense of many of these interpretations. Radiohead's use of ambiguity, however, extends much further into their compositional and performative strategies, encompassing the realms of lyrics, song forms, chord progressions, vocal timbres, imagery, and human-technology interfaces. A full account of the ways these various components intersect, diverge, and play off one another provides many fruitful avenues of research yet to be explored.[38]

Whether one appeals to the "wisdom of the crowds" (Sorowiecki 2004), mass collaboration (Tapscott and Williams 2006), or "crowdsourcing" (Howe 2008), in structure and function the increasing reliance on and participation through the internet by large communities of like-minded individuals signals an era of mass participation and collaborative problem-solving that has come to characterize our age. This is as much a political as it is a pragmatic reality: by reading through and mulling over entries by listeners with highly varied training, education, and life experiences, I was presented with a much broader view of the possibilities—in fact, listener realities—than I would have found on my own. The open-ended, interactive, and inclusive nature of many of these websites has created public forums for debate that to my mind indicates a healthy new direction and long overdue reinvigoration of musical criticism and aesthetics, at the same time suggesting alternative, decentralized analytical approaches to musical works.

Musings on ambiguity remind us that often the best songs are those worth revisiting. These are the melodies, structures, and words that continue to challenge and surprise us over the years, the ones that reward our efforts and personal imprint. They are also a mark of our imagination, of our need for ambiguity and the space it affords our feelings and personal stories:

> [P]opular music—all music—exists *only* by virtue of people's, our, desire for, imagination, and creation of it. And then it exists in rich, complex, and intimate relation to us, calling out for images and discourses that take us deeper into its mysteries—the mysteries of our passions and entanglements in it, all of which begin and end in imagination. Anything less imaginatively or less musically conceived is unequal to the task and to our object, which is after all nothing less than music. (Hubbs 2008: 233)

---

[38]Brad Osborn in his excellent book on Radiohead dedicated an entire chapter to "Pyramid Song" (2017: 175–95). For readers looking to understand how rhythm and meter interact with other facets of this song, Osborn's analysis also addresses form, timbre, harmony and voice leading, and the official music video.

3

Rhythmic Play, Compositional Intent, and Communication in Rock Music

Rhythmic play is an obvious and prominent aspect of the world's musical traditions. Immediately recognizable in its exterior and performative form in percussion and improvisatory-based musics, it manifests itself much earlier and informally around the globe in the games of the playground, campfire, and living room.[1] As a subset of musical play under the broader rubric of creative play, rhythmic play beginning in childhood promotes cooperation in groups through rehearsing the skills of social interaction, at the same time activating higher-level mental processes through the nurturing of "exploratory competence" (Cross and Morley 2009: 73–4; see also Bjørkvold 1989 and Pellegrini and Smith 1998). The source of everything from athletic achievements to scientific discoveries to engaging works of theater and art, we are often at our best when at play (Turner 1982; Donald 1991: 162–200).[2]

Rhythmic play as the confluence of rhythm, motion, and cognition appears early in human development. Almost from the time we are born we begin to engage with our caretakers and the outside world in a rhythmic dialogue that promotes emotional bonding, spatial awareness, and pleasure in the act of play.[3] As has been noted in Chapter 1, it has even been argued

---

[1]Representative examples of musical ensembles include Sargeant and Lahiri (1931), Feldman (2006), and Hesselink (2006); during childhood, Greenacre (1959) and Gaunt (2006).
[2]The first half of this chapter was previously published as "Rhythmic Play, Compositional Intent, and Communication in Rock Music," *Popular Music* 33 (1): 69–90 (2014a).
[3]For a wide range of sources, see Lourie (1949), Papoušek (Hanuš) (1996: 46–8), Papoušek (Mechthild) (1996: 104–7), Ejiri (1998), Jaffe et al. (2001), and Davies (2003: 37–43).

that synchronous movement and the ability to keep a steady pulse (the onset of entrainment) directly contributed to our transition from protohuman to human society and the development of the modern brain. Evolutionary perspectives aside, rhythmic awareness and transformative skills begin to present themselves more formally in children outside of the sphere of games in musical activity, both practically/socially—first instrument lessons, early ensemble and/or choir experiences—and aesthetically/socially through listening (typically to pop/rock, but also other musical genres). For many of us, amateur and specialist alike, these become lifelong pursuits.

In this chapter, I focus on the interior and more subtle, but just as ubiquitous, use of rhythmic play in composition. Firstly I address such play as embodying an *attitude* on the part of the performer-composer, an approach to music as pure structure in which one's skill and imagination can be tried out in sonic reality (Lerdahl and Jackendoff 1996[1983]: 9). Here compositional play feeds into the aforementioned cognitive challenges leading to exploratory competence, as Leonard Meyer noted:

> The relation of artistic creation to play must be mentioned. Many references are made in the literature of music to the playfulness of a particular passage or to the delight taken by musicians in play. It seems very probably that this too is a way of referring to the conquest of self-imposed difficulties. Karl Groos frequently emphasizes that this is an essential feature of play; that, in his own words, "play leads up from what is easy to more difficult tasks, since only deliberate conquest can produce the feeling of pleasure in success." (1956: 70)

And while such rhythmic play is frequently discussed in the literature on classical music and is often marked as contributing to its special quality,[4] I will argue that it is also central to rock music and its practitioners.

A second and perhaps more notable aspect of compositional intent is when such play serves as an attempt on the part of the composer as a special kind of *communication* with his/her/their audience. In this capacity, the musical work becomes an unspoken or hidden challenge to the listeners—the interior play projected outwards—as a kind of in-group or insider knowledge, the challenge resting on an audience's familiarity with the music as a shared body of expectations (Davies 2010: 24).[5] Listening thus becomes a window

---

[4]Richard Taruskin (2010a: 204–8) has identified such conscious reflection within the compositional act as beginning with instrumental music of the early eighteenth century (see also Benjamin 2006: 334).
[5]For a representative sampling of research on music and expectation, see Huron (2006), Ball (2010: 254–321), and Huron and Margulis (2010). Bruford (2018: 128–64) provides an excellent discussion of communication among communities of expert drummers and their appreciative audiences.

into the creative act, something that happens everywhere in the world when performer-composers take their audience's listening and cognitive abilities, their imagination, seriously:

> The notion is similar to Bird's description of the West African Mande, whose performances are so dependent upon aesthetic tension, "the device by which the master jostles the expectancies of his audience, forcing them to participate in his act of creation" (Bird 1976: 91). Jostling expectancies, getting under the surface, reframing usual thought patterns, and evoking a dramatic response are all at the heart of Kaluli poetics, because composers force their audiences to participate in their creations by making them weep. (Feld 1990: 132)

Rhythmic play through expectation is most keenly felt at the beginning of a rock song—its intro, where the "groove" is established—at the nexus of metric understanding and entrainment. Knowing what a song's beat is, its metrical organization, is of central importance to listeners in their understanding and enjoyment of a piece (Povel and Essens 1985; Lull 1992: 20; Temperley 2001: 24, 205–6).[6] Entrainment, however, is not just about intellectual understanding; it represents more fully the reaching out for the emotional content of a song, its bodily feel as we move along both physically and emotionally (Clarke 2005: 62–90). In so doing, rhythmic entrainment has the potential for changing one's personal consciousness, a sense of individual awareness within a collective communal experience (London n.d.[a]: 10; Becker 2010: 149; Juslin et al. 2010: 626).

Two representative and contrasting examples featuring rhythmic play are analyzed in this chapter. The bands from whose work I will sample—the Police and Radiohead—were chosen for a number of commonalities:

(1) They were misunderstood at the beginning of their careers as to what kind of music they were creating, what roots they were drawing on, and what direction their music would take them

(2) They had antagonistic relationships with the press due to initial mixed critical response, at the same time forging close links with an avid and loyal fan base

(3) Unafraid of uncertainty as they looked to forge new sonic ground, they all "played" with different genres, styles, rhythms, and melodic/harmonic material

---

[6]It is also, most likely, based on evolutionary adaptations (Levitin 2006: 168–9, 171–80; Patel 2006; Sacks 2007: 240).

(4) Both groups would go on to create unique sound worlds—almost their own subgenres of rock—to later great critical and commercial acclaim

They also both happen to be British-based bands, though this is more of a coincidence and/or a reflection of my personal listening habits, rather than an exclusive marker of British rock (though see note 8).

The first example is an examination of the intro to the Police's "Bring On the Night" (1979) as representative of what I am calling a "temporary rhythmic fakeout," where listeners cannot help but be misled as to where the beats land, at least temporarily, until a "reveal" moment in which all becomes clear. The second is an example of a "complete rhythmic fakeout" in Radiohead's "Videotape" (2007), such that listeners are led astray from the beginning and then are never provided "proper" musical cues (or they are so subtle) to "correct" the listener's perception.[7] The burden for me as an analyst will be to show not only a consistent pattern of play in these artists' works in musical structural terms, but also in their expressed intent—through interviews, commentary, and/or biographies when available—to employ this play as a strategy to communicate with their audiences via a form of insider knowledge, validating their attention and listening capabilities.

Both musical excerpts are clear examples of what the theorist Mark Spicer has called an "accumulative form," the technique by which a groove is gradually built up from its constituent parts—a conscious choice to withhold structural elements—so that listeners are drawn into the compositional process in real time (playing upon, of course, a knowledgeable listener's expectations; Spicer 2004: 33, 61). His description of another Radiohead song's intro perfectly encapsulates the procedure and its effect:

> Listening to an accumulative beginning is not unlike assembling the pieces of an aural jigsaw puzzle: only when all the layers of the groove are put together can we understand the complete picture. The Radiohead example exploits a procedure that is characteristic of many accumulative beginnings: here, the addition of each new component seems to be a deliberate attempt to surprise the listener—or, at the very least, to toy with the listener's expectations—so that when the groove ultimately does crystallize it sounds as if it has "emerged" out of a state of rhythmic, metric, and/or tonal confusion. (Spicer 2004: 33)[8]

---

[7] My idea of "rhythmic fakeout" is an adaptation of "metric fake out" as conceived by the music theorist Justin London (n.d.[b]). London is interested in metrically ambiguous openings, where in this chapter it will be shown that listeners all get the meter correct, but are unclear or unaware of where the main beat is.

[8] "Examples of accumulative and cumulative forms can be found in songs written and recorded on both sides of the Atlantic, of course, and yet such forms seem to be particularly favoured by

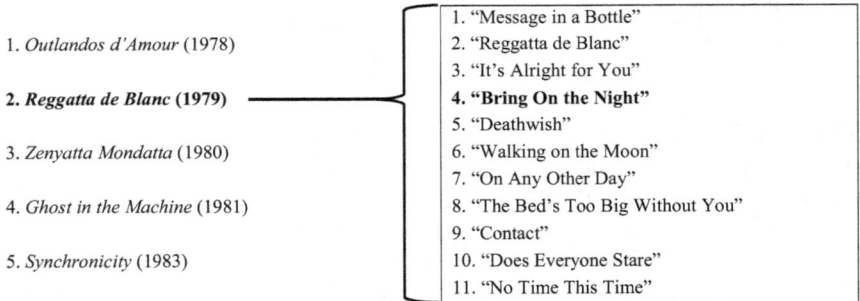

FIGURE 3.1 *Police full-length studio releases (with track listings for* Reggatta de Blanc*).*

It is the nature of this dynamic play between performer-composer and audience that I hope to reveal in the analysis that follows.

Temporary Rhythmic Fakeout: "Bring On the Night"

The brainchild of American-born Stewart Copeland (drums, percussion), the Police was formed in 1977 in London with a lineup that would eventually include British artists Sting/Gordon Sumner (bass, vocals) and Andy Summers (guitar). The coming together of three distinct musical personalities—punk (Copeland), progressive rock and classical (Summers), and jazz (Sting)—the group appeared toward the end of punk's brief but influential heyday. Their historical placement and initial preference for fast and aggressive numbers led early critics to write them off as simply one of many bands trying to break into the punk or new wave scene. With the release of their first album in 1978, and continuing on through to their fifth and last release in 1983, however, a much richer and more complex picture emerged that defied any simple genre classifications (see Figure 3.1). Mark Spicer has mapped out what he calls a "Universe of Style" for the Police, one in which reggae is the largest sphere or planet, surrounded by smaller spheres of punk, jazz, progressive rock, synth pop, music hall, blues, Baroque lament, and "Villa-Lobos" (2010: 126).[9] Such border-crossings and

---

British pop-rock composers throughout the post-Beatles era" (Spicer 2004: 30).
[9] Summers would describe the Police's sound as an entity "for which there is no previous formula, a space jam meets reggae meets Bartók collage with blue-eyed soul vocals" (2006: 192).

difficult-to-pigeonhole music served as sources of frustration for early critics of the band, as did Sting's savvy and frequently intellectual approach to lyrics and formal structures.[10]

What first drew most fans to the music of the Police—and what the band would come to recognize as central to their unique sound—was the rhythmic space they carved out between rock/punk and reggae. It was a creative tension produced by the mixing or blending of two very different approaches to rhythmic construction, often within a single song, that had seldom been attempted before:

> Punk is *rhythmically explicit* because it saturates the rhythmic texture with eight-beat timekeeping. Reggae, by contrast, is *rhythmically implicit*, because the most consistent rhythms are all afterbeats. The other rhythm lines, especially the bass, move freely, creating a rhythmic fabric of unparalleled lightness. (Campbell and Brody 1999: 335; emphasis in original)

"Play" and "space" became common metaphors by band members in interviews and personal writings on their compositional strategy that straddled both of these poles:

> For us it was the blending of rock and reggae and punk, and using the spaces that reggae provides to find a fresh approach to playing as a three-piece, rather than just banging out heavy power chords all night long. . . . (Summers, quoted in Goldsmith 2007: 90)

> Very few of the new bands had the finesse to be able to play reggae, with its complex rhythmic counterpoint that seems to turn traditional pop drumming on its head. This, and the predominance of the bass in the music, allowed Stewart and me to explore subtle areas of interplay that were rarely touched on by less experienced outfits. To create a hybrid using the drag-race horsepower of rock n roll and welding it seamlessly to the rolling stock of reggae music would make for an interesting journey. (Sting 2003: 284)[11]

---

[10]For a clear and concise biographical overview of the founding of the Police and its musical personalities, see Welch (1996: v–xiv). Each band member also wrote an informative (and highly entertaining) autobiography: Copeland (2009), Summers (2006), and Sting (2003) (see also Sting 2007).

[11]Songs that clearly feature both styles within a single composition include "So Lonely" (*Outlandos d'Amour*), "Bring On the Night" (*Reggatta de Blanc*), "Don't Stand So Close to Me" (*Zenyatta Mondatta*), and "Spirits in the Material World" (*Ghost in the Machine*). Sting would express his view on such hybrids even more succinctly in his book on lyrics: "This kind of musical juxtaposition—the lilting [reggae] rhythm of the verses separated by monolithic slabs of straight rock and roll—pleased the hell out of me" (2007: 7).

The idea of rhythmic (inter)play also featured prominently in early reviews of the Police's work (Cohen 1979: 84, 86; Fricke 1980: 104).[12]

The two most prominent aspects of reggae's move away from rock rhythm include the shifting over of the bass drum hits to beats 2 and 4, and an increased emphasis on the hi-hat part, often accentuating the off-beats. The shift away from beat 1 came to be known as the "one drop/one-drop" rhythm, signaling the dropping or emptying of the typical rock placement of the bass drum. Carlton "Carly" Barrett, drummer for Bob Marley and the Wailers (among many other artists), is credited with polishing and formalizing the term and practice, though importantly Carlton acknowledged that such language was in the air years earlier in ska recording studios (Bradley 2001: 165, 204; Potter 2012). For Stewart Copeland, it was *Burnin'* (1973) by the Wailers that really turned him on to reggae drumming and its reorganization of the snare-bass drum relationship: "That's the whole reggae thing, really, where the concept of reggae traps drums turns the patterns upside-down and backwards" (Bosso 2013).

Additionally, it was the subtle manipulation of and unexpected emphases on the off-beats (syncopations) within the hi-hat line—either through dynamic stress or a stroke on the open hi-hat, and often in combination with various crash cymbals—that Copeland drew from reggae and which he found so aesthetically pleasing; it was also what many other musicians would come to recognize as his personal imprint on rock drumming history (Starr 2009: 217–30).[13] Copeland was vocal about the pleasure he felt when engaged in such compositional-rhythmic play. In a 1981 interview with the British interviewer Jools Holland, he spoke about taking familiar rhythms and "turning them around" a bit, "camouflaging" them so that something of one's own personality, something new, might be expressed (The Police 2003).[14] In a much later interview with *Modern Drummer* magazine, Copeland added extra insight into his interest at the sixteenth-note level, co-crediting it to the music he heard when growing up in Beirut:

---

[12]For a discussion of harmonic play and space created by Summers through altered chords and alternate fingerings, as well as Sting's contribution to this sonic palette, see Sting (2003: 163), Friedland (2000), and Gress (2010).

[13]For a sampling of such hi-hat offbeat accentuation from the first two formative albums, listen to "So Lonely" (*Outlandos d'Amour*), "Roxanne" (*Outlandos d'Amour*), "Message in a Bottle" (*Reggatta de Blanc*), "Deathwish" (*Reggatta de Blanc*), "Walking on the Moon" (*Reggatta de Blanc*), and "Contact" (*Reggatta de Blanc*).

[14]Holland: "Why is your drumming different from another drummer?" Copeland: "Longer arms? I play with my feet? I suppose it's because I've stolen all my licks from different sources. You see, all the licks, they all get passed back and forth, most of them. And the trick is to find new ones and *turn them around* a bit, *camouflage* them a bit. And express yourself with the same sticks and the same cymbals and the same configuration of things to bash with new ways of doing it." [emphasis added]

Stewart: One thing that Arabic music does feature prominently is the 16th-note interest. In modern electronic music, the 16th note is not very interesting. It is metronomic. That was true even through pre-electronic pop music. People never thought about the hi-hat as providing anything other than steady 16th notes. . . . One factor is that for a long time it hadn't occurred to anyone else other than your humble servant to make use of various 16th-note interests.

MD: Do you mean as far as breaking up the 16th-note patterns on the hi-hat and splash cymbals?

Stewart: Yes, in terms of considering the inflections and doing interesting things with the accents. (Micallef 2006: 52)

Sting would similarly incorporate a reggae-influenced approach to his bass lines that would often include activity at the sixteenth-note subdivisional level (Spicer 2010: 132), something that becomes apparent in the analysis that follows.

In perhaps the only full-length academic analysis of the musical style of the Police, Spicer noted that metric conflict and play was a common trait of most of their recorded output, regardless of the presence or absence of overt references to reggae melodic and rhythmic gestures. A characteristic manifestation of this approach was the shifting of the various instrumental lines in relation to each other by a quarter or eighth note—similar in manner to the bass drum shift or the accentuation of off-beats, respectively—so that the underlying beat or meter is often obscured: "It turns out that such rhythmic displacement is quite typical of the Police's unique appropriation of the reggae style and therefore a crucial defining feature of the band's idiolect" (Spicer 2010: 133; see also Gress 2010). When such displacement occurs at the beginning of a song, unbeknownst to the listener (as it does with "Bring On the Night"), a temporary but "incorrect" anchor is created and maintained until the song reveals enough critical information, forcing the listener to re-evaluate their initial interpretation—a process which Mark Butler has referred to as "ambiguity of beginning" (2006: 124).

"Bring On the Night" was initially released as the fourth cut on side one of the 1979 album *Regatta de Blanc* (a pseudo-French translation for "white reggae"). The song and record are considered by the band to be some of their very best work (Summers 2006: 208–9; refer again to Figure 3.1 [CD track listings are provided]);[15] the song's intro also frequently elicits such adjectives from fans as "enigmatic" (Kid Charlemagne 2011) and "mysterious" (AlanTubeViewer 2011). I first heard "Bring On the Night" as a high school student and remember being intrigued by why I couldn't tap

---

[15]The title track (track 2) would go on to win the 1980 Grammy Award for Best Rock Instrumental Performance.

my foot properly to the beat during the intro and opening verse (it always came out wrong when the chorus came in). Over the years I occasionally would try out the song on family members and friends, none of whom could hear the opening properly. By the time I was a university professor I took it upon myself to play the song for numerous music history classes composed primarily of music performance majors—as well as for their professors—in an attempt to see if specialist training made any difference. The result was always the same: everyone succumbed to the rhythmic fakeout.[16]

The verse-chorus form of "Bring On the Night" is typical of many pop-rock songs: intro-verse-chorus-verse-chorus-bridge-chorus-outro. The material of the intro, however, features prominently throughout: not only is the initial intro a full twenty-seven seconds in length but both the bridge and outro also morph back into the opening strains (albeit with added guitar improvisations). The intro begins with just an electric guitar figure (modified with a flanger effect)[17] and hi-hat pattern in a four-bar phrase that repeats twice. During the third iteration of this phrase bass drum hits are added, after which the verse commences with the entry of Sting's voice, electric bass, and arpeggiated guitar (the "Villa-Lobos" sound in Spicer's aforementioned Universe of Style).

What is immediately apparent both visually and aurally is the even and regular manner in which the hi-hat strokes organize themselves into groups of four, so that it feels "right" to view the initial eighth/two sixteenths gesture as a beat 4 leading to a downbeat with the onset of regularly occurring sixteenth notes. This interpretation is reinforced by the straightforward, symmetrical divisional relationships of the guitar pitches (two eighths, eighth and two sixteenths, four sixteenths, four sixteenths, etc.) such that the listener is drawn in to treat the guitar's first sixteenth note as a pickup to a strong beat (the first eighth note in the guitar is also louder than the sixteenth note that precedes it).[18] Further metrical/bar accents are provided by the guitar's pitch changes on the sixteenth-note pickup to bars two and three, suggesting harmonic changes that align with these downbeats. Figure 3.2 provides a 4/4 realization of this interpretation, one that fits every listener's impression I have ever met (including my own).

---

[16]Classes were asked to close their eyes, so as not to be influenced by others, then silently tap out where they thought the beat landed. The uniformity of the rhythmic fakeout—the beat misplaced by an eighth note—was consistent across the various years, as was the temporary confusion and quick "correction" that occurred shortly after the beginning of the first chorus (after this students remained tapping on the proper beat, even with the entrance of the second verse). Such "evidence" is, of course, only anecdotal; an experimental study along the lines of Vazan and Schober (2004) would serve such purposes well.

[17]This opening guitar line would be played by Sting on the bass in all live performances of the piece.

[18]In musical-theoretical terms this is an example of metrical structure interacting with grouping structure (see Lerdahl and Jackendoff 1996[1983]: 28).

FIGURE 3.2 *"Bring On the Night" opening four bars (first phrase).*

FIGURE 3.3 *Entrance of bass drum (third phrase) with same metrical realization.*

With the entrance of the "syncopated" bass drum hits in the third phrase (beginning bar nine), this order is generally not disturbed (see Figure 3.3). For perhaps overly sensitive listeners, especially those familiar with Copeland's love of placing bass drum strokes squarely on beats 2 and 4 and/or those familiar with reggae drumming norms, the entrance of the bass drum signals the first clue as to where the downbeat might actually be. For most audiences, however, the continuation of the strongly marked hi-hat and guitar pitch groupings creates a bass drum line that feels syncopated through the entirety of the first verse.

Such a "musicological" listening is potentially bolstered by familiarity with the song "Edge of Seventeen" by Fleetwood Mac's Stevie Nicks from her 1981 solo album *Bella Donna*. Not only was the song released within two years of "Bring On the Night"—with many of the audiences then and now fans of both groups—but Nicks's guitarist, Waddy Wachtel, has admitted that the intro to "Edge of Seventeen" was directly lifted from the Police's composition (Simons 1999). The similarities are numerous and unmistakable, with the "Edge of Seventeen" mimicking the Police's instrumentation and instrumental timbres, organization and accentuation of the hi-hat sixteenth notes and syncopated bass drum hits, and guitar pitches and harmonic changes (moving from C to D to E), such that the "wrong" metrical interpretation (in the context of the Police song) is in fact correct (refer to Figure 3.4). Whether or not Nicks was "faked out" or preferred this metrical shift is an interesting and as yet unresolved question.

Four bars later (bar 13) marks the last change in texture before the beginning of the chorus ("Bring On the Night"). Here Sting's presence is finally felt with his bass taking over the previous guitar line (C-D-E root movement) and his singing of the first line of verse ("The afternoon has gently passed me by"); Summers (guitar) then switches to the distinctive arpeggiated pattern (refer to Figure 3.5). The metrical shift/fakeout that has been felt up to this point, however, is not altered by the entrance of the voice and new instruments. Bass gestures, an interesting mix of eighth- and sixteenth-note activity, all begin squarely on beats, with pitch/harmonic changes similarly falling on the downbeats of measures (C-D-E). The highly syncopated guitar line, which could be bracketed any number of ways, nevertheless supports this metrical interpretation by reinforcing the tonic (E) on the strong beats of every bar (beats 1 and 3). And the vocal line, which almost floats over the rest of the ensemble, starts at the beginning of a beat (beat 2) with its first resting point, the longer pitch F#, falling on a downbeat.

It is only with the onset of the first chorus that most listeners realize they have been tapping exactly one eighth note behind. The metrical reorientation occurs as Sting shifts from what was an offbeat bass line—though interpreted up to this point as on the beat—to the stereotypical reggae rhythmic pattern of <four sixteenths-two eighths-four sixteenths-two eighths> aligned with the beginnings of beats. The deception was maintained this far because of the highly syncopated approach the Police employed during the verse—

FIGURE 3.4 *"Edge of Seventeen," bars 5–8.*

FIGURE 3.5 *Entrance of arpeggiated guitar, bass, and vocal.*

offbeat accentuations in the hi-hat, a guitar part that begins on the "and" of one, and later a bass line that plays primarily on the "ands" of beats—coupled to a stripping away of beat markers for a significant period of time (bass drum hits and later guitar arpeggiations which all fall squarely on the beats).[19] Even with an intellectual understanding of such reggae conventions, the opening pull of the hi-hat and guitar accentuations are too strong for listeners to ignore; Figure 3.6 shows the "correct" way of notating the opening four bars.

I had noted earlier how a listener attuned to reggae drumming conventions might have already heard the "syncopated" bass drum hits beginning bar nine as landing squarely on beats 2 and 4. An aficionado of dancehall—a reggae style that emerged in the late 1970s but became popular in the 1980s—would have also recognized the distinctive rhythmic variant known as the "sixteen note one drop," as notated in Figure 3.7. The transcription is based on the general drum pattern found in the song "Tribulation" (1978) by the dancehall band Tappa Zukie, and while it is played at a much slower speed than "Bring On the Night," the offbeat accents on sixteenth notes played on the closed hi-hat and the placement of the bass drum hits are identical to those found in Figure 3.3 (but played in the correct rhythmic alignment; see further Niaah 2010: 15–16 and Miller 2020).

---

[19]Spicer noted a remarkably similar example in the opening instrumental track of the Alan Parson's Project album *I Robot* (1977) in which a groove opens on the "and" of a beat; here he referred to this compositional tactic as an "aural game of 'hunt the downbeat'" (2004: 35).

FIGURE 3.6 *Correct metrical realization of opening four bars.*

FIGURE 3.7 *"Sixteen Note One Drop" as played in "Tribulation."*

Within the terms set out by the cognitive scientist and musicologist David Huron, the intro to "Bring On the Night" is a classic example of the "garden path" phenomenon, one in which a listener feels they have understood a particular utterance or passage correctly, but must then reanalyze such knowledge in light of later information (2006: 29–81). The experience is also remarkably similar to Daniel Levitin's road map and joke-telling analogy:

> When a joke works, we follow a narrative path and, at the very end, the joke-teller has to surprise us to show us that we are not "where" we thought we were. If you can clearly see the punch line coming and there is no surprise, the joke isn't funny. The joke is, in essence, a joke *on you*: you realize that you *thought* you were going *here* and in fact, in the hands of the storyteller, you've ended up *way over there*. Ha! There are more ways than one to complete this path, this puzzle; this road leads to places I didn't foresee. (2009: 110; emphasis in original)

The published scores to "Bring On the Night," while differing in minor surface details, nevertheless follow the correct contours of the guitar line and, importantly, begin at the correct place (the "and" of beat 4; Luttjeboer 1996: 85 and Farncombe 2007: 66–7). Critically, however, these scores leave out the hi-hat part, so that the rhythmic tension or fakeout that unfolds doesn't show.

That the construction of the intro to "Bring On the Night" and its effect as documented above was deliberately planned by the Police was established in an interview with Copeland in a 2006 issue of *Modern Drummer* (Micallef 2006: 52–3). But do the members of the Police respect the attentiveness and listening capabilities of their audiences, really expect them to "get" such rhythmic play? Again, all three members have been articulate in interviews and print with regard to how they feel about their fans:

> Why underestimate the record-buying public? Why do you imagine that they have to be spoon-fed all the time? Does it have to be so utterly simple? I don't think so. . . . It confirms my belief that sophistication, or intended sophistication, is not the kiss of death. As long as you're grounded somewhere in common sense. (Sting, quoted in Fricke 1988: 117)

> What's characterized the music of The Police is space and the ability to draw audiences in by not playing things. We let it be suggested, so that they can come in themselves. (Andy Summers, quoted in Goldsmith 2007: 158)

> This is how it was always supposed to be. I get to go onstage with two titans of music playing songs that (1) are beautiful songs that beguile and challenge us night after night and (2) are hymns of glory to the gathered masses. Music that is known has a particular potency. If it has cool musical rips and curls, that raises the temperature, but when you get to play challenging and popular music with challenging and inspiring players this is as good as it gets. (Copeland 2009: 300)

This trust in and respect for their audiences was unfortunately dismissed by an early reviewer of the album who felt that such attention paid to compositional craft was "calculatedly middlebrow,"[20] an anxiety other critics would rehearse in their search for a misguided (in my opinion) sense of "authenticity" in rock music. The consistency and sophistication of the Police's music would eventually silence such voices.

Anecdotal evidence suggests that many fans are aware of the subtle play that occurred at the beginning of "Bring On the Night."[21] More important,

---

[20] "The group's approach [in *Reggatta de Blanc*] was relentlessly, calculatedly middlebrow: never identify, never overexplain, flatter your audience into thinking they appreciate cross-rhythms when what's really hooking them is some of the snappiest songwriting since Jerry Leiber and Mike Stoller" (Cohen 1981: 81).

[21] In December of 2011 I posted a query on the "official" video site of YouTube for "Bring On the Night" and received five positive responses within a couple of weeks (and this was on a site not visited that often). Numerous students in my music history courses told me they knew about this opening, with one even using it regularly as a "musical joke" on her friends when asked to DJ at parties, because the whole room would trip over themselves at the entrance of

however, is the attitude that is manifested by the Police in their compositions with the end goal of a special kind of communication with their audiences. It is an approach that celebrates and revels in rhythmic play in the company of their listeners as a kind of insider knowledge, a badge of shared identity. And while of course the same craft is employed in their harmonies, larger formal structure, and lyrics, to my mind it is the rhythmic complexity and interplay that contributes so significantly to the enduring quality of their music. For Sting, such play took on metaphysical dimensions: "When you watch a musician play—when he enters that private musical world—you often see a child at play innocent and curious, full of wonder at what can only be described as a mystery, a sacred mystery even" (quoted in Charlton 2003: 213).

Complete Rhythmic Fakeout: "Videotape"

Unlike the members of the Police who came from differing social circles and regional alliances, Radiohead was formed in 1985 by local friends at the elite Abingdon (Secondary) School in Oxfordshire, England: Thom Yorke (lead vocals, guitars, and keyboards), Phil Selway (drums/percussion), Ed O'Brien (guitars, backing vocals), and brothers Jonny Greenwood (guitars, keyboards) and Colin Greenwood (bass). Radiohead's early splash on the international scene came with the release of their single "Creep" in 1992, its eventual success often credited to its musical and historical proximity to work on Nirvana's *Nevermind* (1991) during grunge's commercial heyday (Randall 2011: 52–3). While Radiohead was initially pigeonholed and misunderstood as a pseudo-grunge band with their first full-length album *Pablo Honey* (1993), beginning with their second album *The Bends* (1995), and continuing on through their most recent release (*A Moon Shaped Pool*, 2016), their compositions reveal a diverse and complex world (as noted in Chapter 2).[22]

The very first strains of the opening song on their first album, "You" from *Pablo Honey*, heralded the central role rhythmic play would serve in Radiohead's overall compositional strategy. Alternating between bars of 12/8 and 11/8 (the last eighth note dropped every other measure), the song quickly and decisively signaled a departure from rock/pop norms

---

the first chorus. The theorist Mark Spicer was also quick to identify the fakeout when I first emailed him (personal communication, 2011).

[22]Further biographical information is readily available on the web (various fan and Wikipedia sites) and in print sources (see, for example, Hale 1999; Paytress 2005; Clarke 2010; and Randall 2011).

that would only become accentuated over the course of their career. Other notable examples include "Pop is Dead," a 1993 non-album single featuring 4/4 verses broken up by 10/4 instrumental breaks: "yet another example of the band's taste for subtle rhythmic play" (Randall 2011: 79); the multipart "Paranoid Android" (*OK Computer*) with contrasting meters within a single song, including phrases of 7/4: "[r]hythmic play comes to the fore once again" (Randall 2011: 151); the rhythmically shifting and unfolding of the intro to "Packt like sardines in a crushd tin box" (*Amnesiac*) in which audiences are temporarily deceived—a kind of rhythmic fakeout akin to the previous Police example—through the use of an accumulative beginning, "a defining feature of Radiohead's style" (Spicer 2004: 33, n.14); and the intro to "2+2=5" (*Hail to the Thief*) which features Thom Yorke's voice floating over a complex meter of 7/8 (refer to Figure 3.8).

Within the larger spheres of meaning Radiohead has created through their lyrics, music, and artwork, however, such rhythmic play is properly understood as part of the broader project of ambiguity and the tacit encouragement of fans to dig below surface appearances. Beginning with *The Bends*, Radiohead has purposefully nurtured a relationship based on trust and creative play with its audiences by creating imagery, sounds, and words—including videos, websites, and clothing—rife with intentional vagueness and/or multiplicity of meanings that reward careful readings and

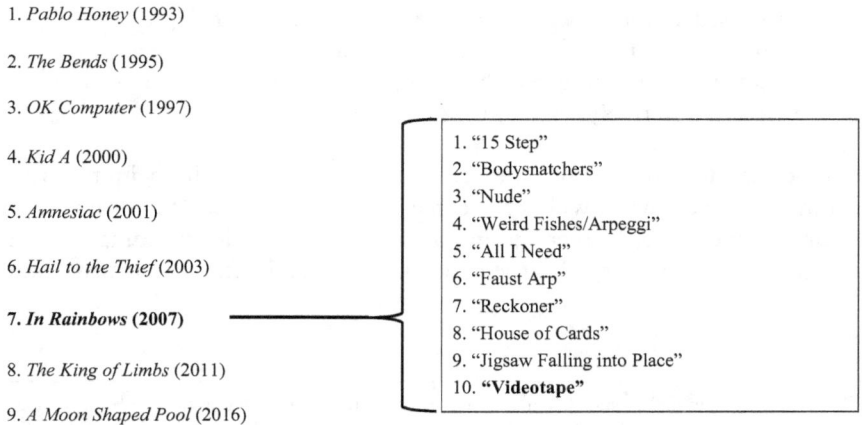

FIGURE 3.8 *Radiohead full-length studio releases (with track listings for* In Rainbows*).*

listenings.[23] As noted in Chapter 2, "The band's reflexive esthetic effectively disrupts naïve consumption, confronting the listener with music and art that adheres to opacity versus authenticity as a guiding principle" (Tate 2005b: 115; see also Forbes and Reisch 2009; Randall 2011: 106).

After what seemed like a four-year recording hiatus to its fans, Radiohead independently released *In Rainbows* in 2007, initially as a pay-what-you-want download (more on this later in the chapter). Having ended their long-term contract with Parlophone/EMI in 2003, the album came as a welcome relief amid rumors that the band had split up. In the interim Thom Yorke had released his first solo album, *The Eraser* (2006), while Jonny Greenwood composed music for two soundtracks (*Bodysong*, 2004, and *There Will Be Blood*, 2007), heralding the beginning of a long and successful "second" career. Nevertheless, the album reached #1 on the album charts in the United Kingdom, the United States, Canada, Ireland, and France, and to date, it remains one of their best-selling and critically acclaimed releases (it won Grammy Awards for both Best Alternative Album and Best Boxed or Special Limited Edition Package).[24]

Compared to the fanfare that surrounded the "controversial nature" of the album's sale and distribution—later to be drowned out by widespread, glowing reviews and the release of five other of the ten tracks as singles—"Videotape" seemed almost an afterthought, snuck in at the end of the album. The piece was important to Yorke, however, as revealed in a BBC Radio 4 interview held on February 2, 2008, just one month after the physical album's US release:

> Interviewer: Do you have a favourite song on the record [*In Rainbows*]?
> Thom: "Videotape." I wanted to put it first, ... Personally speaking, that's my favourite thing we've ever created, because it has this inexpressible substance thing going on behind the specifics of the song. So I'm really, really proud of that.

Internet chatter and a few sentences in print interviews both immediately before and after the download became available spoke to the difficulty of recording the piece, further hinting at some kind of hidden compositional or performative mystery. But the general public made little or no fuss about

---

[23]Where in certain fields such as literature, philosophy, and mathematics ambiguity refers only to passages or events that have two or more possible meanings or interpretations (e.g., Blackburn 2006: 12), I include along with this understanding the secondary ideas of uncertainty and opacity.

[24]*Rolling Stone* magazine called *In Rainbows* "their most expansive and seductive album, possibly their all-time high" (Anonymous 2011); *The Guardian* felt "that it may represent the strongest collection of songs Radiohead have assembled for a decade, ... ventur[ing] into new emotional territories" (Petridis 2007).

> "The Hidden Syncopation of Radiohead's 'Videotape'" [38:15]
> December 15, 2016 by WARRENMUSIC [https://www.youtube.com/watch?v=RvKhtFXPswk]
>
> "The Secret Rhythm behind Radiohead's 'Videotape'" [10:14]
> August 4, 2017 by VOX [https://www.youtube.com/watch?v=p_IHotHxIl8]
>
> "The Author Is Both Dead And Alive, or the Vox 'Videotape' Aftermath" [29:39]
> August 11, 2017 by WARRENMUSIC [https://www.youtube.com/watch?v=p_IHotHxIl8]
>
> "Rhythmic Displacement in Radiohead's Videotape" [1:06]
> August 12, 2017 by Jonathan Palmquist [https://www.youtube.com/watch?v=7M7FRpvUf8M]
>
> "Radiohead and the Rhythmic Illussion [sic]" [9:51]
> November 23, 2017 by David Bruce [https://www.youtube.com/watch?v=kBNvPb331SQ]

FIGURE 3.9 *Fan-created YouTube content related to Radiohead's "Videotape."*

the song, especially when compared to the work it is often associated with, "Pyramid Song." That would all change dramatically, however, nine years later.

On December 15, 2016, a YouTube video with the title "The Hidden Syncopation of Radiohead's 'Videotape'" was posted by WARRENMUSIC, the internet handle of Warren Lain, a 2005 graduate of UCLA's undergraduate program in ethnomusicology (Warren reveals this personal information in a later posting). Clocking in at roughly 38 minutes, the video is a beautiful testament to one fan's creative and passionate engagement with the band and this song, and he approaches the task like a detective trying to solve a complex riddle. While I will say more about the content of this video later in the chapter, the main discovery he makes is that Yorke and Radiohead have apparently written a piece in which the piano chords as rhythmic anchor of the song sound like they're all on the beat, but are actually all syncopated, such that they sound an eighth note before it.

Even with the typically rabid and vocal Radiohead fan community, not even Warren could have predicted the heated debates and flurry of videos that would be produced to respond to his work. Figure 3.9 shows Warren's initial posting, followed by YouTube content generated specifically addressing his claims. While all the videos caught the basic facts confirming what Warren had indicated, none of them explained the phenomenon from start to finish with all of the required steps, illustrated by clear notational examples. And so I take us back to the beginning to make sense of this all, even before the release of the album, though not without first introducing the "official" sheet music with a few comments on what the studio recording of "Videotape" presents the first-time listener.[25]

---

[25] As noted in Chapter 2, commercially released scores are generally prepared by professional editorial teams, not by the artists themselves.

FIGURE 3.10 *Score version, (a) one cycle of piano part, core cell; (b) entrance of electric bass, one cycle.*

The commercially released score of "Videotape," what I will henceforth refer to as the "score version" of the song, is set in 4/4 with piano chords landing on every beat (Weeks and Davis 2011: 128–31; see Figure 3.10). From the beginning up through the entrance of the drums at 1:20, the piece evokes a floating or dreamy state, achieved through rhythmic and tonal ambiguities. As a listener and/or score reader, one first notices that the piano part features a 3-bar phrase—an unusual phrase length rhythm for rock music—which serves as a core cell, repeated over and over with occasional slight variations (later in the piece it moves to 4-bar phrases). The top line of the piano, however, repeats every bar, creating an internal asymmetry within the right hand (1 bar + 1 bar + 1 bar, versus the lower line of 1 bar + 2 bars), and if one charts the entrance of the voice phrases against the beginning of the piano core cell, we see during the fourth repetition of the cell Yorke singing only 2 bars, then restarting "early," creating a further blurring of phrase lengths. Tonally this is set against passages that can be felt either individually or in combination as F♯ minor, F♯ Dorian, or A major, the A major feeling frequently reinforced by the electric bass line.[26]

The score indicates 84 beats per minute to the quarter note—though I believe 78 beats per minute is more accurate—with every piano chord

---

[26] The score is set in E major, which is almost certainly a mistake. D♯ only appears for a few seconds in a wordless, descant background vocal part, where it sounds chromatic or "odd"; and it shows up again toward the end of the piece buried in a couple of piano chord clusters. The content and movement of the voice and piano parts strongly suggest F♯ minor (or F♯ Dorian if one accounts for the D♯), and occasionally A major.

FIGURE 3.11 *Score version, entrance of drum set, one cycle (1:20-).*

occupying a beat (true for the entire piece). This falls on the low end of the spectrum of preferred beat speeds between 70 and 125 beats per minute (De Clercq 2016: paragraphs 2.1-2.5), though I suspect almost everyone would hear the piano chords as quarter notes.[27] This orientation is not called into question when the drums enter at 1:20 (refer to Figure 3.11), which features bass drum hits (floor tom?) on beats 1 and 3 at this speed—very typical of rock music—preceded by what sound like sixteenth-note snare rim shots. It would be easy to imagine these snare hits as syncopated backbeats, especially as all other instrumental parts are landing "on" the beats (piano, bass, and bass drum). A secondary electronic percussion line then emerges that initially has a distinct onset, but soon elongates and blurs; I have not included this in Figure 3.11.

Well into the second half of the song at 3:05, a new percussion texture appears with softer bass drum hits on every beat, and a new syncopated hi-hat that elaborates on the original snare part (refer to Figure 3.12). Roughly 30 seconds later the snare rim shot returns, still sounding before every bass drum hit, but now four times per bar. Even with the entrance of the various drum parts, there is little or nothing in "Videotape" sonically that would suggest to a "regular" listener, myself included, that there was anything else going on rhythmically behind the scenes.

This is where many general fans found themselves when Warren's video of late 2016 appeared, making the bold claim that the piano, electric bass, and bass drum were all syncopated in relation to the rest of the drum lines, landing an eighth note before the masked or "real" beat. For the few that had been trolling the various Radiohead websites and YouTube videos since 2005, however, the clues were all revealed by the band as to their compositional intent, though it takes a bit of work to properly put the entire puzzle together. We now go back to the beginning to briefly but logically

---

[27]De Clercq goes into more detail outlining this wide range of speeds, though he settles on 120 beats per minute as "the best available approximation of ideal tempo, given a time signature of 4/4" (2016: paragraph 2.6).

FIGURE 3.12 *Score version, (a) addition of hi-hat (3:05-); (b) addition of snare (3:37-).*

show how the song evolved, and how to the band, at least, the piece is conceived and embodied in performance.[28]

The title of the song appears on a blackboard outlining the band's two weeks of rehearsals from September 19 to 30, 2005, and again on March 8, 2006, suggesting it will be part of their setlist for an upcoming tour (a portion of the lyrics are posted online on April 5, 2006). Sometime in May (?) of that year the band posts a photo of Thom Yorke outside with his head down and right hand over his face looking dejected or tired; initially

---

[28] I'd like to acknowledge the two citizeninsane websites related to "Videotape" that helped me locate most of the general details in the discussion that follows (https://citizeninsane.eu/music/inrainbows.html, and http://citizeninsane.wikia.com/wiki/Videotape). All interpretive comments and analysis, however, are my own.

the photo was titled "Videotape!Again!" There is not much to go on here, but one immediately questions why this image was associated with this particular song.

On May 18 "Videotape" is premiered by Radiohead at London's Hammersmith Apollo, where it opens their set. The drum set playing is different from the studio version, though some of the elements are already here (such as the syncopated hi-hat part). Crucially, however, about 3/4 of the way through the song there is what I would call a "Pyramid Song" or "reveal" moment where Phil Selway suddenly switches from a syncopated or rhythmically ambiguous line to a more traditional rock music texture with strong backbeats in the snare. That moment immediately reorients the listener, with two important discoveries: (1) the piano chords and electric bass now land on the "ands" of the beats, and (2) the piano chords are half notes, occurring two to the bar. Had Radiohead chosen to stick with this arrangement, none of the material or mystery I introduced in this chapter would exist.

The band is clearly not happy with this rhythmic setup, as revealed in an interview for *Rolling Stone* online between David Fricke and Thom Yorke on June 1:

> [David Fricke]: How would you describe the status of the next Radiohead album?
>
> Thom: We have roughs of things. We have maybe half of something so far. There's another six tunes we haven't started playing live yet. There's one called "Videotape" that's really cool. It's got lots of cyclical melodies. It's one of the first things we had. We were smashing our heads against the wall, trying to figure out what to do with it. Sometimes that drives me crazy.[29]

It's unclear why the more obvious version doesn't satisfy Yorke and company. Perhaps it gives too much away? Maybe it isn't challenging enough to perform? But later that month, almost exactly a month after the premiere of the piece, Radiohead plays it again at their June 17 performance at Bonnaroo in Manchester, Tennessee. This time Selway maintains a syncopated approach throughout, sometimes playing the snare "on" the beat (according to the score), other times "off."

Later in 2006 in November Yorke performs "Videotape" with only a piano for the first episode of his producer Nigel Godrich's *From the Basement* program (it was later released in 2008 as a B-side to the 45 SP "Jigsaw Falling Into Place"). Though you can't see below his waist initially,

---

[29] This interview was also published in print in the *Rolling Stone* June 15 edition, but these comments on "Videotape" were not included.

you can hear him tapping his foot against the piano, always preceding a piano chord (as a backbeat?). And at 2:05 into the performance, as the camera pans outward, so you can see he's clearly moving one of his legs at the faster, double speed (compared to the score) so that the piano chords are indeed half notes and are syncopated against a beat that Yorke is feeling in his body, but which is not sounding. He follows up on this performance in a posting on Radiohead's site on December 18:

www.from thebasement.tv

> this site is up now . . . and luckily they have the facts straight about the songs . . . so no beef do i have no more.
> so that's alright then.
> "videotape" i was very proud of. and it doesn't sound the like the version that we are working on now..
> which is even better . . .
> they are sketches obviously just me on the piano. check it oot.

In Rainbows is released online on October 10, 2007; the physical release comes out on December 3, 2007, in the United Kingdom and January 1, 2008, in the United States. On November 9, 2007, Yorke is again interviewed, this time by David Byrne for *Wired* magazine and published on December 18. The pertinent excerpt reads as follows:

> TY: Oh God we tried torturously many—. I mean, I can't think of an example. I mean "Videotape" was the absolute—uh, the last track—the last track was the absolute agony, because that went through every possible parameter. I had an absolute obsession that it should be umm—like Surgeon, which is really hard, you know, uh, post-rave trance track. [Laughs.]
> DB: [Laughs.]
> TY: And umm . . . Tried endlessly, you know? [Laughs.]
> DB: [Laughs.]
> TY: And to be fair to the others, they didn't—they didn't—as they possibly should've done—kick me out of the room. Uh, but—uh, you know—we tried and possibly we got something out of it but probably not. But you know, and the other thing was that—with that track—was that Jonny was absolutely obsessed about the fact that the piano was in the wrong, you know, the piano was ahead—it's an eighth ahead of where the one is. [Laughs.] The one is an eighth ahead. And he wanted to just stuck to the whole rhythm an eighth ahead. So you—but it didn't. It was a constant argument about where the one was. [Laughs.]
> DB: [Laughs.] Yeah, yeah!

TY: And shifting it and blah-blah. And then we ended up with something really, really bad, you know. And what happened was I left the—funny enough, I left the studio—. [Laughs.]

DB: [Laughs.]

TY: —for, like, most of the day. [Laughs.] Came back in the evening, umm, and Jonny and Nigel had stripped everything away. And what we were left with is what was on the record. So there you go[30]

Here we finally have Yorke saying out loud that "the piano ... is an eighth ahead of where the one is," which only makes sense if the piano chords are half notes since otherwise, everything is a sixteenth note off (such as what we saw in Figure 3.11).

On New Year's Day, 2008, Radiohead surprises their fans by releasing a live performance of *In Rainbows* from an undisclosed location in Oxfordshire (the "Scotch Mist" version) on the internet. From here on out the masked beat approach, like the studio release, became the norm for "Videotape" in live performances. Two follow-up comments over the next couple of years also cemented the band's commitment to this hidden downbeat and proper sense of pulse. The first is by Selway in an online interview for <exitmusic.com.ar>, posted April 7, 2009:

> From rehearsals, right through to the studio, it took me about two years to find the "1" in the bar—and even then, someone had to hit me round the head to show me where it was.

The second is by Godrich, most likely posted in 2012 on an AtEase online Radiohead discussion list:

> Well frankly like everything in life it depends how you look at it, but technically speaking the piano chords are all pushed—ie. before the beat ... that's how thom hears it in his head even if it's possible to think of it as on the beat. I hear it both ways. ... You? Begs the question ... if you hear the chords on the beat and you love the song does it matter? I don't think so!

Visual confirmation of this all is provided by the bass player, Colin Greenwood, who can be seen in any video footage on YouTube to be bouncing his head and body to the faster speed.

---

[30]The online version included accompanying audio files of the entire interview; excerpts were released in hard copy in January, 2008, under the title "The Radiohead Revolution," though again (interestingly) no comments on "Videotape" were included in the print version. A transcript of the entire interview can be accessed at: https://citizeninsane.eu/media/usa/etc/07/i01t_2007-11-09_wired.htm

FIGURE 3.13 *Radiohead version, entrance of drum set, one cycle (1:20-).*

To help understand why Selway (and the rest of the band) had trouble with the percussion part, I've created the "proper" notation of the entrance of the drum in what I'm calling the "Radiohead Version" (see Figure 3.13). The snare rim shots can now be seen to land on every beat 4, typical of rock drumming when interpreted as half of the backbeat, but the bass drum hits are placed an eighth note early (before beat 1), coinciding with every other piano chord. I should point out that only the August 11, 2017 video by Warren Lain clearly identifies why the piano chords should be half notes as we see here, and hence why the official score is incorrect (all the others essentially get it right, but don't explain how they came to their conclusions).

Figure 3.14 shows the next two major entrances of the drum set, analogous to Figure 3.12, but with this new configuration we now feel the hi-hat as unsyncopated, landing on every beat 2, 3, and 4 (3.14a), and the later return of the snare as landing on beats 2 and 4, the full rock backbeat now fully realized (3.14b). It's fascinating to consider that Selway might have borrowed the rim shot backbeat with bass drum syncopation we see in Figure 3.14 from the previous album, *Hail to the Thief* (2003), where he plays this exact part in the song "There There." It's also clear that Yorke enjoyed this feeling of playing an entire song with the keyboard playing on the off-beats, an approach that reappears in the song "The Mother Lode" on his solo release of 2014, *Tomorrow's Modern Boxes*.[31]

As the music theorist Leonard Meyer already documented more than fifty years ago, the expectation that results from a doubtful or ambiguous musical

---

[31] With "The Mother Lode," however, Yorke has bass drum hits that enter relatively early in the song in the "correct" place, giving an early cue as to where the beat proper might be.

FIGURE 3.14 *Radiohead version, (a) addition of hi-hat (3:05-); (b) addition of snare (3:37-).*

passage—a feeling of suspense—is often pleasant for a listener, depending on how long it takes for such clarification or resolution to occur (1956: 26–8). With "Bring On the Night" by the Police this "eureka" moment is obvious and predictable, while with "Videotape" it might not ever happen, or it will encourage curious listeners to dig deeper into what the band and other fans have said. For Warren and the legion of Radiohead fans who chimed in on the hidden syncopation, the withholding of metrical cues at the beginning of the song created a fertile space to construct their own rich body of meanings, foregrounding uncertainty and mystery over predictability:

> Delaying a cadence, or creating uncertainty about any other learnt musical pattern, boosts the eventual reward (assuming that it comes at all). And

the hiatus sharpens our attention, obliging us to concentrate and search for clues about what the music will do, rather than riding on a wave of tepid, blithe predictability. The music, in short, becomes *more interesting* when it is *less predictable*. And when the final tonic chord arrives [or the proper placement of the beat becomes apparent], what would have been a mildly pleasant sense of completion becomes a flood of delight, even awe. (Ball 2010: 285; emphasis in original)

As I've noted in both this chapter and Chapter 2, Radiohead is clearly aware of the curiosity and passion with which their fans pore over their often cryptic comments and ambiguous references spread out over websites, interviews, videos, and their published work. They have also been quite clear in print and media interviews about their trust in their fans' ability to "get" the subtlety of their work:

People underestimate what the general public is capable of listening to. . . . It's not above people's heads. People get it. We're [just] people making it, [so] other people are capable of getting it. (Ed O'Brien, quoted in Randall 2011: 182)

You want to slap [industry] people and say, "Why don't you go back and look at all the beautiful things that have been made in the music business and realize that you have to have faith in people?" In the long run, the industry wants to make money, but if a company wants to make money then it has to take a risk. These people don't take risks. They make quick money and then that's it. And the world isn't a nicer place for it. (Thom Yorke, quoted in Ross 2010: 100–1)

But the real proof is in the ongoing relationship that has been nurtured and maintained between Radiohead and its audiences from the very beginning, how the members have placed their trust in the fans' interpretive insights, ruminations, and, critically, their ability to make the right ethical choices. As has already been amply documented, *In Rainbows* was initially released digitally with the option left open for what to pay for the download, including nothing at all. Fans were also encouraged to create and donate their own music videos, were provided access to original music files to create their own original works, and were given outlets to write their own reviews before the press was sent the standard media packet (see Lawson 2009: 61–79 and Randall 2011: 235–40, 254–6). Since that time Radiohead has also released a concert DVD free of charge in which the band donated the audio masters and cover art, but the fans were responsible for providing all of the video footage ("Strictly Not for Sale—By the Fans for the Fans,

Please Share and Enjoy"),[32] and in 2011 various DJs around the world were given masters to their next record *The King of Limbs* to produce their own mixes, released later as a collection titled *Radiohead TKOL RMX 1234567*.

Conclusion

The theorist David Temperley in an article on syncopation in rock music argued that metrical ambiguity and the blurring of an underlying pulse was common in classical music, but was infrequent in most kinds of rock (1999: 35). While I understand the importance he placed on metrical regularity and identification in rock and popular music, I believe that the examples provided in my analysis—while perhaps exceptional in the degree to which they are challenging—are nevertheless indicative of a broader trend. Rhythmic play through metrical-structural manipulation was a central and defining feature of not only the two songs examined here but of most of the output of both the Police and Radiohead, as it is of many bands who achieved great commercial and critical success (not to mention the realms of jazz-rock and "math metal"). Entire books could be filled with examples of rock music in which rhythmic-metrical ambiguity takes place in different parts of the song, instrumental and vocal lines overlap while sectional markers become unclear, or two (or more) different meters occur at the same time.

With "Bring On the Night" it was Spicer's accumulative form, achieved through a temporary rhythmic fakeout, that came to the fore. The opening groove provided only snippets of the forthcoming texture, the compositional process laid bare as listener expectations were toyed with until clarification finally occurred. For such a process to take hold, I believe, a delicate balance must be achieved between complexity and intelligibility: expectations and interest must be aroused, whether or not listeners are cognizant of such play, without excessive deception that leaves audiences frustrated or merely confused. In the example provided by "Bring On the Night" a full (but relatively brief) verse must pass before aware listeners realize they have been tapping their foot exactly one eighth note off the main beat. Part of the fun of this track for myself—as it must be for others, including members of the Police, I would imagine—is that a number of audience members are not entirely aware of what has just happened. As the chorus enters they might interpret the "new" beat as a kind of hiccup, perhaps even a skip in the CD player.

---

[32]Fans were specifically invited to bring their own video cameras to a performance on August 23, 2009, in Prague to collaborate on the project. A website has been created with the final results (http://radiohead-prague.nataly.fr/Main.html).

The same phenomenon, feeling the proper meter but being thrown off by an eighth note, is realized in a very different way with "Videotape." For most listeners, the delayed entrance of the various drum sounds does not alter their sense of where the main beats are, and so I have described this as a complete rhythmic fakeout. And yet it is clear that Yorke and other members of Radiohead's inner circle wanted for their fans to understand what they were doing, if they so chose, and perhaps to at least attempt to hear and feel the song the way they do. As Nigel Godrich noted above, however, in the end, the choice to hear the chords on or off the beat is up to the listener, with both ways equally valid and potentially enrapturing.

The significance of such play beyond the structural-compositional interest is the special form of communication that takes place between the composer-performer and the listener. When artists engage in such activity with their audiences specifically in mind, as did the Police and Radiohead, the act reflects the unfolding of a collaborative aesthetics, one in which the concerted effort of the fans is rewarded with a kind of shared insider knowledge. Bands and their audiences thus become joined through an understanding of such compositional-performative play, an extended community based on trust, respect, and shared ownership. Distances that are otherwise inherent to the modern listening experience—those of space, time, and context—are brought that much closer, even collapsed, when such communication is the goal. Expanding our gaze outward, this celebration of rhythmic play further links us with music-making around the globe, even with humanity itself.

4

The Backbeat as Expressive Device in Rock Music

Introduction

The backbeat, generally understood as when beats 2 and 4 in a quadruple meter bar are accented or marked in some way, remains the most common and distinctive rhythmic feature of post-1950s popular music. Growing up, it was the prominent snare backbeat that could be heard all over the house that drove my mother crazy, and she would have been sympathetic to the following perspective:

> It [the backbeat] stalks the desolate landscape of pop, stamping its jackboot of conformity upon all those who oppose its rules of metrical oppression. Twice in each bar. (Bennett 2013)

While the author of this quote is speaking a bit tongue-in-cheek, he does highlight common perceptions about the perceived banality and straightjacketing effect of the backbeat. Its ubiquity and apparent simplicity perhaps account for why commentators tend to relegate the backbeat to purely a time-keeping role, and why variations in its employment and the resultant meanings that have accrued over multiple decades and genres have only recently drawn concerted academic attention.

The importance of the backbeat in drawing in listeners and/or dancers physically and cognitively cannot be overstated. In addition to providing moments in which participants can clap along in synchrony with others, the backbeat also sets up perceptual anchors for understanding at what speed level an artist is most likely feeling their work, creating a framework for understanding and enjoying other compositional strategies and subtleties

(Abel 2014: 49–59; Laing 2015: 79; Hanenberg 2018). Even if the backbeat does not always reveal the "proper" way to understand measure lengths and meter as conceived of by the composer/artist (see de Clercq 2016), it does provide key moments for listeners to entrain regardless of compositional intent. In the case studies that follow, it is by paying close attention to the placement of the backbeat in relation to rock music norms that will reward us with a much broader and richer perspective on the backbeat than as merely a timekeeper.

This chapter focuses on the creative use of the backbeat as an expressive device to create considerable intellectual and emotional interest. Numerous and detailed studies have explored microtiming fluctuations in the placement of the backbeat as an expressive device, which is standard in academic studies of the backbeat and expressivity (Butterfield 2010: 164, 168–72; Iyer 2002: 398; Frühauf et al. 2013). My use of the term "expressive," however, expands from this micro-level focus to the broader and more interpretive understanding of conveying a quality, idea, or mood. In locating examples of the manipulation of the backbeat to achieve these effects, I've chosen well-known, common/popular artists and songs with a "regular" listener and average listening disposition in mind—the unusual but readily comprehensible hiding in plain sight. The chapter closes with a brief Coda where I explore backbeats in non-4/4 time (considered irregular in a rock music context).

The backbeat raises a number of challenges to Western historical and musicological norms or assumptions with regard to meter. And as the backbeat became prominent and associated with early rock 'n' roll, its feel fueled racialized (and hence racist) understandings of its origins and significance. These theoretical and sociocultural contexts need to be laid bare first before moving to the case studies that make up the bulk of this chapter.

Western Metrical Hierarchies

In 1968, the esteemed conductor, composer, French horn player, and music historian Gunther Schuller published his highly influential book *Early Jazz: Its Roots and Musical Development*. Now considered one of the first serious musicological treatments of the subject, it represents perhaps the earliest challenge to Western music theory's insistence that meter is based on internal hierarchies, with beats 1 and 3 stressed or marked more than beats 2 and 4:

> By the "democratization" of rhythmic values, I mean very simply that in jazz so-called weak beats (or weak parts of rhythmic units) are *not* underplayed as in "classical" music. Instead, they are brought up to the level of strong beats, and very often even emphasized *beyond* the strong beat. The jazz musician does this not only by maintaining an equality of

dynamics among "weak" and "strong" elements, but also by preserving the full sonority of notes, even though they may happen to fall on weak parts of the measure. . . . Another manifestation of the same principle is the so-called drum backbeat on the second and fourth beat of a bar. (Schuller 1968: 8–9; emphasis in original)

A few pages later, Schuller directly credits this "democratization" or equalization of rhythmic values to the Africanization of Western popular music (Schuller 1968: 16).

While the backbeat arose independently of African cultural influences (to be addressed further in the subsection that follows),[1] Schuller did anticipate later research by ethnomusicologists such as David Locke who in the 1990s introduced the idea of accentless meter in African music, with every beat receiving the same accent (Locke 1998: 19; see also London 2012: 137). Whether one agrees with this position or not, on philosophical grounds—at least from a Western musical-theoretical perspective—meter cannot exist without at least implied accents or strong positions within a bar (and, as Mark Abel has raised, it also negates the possibility of syncopation, at least as conceived of in the West; 2014: 89–91). Accentless meter has been criticized numerous times by Kofi Agawu, who reminds us that most West and Central African rhythms are also danced, such that even when "just listening" the participant is either moving or imagining the movement of the feet (Agawu 2003: 73; see also London 2012: 132). This is an extremely important and often overlooked point in musical studies: with dance, we immediately have (at the very least) a binary division of perception and organization, which automatically distinguishes or marks the beats.

Even without this search for cross-cultural influences or resonances, the backbeat in Western popular music genres presents a challenge to the traditionally understood relationship between strong and weak beats in a 4/4 bar. For many generations of listeners, performers, and composers born from the 1950s on, the backbeat has been heard in almost every genre and song they have ever encountered, running into astronomical numbers of occurrences. To suggest that they can only hear these beats as "syncopations" seems unlikely, if not incomprehensible. And yet leading popular music scholars, when addressing metrical accents and syncopation in rock and pop music, accept (and sometimes even quote) the model of a four-beat bar with strong beats on 1 and 3 as theorized in Fred Lerdahl and Ray Jackendoff's now-classic *A Generative Theory of Tonal Music*, even though the latter's work is based almost exclusively on common-practice classical music (1996[1983]: 68–104).

---

[1] See Abel (2014: 54), Tamlyn (1998: 157–9), Jasen and Tichenor (1978: 4), and Floyd and Reisser (1984: 36).

And so David Temperley in a highly cited article on syncopation in rock music (1999) can speak of strong beats on beats 2 and 4 as syncopation, as it involves a deviation from a "normal" placement of an accent, even though the accented backbeat has been the norm for more than 70 years, or even 120 years if we allow marches into our historical overview. Or David Huron and Ann Ommen in an article specifically on syncopation in American popular music from 1890 to 1939 can similarly look at beats 2 and 4 as "weak" beats, even though no mention is made of military band music or its "backbeats" being played and enjoyed everywhere in America during that time period (2006).[2] Or Walter Everett in his impressive book on the foundations of rock music nevertheless identifies the backbeat as a common form of syncopation, "working against the regular underlying strong-weak pattern of the *natural* metric accent" (2009: 10; emphasis added).

A middle ground is suggested by Justin London, when he suggests that the backbeat represents a normal and recurring dynamic accent, versus a metric accent on beats 1 and 3 (2012: 19). Nicole Biamonte in her work on metric dissonance in rock music takes this a step further, suggesting that the backbeat is an example of a "displacement consonance":

> Because it is an essential component of the meter, functioning as a timeline—a rhythmic ostinato around which the other parts are organized—I consider the backbeat in rock music to be an instance of displacement consonance rather than dissonance. I hold this view in part because there is still an accent on beats 1 and 3, as demonstrated by the propensity of musically untrained listeners to clap on beats 1 and 3 of a backbeat rather than 2 and 4 (see Hein 2013). More importantly, the backbeat is contextually consonant because it is a basic rhythmic unit that typically continues throughout the song, with no expectation of a resolution to a consonant pattern. (2014: paragraph 6.2)

Mark Butler gets even closer to where I think we should be: "In rock, funk, and other traditions with roots in African-American musical practice, strong phenomenal accents on the second and fourth beats of the measure are so pervasive that this trait can be regarded as normative . . . there is little reason to regard the attacks on beats 2 and 4 as belonging elsewhere" (2006: 87).[3] And for Anne Danielsen, the traditionally understood strong-weak relationships are completely inverted:

---

[2] The authors do openly question the assumptions about relative weights or strengths of the different beats, but then for reasons that are unclear to me choose to analyze the frequency distribution of note onsets in Germanic folk melodies, not military-marching band music that was much more prominent and popular (2006: 214).

[3] A related issue, though one I will not pursue here, is whether or not backbeats are anacrustic or continuational in nature; see Attas (2011: 36–9), Biamonte (2014: paragraph 6.1), and Butterfield (2006: paragraph 40).

As mentioned, it is important to emphasize that in this context [West African cross-rhythms] the time signature 4/4 does not imply a beat sequence of strong-weak-strong-weak, as is often the rule within classical music. How the beats are weighted varies from genre to genre. The sequence might well be quite the opposite: weak-strong-weak-strong, as in a typical backbeat. Every beat might also be equal in weight, as Arom claims for African rhythm in general, or, as with much funk, the first beat might be the only quarter that stands out as a really heavy beat. (2006: 45)[4]

The real revelation for me, however, came with my discovery of Mark Abel's *Groove: An Aesthetic of Measured Time* (2014), a book I have already cited liberally in this chapter. Possibly the best scholarship I have read on groove, meter, and rhythm in popular music, it is with his interpretation of Victor Zuckerkandl's work (1973[1956]: 169) that I feel we get the closest to what the backbeat achieves within a metrical context:

> For beats "two" and "four" to become the emphasized beat without becoming the strong beats would seem to require a radical revision of our understanding of what constitutes meter.[5] A key insight here is provided by Zuckerkandl who argues that the conventional view of meter is erroneous. Meter is not produced from a pattern of strong and weak accents but is much better understood as oscillation, as a 1—2—1—2 etc., where "2" is not weak but "away-from-one." At the heart of meter is a cyclical motion or wave comprising a motion of "to-fro" or "away-back," and the standard understanding of causality in meter must be reversed: "it is not a differentiation of accents which produces meter, it is meter which produces a differentiation of accents." (Abel 2014: 50)

This argument is persuasive to me for two key reasons: (1) this view allows for the backbeat to occupy a metrical position that does not automatically afford it a "syncopated" status (how can one interpret the backbeat as a "displacement" of a normal musical accent, when it is omnipresent and omniaccented); and (2) it brings to the fore our embodied engagement with popular music through metaphors of motion in which dance and the movement between our two feet is central to its understanding and appreciation (while simultaneously reinforcing one of the key features of entrainment).[6]

---

[4]While Danielsen will dedicate an entire chapter to the importance of beat 1 in funk music (Chapter 5: 73–91), she doesn't discuss the inverted weak-strong of the backbeat anywhere else in her book and how it might challenge the beat one dominance hypothesis, even though it is present in most of her analytical samples.
[5]This is a reference to Gracyk (1996: 134–5), who makes the argument that because of the prominence of the backbeat, beat 1 is no longer the strongest.
[6]See also Blom (1981).

Throughout the rest of this chapter, I will assume that a percussion backbeat that lands squarely on a beat 2 or 4 in a four-beat bar is a consonant gesture and that strokes that occur before (early) or after (late) these positions will constitute syncopation.

The Big Beat

By 1955 the "Big Beat"—aka rock 'n' roll—had planted its roots firmly on US soil. Whether or not one places the advent of the genre at the feet of Alan Freed and his misattributed coining of the term in 1951 in Cleveland, or with Sam Phillips and his discovery of Elvis in 1954 in Memphis, or (more accurately) with the convergence of numerous artists, musical styles, and commercial practices from the previous decade, the large-scale recognition and wildfire-like spread of the new musical form brought forth a universal commentary that focused on the power of the music's "beat," its tendency to inspire dance, and its often "crude" or corrupting lyrics.[7]

Freed's focus on rock 'n' roll's beat and its connection to movement was a sensitive response to what was being expressed around him in person and in print (he was also, unwittingly, supporting a key feature of entrainment). A wide variety of magazines and newspapers from the mid-to-late-1950s heralded the new craze and its rhythm:

> The present generation has not known the rhythmically exciting dance bands of the swing era. It therefore satisfies its hunger for "music with a beat" in the Earl Bostic, Buddy Johnson, Tiny Bradshaw bands or uses the rhythmically pronounced recordings of the Clovers, Ruth Brown and others, as its dance music. (*The Billboard*; Rolontz and Friedman 1954: 1)

> The insistent, galvanic beat which is the heart of rock 'n' roll apparently has ensnared teeners and a good many who are past their teens. It electrifies its devotees and exhausts those who provide it. (the New York City *Daily News*; Sullivan 1955: 88)

> The heavy-beat and honking-melody tunes of today's rock 'n roll have a clearly defined ancestry in U.S. jazz going back to Louis Armstrong and Bessie Smith of 30 years ago. . . . Admiration shows on the Murrays'

---

[7] See further Jackson (1991) and Guralnick (2015). A similar diffusion in origin theories is found in the identification of the "earliest" rock 'n' roll recording: the 1951 single "Rocket '88" by Jackie Brenston and His Delta Cats (Covach and Flory 2012: 8), the 1954 single "Sh-Boom" by the Chords (Belz 1972: 25–6), and Bill Haley's "Crazy Man, Crazy" (1953) or "Rock Around the Clock" (1954), which became the first official #1 rock 'n' roll record in 1955. "Rocket '88" was one of the first six singles (45s) inducted into the new category of "Singles" by the Rock and Roll Hall of Fame in 2018 (Bowman and Schwartz 2019: 79).

[Arthur and his wife] faces as they watch rolling dancer rock partner. Murrays concluded that new craze is a healthy dance for teen-agers. (*Life*; Anonymous 1955: 168)

In the streets and in the theatre the youngsters gave a lot of evidence of fierce enthusiasm for the rhythm. (*The New York Times*; Asbury 1957: 12)

Rock 'n' roll was discovered by the kids themselves. . . . The ballad-type music they'd been hearing was too soupy and languid for dancing. Television offered very little musical variety for them. So when they encountered the powerful, affirmative jazz beat of rock 'n' roll, it was like making an exciting discovery. (*Pageant*; Freed cited in Irwin 1957: 59)

Dick Clark's American Bandstand television program (1957–89) provided fuel for many of these observations; on the Rate-a-Record segment the phrase "It's got a good beat and you can dance to it" became a running joke (and was chosen by Clark as the subtitle to the book he penned about the history of the show; Clark 1985).

Freed was so enamored with the idea of the Big Beat that he used the moniker for his 1957 prime-time television show and his subsequent 1958 national concert tour (Jackson 1991: 167). Importantly in the context of this chapter, however, Freed went further in defining what was special about this beat: "[R]ock 'n' roll has added something of its own: the rolling two-beat rhythm *with the accent on every second beat*. Only the young in heart can dig that socking syncopation. For those who hate it, I think it's too much excitement for their tired arteries" (Irwin 1957: 61; emphasis added). Others would refer to this phenomenon as the "backbeat/back beat," immortalized in the first refrain to Chuck Berry's 1957 classic "Rock and Roll Music."

While the commentary I've provided so far has been essentially positive, there is also a large and well-documented body of criticism running parallel to these accounts that condemned rock 'n' roll—especially its rhythm—from a decidedly racist perspective. Drawing on such tired stereotypes as the "natural" affinity between "African" culture and rhythm, and because of the strong African American cultural underpinnings of the tradition, rock 'n' roll was an easy target for white supremacist groups. After the Birmingham, Alabama-based White Citizens Council disrupted the April 10, 1956 performance of Nat King Cole, its spokesperson provided the following rationale for *Newsweek*: "Rock-and-roll music . . . is the basic, heavy-beat music of the Negroes. It appeals to the base in man, brings out animalism and vulgarity" (Anonymous 1956: 32).[8]

---

[8]Quotes from a similar perspective include Larner (1964: 46), Anonymous (1982: 10), and Bloom (1987).

Putting a finer point on it, later conservative Catholic writer and sacred music composer Peter Kwasniewski specifically identified the backbeat as "unnatural" and morally corrupting:

> The fundamental problem with rock music, many of its antecedents, and nearly all of its offshoots, can be summed up quite simply: its rhythm is unnatural and morally tainted. . . . The normal pattern for almost all music in the world, from all periods of history, whether genuine folk music or the art music of high cultures, accentuates the odd beats, that is, the downbeat (the first) and, to a lesser extent, the third. . . . Rock music, on the other hand, generally uses a constantly syncopated or *off*-rhythm, accentuating the even beats instead of the odd. (Kwasniewski 2013)

Even more balanced authors such as Richard Aquila could not escape characterizing the backbeat as "raw" and "primitive":

> Rock & roll did not sound like traditional pop music. It was more raw and primitive, usually played by small combos featuring guitars, drums, and saxophones. And, significantly, it had a beat kids could dance to. That beat gave rock a special, identifiable sound. Rock & roll, like its forerunner rhythm and blues, stressed the second and fourth beats of a measure, unlike traditional pop music which stressed the first and third beats. (Aquila 2000: 18)

In 2013 Ethan Hein self-published a presentation online with the title "Friends Don't Let Friends Clap on One and Three." The following paragraph is taken from his abstract:

> The backbeat is a form of syncopation. Naively, one might always clap on the strong beats. Accenting the weaker beats creates "rhythmic dissonance" akin to harmonic dissonance in western tonal music. The dominance of the backbeat is a significant factor in the broader Africanization of American popular music, manifested in part by a steadily greater prevalence of syncopation. Despite its ubiquity, the backbeat has faced considerable cultural resistance in America, due in part to racial anxieties. (Hein 2013)

While I have already addressed the metrical implications of these statements in the preceding subsection, Hein's writing goes on to reinforce more than a century of racial stereotypes about the perceived rhythmic abilities and perspectives of "Black" audiences versus "white" ones. This is made clear in the opening slide of Hein's presentation, where he describes a 1993 concert by the Black blues musician Taj Mahal in Bremen, Germany for a predominantly (we can assume) white audience. Taj Mahal becomes upset when his audience claps in the "wrong" place, on beats 1 and 3, and then educates them by stating that what they're doing is influenced by (white) classical music, in contrast to Black (*schvartze*) music where you clap on beats 2 and 4.

Furthermore, Hein is not alone in his misattribution of the backbeat to "African" influences,[9] and he is in distinguished company when he assumes incorrectly that the backbeat as syncopation is an African contribution to Western popular music, emerging with early jazz (to be discussed below). It is not just that the backbeat does not exist in traditional West and Central African musical cultures, at least the practices that were brought over during the time of slavery. Rather, there is a long and recorded narrative in scores and other historical documents that clearly demonstrate the existence of "offbeat" accentuations in four- or duple-beat bars in nineteenth-century classical music and European-derived popular music accompaniments (Abel 2014: 54; Tamlyn 1998: 157–9).[10]

As Gary Tamlyn noted in his magisterial Ph.D. dissertation—an entire work dedicated to the history of the backbeat in Western popular music—such a contrast between low pitches and dark timbres on beats 1 and 3 and higher pitches and lighter timbres on beats 2 and 4 defined the "oom-pah" style of military/marching bands, the most popular form of music in North America during the late nineteenth and early twentieth centuries (1998: 159). Bass drum hits on beats 1 and 3 and snare drum hits on beats 2 and 4 were a part of this sonic palette, later becoming the template of the rock-pop snare backbeat thought to have emerged in the mid-twentieth century with R&B, rock 'n' roll, and urban blues. Theodore Brown in his dissertation on the history of jazz drumming up to 1942 confirms that this is the most common drum pattern found in turn-of-the-century military march accompaniments (1976: 145), and leading scholars of ragtime directly link the "oom-pah" rhythm and low-high pattern in the left hand of early ragtime music to military marches (Jasen and Tichenor 1978: 4; Floyd and Reisser 1984: 36).

The marked or accented snare backbeat does nevertheless become a defining feature of popular music from the mid-twentieth century onwards, felt all the way through contemporary EDM and hip-hop. And while it is tempting to suggest we might have different relationships with how we hear and react to the backbeat (and sound more generally) depending on our

---

[9]Examples include the "Beat" entry in Wikipedia; certain backbeat blogs (http://www.ethanhein.com/wp/2013/the-backbeat-a-literature-review/); and the "Backbeat" entry in the online *Grove Dictionary of American Music*. Mark Abel in his excellent book on groove dedicates an entire chapter to discussing the racialization and essentializing nature of discourse associating groove with African-ness or Blackness ("Is Groove African?"; Abel 2014: 61–91).

[10]And so in an otherwise excellent cultural history of the backbeat and its significance to African American audiences beginning in the twentieth century, author Steven Baur misses this important historical link (2021).

cultural backgrounds and upbringing, such possibilities are unfortunately beyond the scope of this chapter.[11]

"Darkest Light": The Backbeat as Providing Clarification and Resolution

What came to be known as the Lafayette Afro Rock Band began as an artistic collective on Long Island, New York in 1970 under the leadership of vocalist Bobby Boyd. Originally nine members strong, the group's characteristic sound began with its powerful and tight horn section, in the vein of similar 1970s funk/R&B/soul bands Earth, Wind & Fire and Tower of Power. Believing at the time that there was a glut of such artists in North America with which to compete, the decision was made to relocate to Paris, France in 1971 to break into the European market.

While in Paris the group began to perform regularly in the Barbès district, a multiculturally rich area settled by mostly North African immigrants. Their lineup and novelty status caught the attention of harmonica player and producer Pierre Jaubert (who had worked with Berry Gordy in Motown) and Cameroonian jazz-funk saxophonist Mani Dibango, both of whom began to collaborate with the band. In combination with such support and the integration of African and Afrobeat musical influences heard in the neighborhood, the group in 1973 became the Lafayette Afro Rock Band to better reflect their sound and new identity (Anonymous 2007; Weiss 2018). While they would disband in 1977, numerous singles and nine full-length studio albums were produced during this fertile period.

The excerpt for analysis in this section is taken from the band's fifth studio album released in 1975, titled *Malik*. While the album and band did not become household names back in their native United States, the opening of the fifth track "Darkest Light" became well-known in rap/hip-hop circles with its prominent sampling by Public Enemy in "Show 'Em Whatcha Got" (1988) and Jay-Z in "Show Me What You Got" (2006), among a host of other artists.[12] (The song "Hihache" [1974] from their previous album *Nino and Radiah* was sampled by Janet Jackson, LL Cool J, De La Soul, and Wu-

---

[11]Here I draw attention to Maureen Mahon's work on the sound of race and gender in Willie Mae "Big Mama" Thornton's voice (2011), and more recently to Nina Sun Eidsheim's *The Race of Sound* (2019) and the careful attention she pays to timbre and vocality in African American musics.

[12]A much slowed down and lowered pitch version of the sax intro opens the unreleased "Mad Love" (2001) by Britney Spears, though interestingly its syncopated nature is flattened out in the mix (it follows the implied rhythmic organization of Figure 4.1).

FIGURE 4.1 *Introduction to "Darkest Light," implied rhythmic organization.*

FIGURE 4.2 *Introduction to "Darkest Light" (after entrance of drum set), actual rhythmic organization.*

Tang Clan, to name just a few of the many artists who knew of the Lafayette Afro Rock Band's work.)[13]

"Darkest Light" opens with a solo sultry saxophone gesture that immediately provides a sense of what the tempo might be and where the beat will be felt (at roughly ninety-six to the quarter note). Because every note is played strongly without any apparent accents, it gives the strong impression of four eighth notes leading to the downbeat of a bar (refer to Figure 4.1). The first time this passage is heard the sustained pitch (D#) feels like a fermata; as we hear the same passage a second time through many listeners will most likely start to count the potential number of beats between these pickup gestures, and to begin to form a sense of the meter. The third time through the passage the long D# is interrupted by a bass drum hit as the drum set enters, creating a quick but noticeable rhythmically dissonant moment as listeners must suddenly shift their tapping over an eighth note to lock in with the strong backbeat, as shown in Figure 4.2. Once established, the "correct" way of hearing this passage—as syncopated

---

[13]For an excellent (if now somewhat outdated) glossary of Black rock artists, including the Lafayette Afro Rock Band, see Crazy Horse (2004: 203–14).

beginning on the "and" of a beat—is not challenged or interrupted for the remainder of the song. (This phenomenon of tapping the foot in the wrong place has been called a "rhythmic illusion" by Gavin Harrison [1996: 5].)

"Darkest Light" is another simple and clear example of Mark Spicer's "accumulative form" as introduced in Chapter 3, the compositional technique by which a groove is gradually built up part by part, with the effect that we often don't have the complete picture of the meter and/or rhythmic organization until a number of (or all) instruments are sounding. It is also an example of "turning the beat around," a phrase coined by Mark Butler with regard to electronic dance music (Butler 2001: paragraphs 7 and 8). In this particular example, we were initially misled because of a saxophone line that would generally not be felt as syncopated in the absence of the percussion part. The sustained D# also temporarily created a feeling of a fermata, obscuring (for the moment) a strong sense of meter.

"Just What I Needed": The Backbeat as Creating a Sense of Play, Fun, and/or Deviance

Boston-based the Cars was one of the best-selling and critically acclaimed of the so-called "new wave" groups to emerge in the late 1970s. John Covach has placed them in a compositional space balanced between a romanticizing and sonic referencing of pre-*Sgt. Pepper*, pre-psychedelic rock, and harmonic and rhythmic play that draws directly from such late 1960s, early 1970s work (2003: 174–9, 188–94). Others have characterized them as both exploratory or avant-garde and meat-and-potatoes rock music,[14] while I personally think in terms of simplicity masking complexity as a useful, if not slightly reductionist, way to describe the output of this highly creative band.

"Just What I Needed" is the band's debut single from their first and self-titled release, *The Cars* (1978). As previous commentators have noted, the song heralded the entrance of new wave music into the North American mainstream, and it remains a favorite among the band and its many fans. A sense of play and fun is already established at the beginning of the song, which features the pattern of an electric guitar playing muted eighth notes for three beats, followed by a loud chord occupying a quarter note (this repeats). The music theorist Nicole Biamonte believes the dynamic accent placed on the chord draws many listeners into feeling beat 4 as beat 1 (2014: paragraph 7.3 and example 10b); for me this rhythmic fakeout only works when I hear the song on my car radio, because it's difficult to hear when the muted guitar begins due to its volume, and because radio stations often elide

---

[14]Guarisco (n.d.); Altman (1978); Palmer (1978).

the end of the previous song with the beginning of this one (further masking the sense of where the beats are).

A continued sense of play and fun, now coupled to deviance, emerges with lyrics that many have interpreted as sarcastic, ironic, or just downright entertaining through the violation of the norms of a romantic text (Cateforis 2011: 31–2; Guarisco n.d.). With phrases like "I don't mind you standing here / And wasting all my time," or "I guess you're just what I needed / I needed someone to bleed," one could forgive the object of his affection from committing fully to a relationship, long-term or otherwise. Harmonically this ambivalence is supported by verses and a chorus that never fully commit to the major or relative minor key (to be discussed further below).

In the context of this chapter, importantly, such play is extended to the placement of the backbeat. For the first two verses and the chorus, the norms of rock drumming are followed: bass drum hits or a combination of hits occupying beats 1 and 3, and snare drum hits falling on beats 2 and 4. Instead of moving to a new third verse, the Cars chose to repeat verse 1, with the basic structure of the opening four bars shown in Figure 4.3. Up to this point, listeners have encountered three iterations of verses, all with the proper snare backbeat placement. There is little or no reason to expect, therefore, what comes next, which is the temporary misplacement of the backbeat on beats 1 and 3 (refer to Figure 4.4).

While there is almost no record of this interesting rhythmic construction in the academic literature, one key discussion that does exist links this backbeat placement to the support of a lyrical and harmonic playing out of ambivalence and confusion:

"Just What I Needed" borders on the cynical, highlighting the conflict that many new wave musicians felt in dealing with rock's well-worn tropes

FIGURE 4.3 *Return of verse 1, "Just What I Needed," first four bars (2:05-).*

FIGURE 4.4 *Return of verse 1, "Just What I Needed," second four bars (2:12-).*

of sex and love. This lyrical tension and ambiguity is deftly mirrored in the song's harmonic construction as well. Each verse is based on a repetitive four-chord cycle that begins with a tonic–dominant statement in E major, but then shifts directly to the tonic–dominant in the relative key of C# minor, refusing to commit to either fully. The turn to the chorus appears at first as if it is securely in E major, but its phrases cadence on the C# minor chord, a gesture that further emphasizes the song's harmonic ambivalence. By the third verse, the drummer has even joined in as well, as he periodically flips the backbeat onto beats 1 and 3, a final complementary nod to the song's lyrical air of hesitancy and confusion. (Cateforis 2011: 31–2)

I chose "Just What I Needed" as a prime illustration of how a sense of play, fun, and/or deviance can be created through the temporary misplacement of the backbeat on beats 1 and 3, violating (in a positive way) a listener's expectations.[15] This sentiment was reflected in an interview I conducted with Mike Frondelli, LA producer and former vice president of Capitol Records:

And that's what "Just I Needed" sounded like—sounded like somebody screwed up an edit and turned the time around. Because I've done that! But somehow or another, to *think* to do that is the interesting part. You have to come up with the idea. Sometimes it's an accident, but sometimes it's genius. (personal communication, 2019)

The song is not, however, an outlier in rock music history, as a number of solo artists and bands have used the effect over the decades.[16] Perhaps the earliest, if not most famous, example of the switched backbeat is found in the iconic track "Sunshine of Your Love" by Cream (from *Disraeli Gears*, 1967). Cream's now legendary drummer, Ginger Baker, is credited with some of the earliest experimentations with rhythmic patterns and styles, including placement of the snare and bass drum that went against rock norms. Ginger himself came to Cream with a strong background in jazz, as well as playing blues-rock, and like many jazz drummers, he had

---

[15]The recorded cover version of this song by the band Poison (on the 2007 release *Poison'd!*) does not switch the backbeat anywhere in the song, leading the following blogger to write the following: "Very cool topic and examples. I'm reminded of Just What I Needed by The Cars, where the snare switches from the backbeat to on-the-beat in the second half of the verse after the guitar solo as well as later in the pre-chorus. To me, it's such a signature part of the song that I don't consider a cover a TrueCover unless it makes the same change" (Doctor of Rock 2015).

[16]Other select examples include Peter Gabriel, "In Your Eyes" (*So*, 1986), Thursday, "Cross Out the Eyes" (*Full Collapse*, 2001), The 1975, "Talk!" (*The 1975*, 2013), and Decemberists, "Make You Better" (*What a Terrible World, What a Beautiful World*, 2015). I thank Brad Osborn for pointing me to the Thursday and Decemberists tracks.

FIGURE 4.5 *"Sunshine of Your Love" opening guitar riff and basic drum part.*

dabbled in numerous African rhythms (see Micallef and Marshall 2007: 9–18). As Murray Bramwell noted, "Ginger Baker produced polyrhythms, counterpoints, and cymbal and bass drum dialectics which made you want to double-check the number of his arms and legs" (2005: 13).[17]

Figure 4.5 reproduces in skeletal form the opening electric guitar riff and drum part to "Sunshine of Your Love." In addition to most readers immediately recognizing this iconic guitar line, it is also clear how Baker has exactly switched the snare and bass drum roles, such that the snare plays on every beat 1 and 3, and the bass drum plays eighth notes on beats 2 and 4 (Micallef and Marchall call this reverse backbeat "backwards beat"). The "heaviness" of this feel is bolstered by the floor tom which plays even eighth notes on every beat, akin to the hi-hat part in traditional rock drumming.

The significance of this approach to the backbeat cannot be overstated; it would be easy to fill pages with testimonials by drummers, from world-famous to the unheard of, that credit their sense of creativity and possibility to Baker's approach to the placement of the snare and bass drum, including the reversal of the backbeat or playing the snare on beats 2 and 3, two simple examples of his artistry.[18] I conclude this section with a quote by the Canadian drummer Matt Frenette of Loverboy fame, who not only shaped his career goals as a teenager on Ginger Baker's example, but was also impressed by Baker's frequent "turning the beat around":

> Ginger Baker really made a big change in my life. I saw him with Blind Faith. They were real hot that night. I saw Ginger's pink champagne Ludwig drums and I freaked. That week my dad and I got a loan, that I worked to pay off at about $100 a month, and bought a pink champagne

---

[17]According to Mike Frondelli, it was Cream's producer Tom Dowd who came up with the rhythm: "Tom was an interesting character because he was working with Cream. And Cream was making that track 'Sunshine of Your Love' and they couldn't find the right beat. And Tom came up with this idea of playing this Indian [Native American] beat [he beats it out on his thighs]. So he adapted this traditional Indian beat and it became this really intricate kind of patchwork that he put together with that song" (personal communication, 2019).
[18]Baker plays the snare backbeat predominantly on beats 2 and 3 in "Politician" (from *Goodbye*, 1969).

set of Ludwig drums. It was a small, little set. I still have that kit sitting in the basement.

I liked Ginger for turning the beat around, and playing the "1" and "3" on the snare. Ginger, Keith [Moon] and Mitch [Mitchell] were all great for their snare drum work—a lot of "shots" playing. It would be a bit too much in today's rock music. I've tried applying it sometimes when we're jamming or working on a new song. The guys kind of look back at me and say, "Ah, it's a little busy, Matt." But Keith, Ginger and Mitch were great for that. (Fish 1984: 11)

"Northshore" and "Cult of Personality": The Backbeat as Creating Ambiguity and Uncertainty

Tegan and Sara Quin are identical twins born in Calgary, Alberta. Self-taught multi-instrumentalists and songwriters, the sisters formed their first band at age fifteen under the name Plunk (an inside joke referring to "light punk"). Their earliest musical influences came from attending punk gigs in and around Calgary, and while that sound and attitude continued to inform their work over the years, to date the duo has released nine studio albums and numerous EPs that demonstrate a diverse palette of sounds, textures, song forms, and lyrical content. After signing their first record contract they changed their band name to Tegan and Sara.[19]

A large part of the sisters' and band's identity in their music, lyrics, and public persona has been as queer and feminist advocates for equity and social justice. In addition to years of activism since the beginning of their career, in 2016 they founded the Tegan and Sara Foundation, with the following goals identified on the foundation's website:

> Tegan and Sara have openly identified as queer since the beginning of their career in 1998, and have been outspoken feminist advocates for LGBTQ equality and gender justice. The essential message that underpins their worldview and identity is inclusion. The Tegan and Sara Foundation is an extension of their work, identity and longstanding commitment to supporting and building progressive social change. (Tegan and Sara 2021)

The specific mission has been to improve the lives of LGBTQ+ women and girls, with the duo presenting such views in all of their concerts and nearly

---

[19] The sisters recently released an autobiography titled *High School* that revisits and examines many of their formative memories from that time period (Quin and Quin 2019).

FIGURE 4.6 *Introduction to "Northshore," potential rhythmic organization.*

all of their mainstream media interviews, as well as in a number of high-profile gay and lesbian magazines.[20]

In 2009 Tegan and Sara released their sixth full-length studio album, *Sainthood*. Recorded in part at Sound City, the iconic independent studio opened in Los Angeles in 1969 that became one of the most famous sites for rock and pop music of the twentieth century (discussed further in Chapter 6; see Figure 6.1), *Sainthood*, according to the sisters, "addresses secular themes of devotion, delusion, and exemplary behavior in the pursuit of love and relationships. Inspired by emotional longing and the quiet actions we hope may be noticed by the objects of our affection, *Sainthood* is about obsession with romantic ideals" (Tegan and Sara 2009). The album is mostly lean and mean in instrumentation, in the spirit of post-punk or new wave with catchy hooks and lyrics, but electronic textures also feature prominently on a number of tracks (see further Gudino 2009 and Tegan 2014).

The first song for analysis in this section is track #7 from *Sainthood*, "Northshore." Like the excerpt that will follow by the band Living Colour, I examine the use of the backbeat to create a sense of ambiguity and uncertainty in an excerpt where the drum set—providing the traditional accents on beats 2 and 4 within a 4/4 bar—plays in distinct contrast to the melodic lines which are grouped in implied bars of 3/4 (or 6/4). At the end of this section, I will discuss the precedent for this rhythmic alignment, and what it might mean for backbeat placements in non-4/4 meters.

"Northshore" is upbeat and adrenaline-infused at 107 to the quarter note, providing the most "punk" feel on the entire album (instrumentation is just guitars, bass, and drums). The intro features two electric guitars playing a series of power chords grouped into blocks of two quarter notes and two muted eighth notes, which immediately suggests a song in 3/4 meter as I have rendered it in Figure 4.6. There is also the possibility that the first two quarter notes will trigger a sense of 4/4, but will quickly be readjusted to 6/4 because of the syncopated feel and placement of the muted chords.

Listeners have very little time to make up their minds, however, as the intro is only four bars long (conceived of in 3/4), followed by the entrance of the drums with the standard rock alternation of bass drum and snare on

---

[20]See, as examples, Macneal (2010), Raziel (2013), and Cruikshank (2014).

FIGURE 4.7 *"Northshore,"* entrance of drums.

every other beat (refer to Figure 4.7). For the first two bars, there is a very strong feeling of 4/4 created by the drums pulling against the grouping of the electric guitars, though an attuned ear will pick up the potential closing gesture of the double bass drum hit on beat 3 of the third bar which creates a larger organization of 6/4 (the drum pattern notated in Figure 4.7 then continues to repeat throughout the verse).

This rhythmic play of 3s, 4s, and 6s is variously reinforced or thwarted by the text of the first verse that also marks its entrance with the drums. The lyrics begin with a series of six "don'ts" grouped into two quarter-note units which, paired with the drums, support a 6/4 interpretation ("Don't bend / don't blink / don't beg / don't scream / don't whine / don't fight"). The next series of don'ts, however, group naturally into 3s in alignment with the chord changes in the guitar lines ("don't tell me / don't tell me / don't tell me"). The second verse begins like the first, except that there are only five "don'ts" grouped into two quarter-note units ("Don't feel / don't tear / don't kiss / don't care / don't touch"), followed by an "early" entrance of a three quarter-note unit that misaligns the 3s of the text with the 3s of the guitars ("don't / want me don't / want me don't / want me []"). This conflict or competition between different meters being played simultaneously sets up a feeling of ambiguity or uncertainty that is resolved in the metrically consonant chorus that follows when all instruments and the lyrics group neatly into a steady 4/4 stride.

A further example of metrical ambiguity and uncertainty is found in the music of Living Colour. An all-Black rock band hailing from New York City, Living Colour was formed by English-born American guitarist and songwriter Vernon Reid between 1984 and 1986 as a response to music industry racism and the ghettoization of Black musicians into more stereotypical genres such as R&B or rap. Partly in response to the place and age, Reid along with Konda Mason and Greg Tate cofounded the Black Rock Coalition in New York in 1985, with a manifesto that opened with the following text: "The Black Rock Coalition (BRC) represents a united front of musically and politically progressive Black artists and supporters" (Black Rock Coalition 2021). Living Colour and the BRC challenged persistent and racist "norms" about who could play and define the sound of rock music, and over the past 36 years the collective has produced a heady, multifaceted, politically savvy, and powerful oeuvre.[21]

After solidifying the lineup that would soon become famous, Living Colour released their debut album in 1988, titled *Vivid*. Recorded in New York City with cameo appearances and co-production credits by Mick Jagger, the album went on to sell more than 2 million copies. A stylistically diverse work that ran the gamut from rock to funk to rap, it was the hard rock, opening track "Cult of Personality" that catapulted the band to international stardom while garnering them the first Grammy ever awarded for Best Hard Rock Performance (1990), as well as three MTV Video Music Awards.

"Cult of Personality" serves as an excellent microcosm of the band's overall technical and compositional prowess. As Maureen Mahon noted with regard to Living Colour (and BRC groups in general): "Players with serious 'chops,' that is, formidable technical ability, were especially appreciated. For the most part, band members could keep time, handle mid-song time signature changes, and play through song structures that are more complicated than the simple three-chord, 4/4 time rock 'n' roll standard" (Mahon 2004: 125). More simply put, and in specific reference to guitarist Vernon Reid, such work was characterized by "blazing, razor-edged solos and expansive compositions" (Prasad 2007: 64).

Rhythmic-formal play is abundant in "Cult of Personality," beginning with the intro. Preceded by a sample of spoken text by Malcolm X, the song begins with a 2-bar 4/4 riff that feels unsettled as the drummer comes in with a fill that intentionally avoids references to the standard rock backbeat. The intro proper then begins, with the 2-bar (4/4) riff played, an inserted 3/4 bar with an extended riff, and a return to the opening 2-bar riff. Not only does this create an "unusual" intro in terms of bar lengths and meter (4 and 8 bars are the norm, as is a single meter), but the material presented in the 3/4 bar will return as the lead-off riff of the metrically ambiguous pre-choruses.

After the first verse we are presented with the pre-chorus, a series of four 3/4 bars with the riff from the inserted bar from the intro played in bars 1 and 3. This would be the standard interpretation if we only listened to the guitar line; the drum set, however, locks into an unambiguous 4/4 rock backbeat, a different approach taken from the inserted 3/4 bar of the intro (see Figure 4.8). Such use of multiple meters in the pre-chorus is an analogous example of "tactus-preserving polymeter" as defined by Keith Waters in reference to jazz improvisational practice (Waters 1996: 25).

---

[21]For more detailed historical, political, and cultural context of the BRC, as well as the aesthetics of "Black rock," readers are referred to Maureen Mahon's excellent and comprehensive *Right to Rock* (2004), especially Chapters 1 and 5; for detailed interviews with founding member Vernon Reid, including his thoughts on the origins and characteristics of Black rock music as well as more current recording projects, see Fricke (1990) and Prasad (2007).

FIGURE 4.8 *Pre-chorus to "Cult of Personality."*

Throughout this passage, the listener is challenged to choose one meter over the other or to hear the two parts as a composite whole (perhaps listening for hypermetric convergences).

The chorus comes next, followed by a 4-bar guitar solo that feels too early to be a bridge or proper extended solo (further playing with listener's expectations). Verse 2 then appears, with the same pre-chorus and chorus dyad heard before the guitar solo proper begins. An explosion of sound and motion, the solo was ranked #87 in Guitar World's "100 Greatest Guitar Solos." Even here, however, the solo finishes thematically at 16 bars (a standard length), then introduces new material for another 4 bars as a kind of winding down or settled catharsis for listeners to prepare for the third and final verse. The song ends with an outro that is sandwiched between sampled spoken text by John F. Kennedy and Franklin D. Roosevelt; what completes this impressive composition is the return of the music (guitar riff) from the pre-choruses, but this time with the drums playing at double speed, creating a clear feeling of a fast 6/4 in which guitar and percussion align. (Unlike the drummer in Tegan and Sara's "Northshore," the drummer here commits to passages in both 4/4 and 6/4.)

The precedent for such examples of drums playing in 4/4 against melodic material in 3/4 (or extended 6/4) was, of course, established by Led Zeppelin in their track "Kashmir" (from *Physical Graffiti*, 1975); it's also significant that Led Zeppelin is frequently cited by BRC members as a central influence on Black rock, and by Living Colour specifically in reference to the opening riff of "Cult of Personality." While scores can be found that notate the song in 3/4, 4/4, or even 6/4—transcribers are making choices as to which parts are more metrically dominant to their ear—there is a clear grouping dissonance between the drums playing the standard backbeat

FIGURE 4.9 *"Kashmir" opening.*

in 4/4 and the guitars and strings playing in what can be clearly felt as 3/4,[22] as reproduced in Figure 4.9.[23]

The main difference between "Kashmir" (and a number of later songs that similarly pit the drums against the guitars[24]) and "Northshore" and "Cult of Personality" is that Led Zeppelin maintains the multiple meters throughout their entire track, such that it could be possible to entrain on a much larger hypermetric level. Interestingly, in all of these examples, the drum "insists" on staying in the classic 4/4 (or duple) backbeat setup. I don't know of any rock (or pop) songs where the melody is in 4s (4/4) while the drum plays in 3s (3/4), perhaps because a precedent hasn't been set as to where the snare backbeat "should" land in bars of 3/4 or 9/8 (more on this in the Coda to this chapter).

"Dazed and Confused": The Backbeat as Creating Ambiguity and Providing Clarification

Much has been written about the diversity of musical styles, textual references, and visual imagery employed by Led Zeppelin over the course of their storied career. A unifying thread, however, that has held the imagination of fans and professional commentators alike is the band's willingness and

---

[22]Nicole Biamonte makes an interesting argument for hearing the guitars in 6/8, "creating a complex hemiola" (2014: paragraph 7.10).
[23]I have chosen to notate "Kashmir" in 4/4, with added brackets in the guitar and string lines showing their groupings in three; I have also indicated single bass drum strokes in the drum set, understanding that John Bonham might be double-stroking on some beats, and/or the producer employed a delay on some of these strokes (internet chatter argues for both options).
[24]A sampling of such songs includes "Say Hello" by April Wine (*Harder . . . Faster*, 1979); "Limelight" by Rush (*Moving Pictures*, 1981); and "Leave It" by Bombay Bicycle Club (*A Different Kind of Fix*, 2011). The Bee Gees in their well-known "Jive Talkin'" (*Main Course*, 1975) create an even more complex texture at 1:17 into the track by having the melodic instruments play alternating measures of 4/4 and 3/4 while the drum continues playing backbeats in 4/4; the result is a reversed backbeat—on beats 1 and 3—every two measures.

FIGURE 4.10 *One possible grouping of opening bass riff, "Dazed and Confused."*

ability to explore alternate compositional possibilities and/or improvise, both in the studio and live on stage. A central ingredient in this mix has been the consistency and creativity with which they have integrated metrical and rhythmic irregularities into their already frequently complex and challenging music (Moore 2001: 82; Ball 2010: 218–20).[25]

Understood in this light, "Dazed and Confused" from Led Zeppelin's debut album (*Led Zeppelin*, 1969) serves as a microcosm of such activity, as Susan Fast has noted: "'Dazed and Confused' was arguably the most important locus for musical experimentation from the group's early inception in 1968 through their live appearances in 1979—in other words, for the entire life of the band save the last tour" (2001: 18; see also Headlam 1995: 314–15). The song is worth a close reading on many fronts, everything from its inception to musical quotation, to its metrical sensibilities, and its use of improvisation within a psychedelic context. For this reason, and many others, the song has received significant article- and chapter-length treatments of its many facets (Fast 2001: 17–47; Brackett 2008: 67–72; Wall 2008: 62–5).[26]

In this last formal section of the chapter, I have chosen to examine the placement of the snare backbeat to create both a sense of ambiguity and a means to provide clarification, such that an electric bass riff (later doubled by electric guitar) with two possible rhythmic interpretations is realized in both versions over the course of two subsequent verses. From the introductory strains of "Dazed and Confused" a sense of mystery and ambiguity is set up by a walking electric bass line played in the absence of percussion or voice. If we look at Figure 4.10, a reproduction of the central repeating figure, there are at least two logical ways to group and hear the passage. The first as I've presented it here is the way a listener would interpret these strains if they felt that the first strong pitch they heard (the G) was beat 1; this organization also highlights the two parallel sets of descending chromatic lines (G down to E in bar 1, and D down to B in bar 2).[27] As the voice enters with the first

---

[25] A balanced view of the band and its activities is found in Yorke (1999) and Wall (2008).
[26] For a substantive academic analysis of authorship and compositional identity in the music of Led Zeppelin's first four albums, see Headlam (1995).
[27] While I hesitate to cite Lerdahl and Jackendoff here, because of their reliance on Western common-period classical music as source material, the interpretation provided here does

FIGURE 4.11 *Beginning of verse 2, "Dazed and Confused."*

FIGURE 4.12 *Beginning of verse 3, "Dazed and Confused."*

verse this interpretation is not called into question, and with the entrance of the drums the strong snare backbeats confirm this interpretation (refer to Figure 4.11).

For other listeners, however, it makes more sense to hear the bass line as organized around the (implied) strong harmonic pitches, namely the tonic and dominant in E minor. If we look at Figure 4.12, the bass line would then realign itself so that the dominant pitch B would fall on a first beat, followed by the tonic E on the next beat 1. And, in fact, this is exactly what happens with the entrance of the third verse, and then continues throughout the remainder of the song.[28]

This switching or realignment of the backbeat under identical melodic material, a kind of playing out of alternate realities, is almost certainly unique in rock and pop music history. While little has been written about the phenomenon in this song, there are two analysts who recognized it and commented on its significance, though they approached the dilemma through slightly different lenses. Joe Bergamanini in a book documenting and analyzing John Bonham's classic drum tracks assumed that the backbeat shifted to beats 1 and 3 in verse 3 so that the riff played by the bass and later doubled by the electric guitar does not change its metrical placement (Bergamanini 2005: 8). What Bergamanini did not seem to consider was

---

adhere to their grouping preference rules #2 and #3 because of the proximity of these groups of pitches and their parallel descending motion of ½ steps, and the change in rhythm and register for the E eighth notes signaling a boundary change (1996[1983]: 45–6).

[28]While not a direct analog, the verses in Prince's "Diamonds and Pearls" (*Diamonds and Pearls*, 1991) feature a similar evocation of a repeated melodic passage that can be heard in one of two ways that are only one quarter note apart, supported by both a displaced tonic (on beat 2 in this case) and a kick drum part that shifts to beat 4 (or beat 3 in the alternative interpretation) every third bar of the four-bar figure.

that the first two verses could be interpreted as having the backbeats on beats 1 and 3 and that it was only with the third verse that the drums "corrected" themselves. In John Brackett's article on Led Zeppelin's musical style he entertained both options, though he could only conclude with the following observation:

> As a result, we are unable to clearly identify what has moved or changed: has the metric position of the riff shifted or has the backbeat been inverted? "Dazed and Confused" indeed. (Brackett 2008: 72)[29]

For me, ambiguity is created through snare backbeat placement if you are not sure as a listener if the backbeats have remained on beats 2 and 4 throughout the song. Conversely, I feel that clarification is provided by the backbeat if you believe the band was trying to explore both possibilities for the bass/guitar line, so that you could choose which one "felt" better to groove along with.[30] In this latter context, the effect is remarkably similar to the way Daniel Levitin has described an ambiguous harmonic sequence:

> [L]isteners reappraise the entire sequence, subconsciously of course, and realize that there exists a *plausible alternative* to the overlearned sequence they expected to hear. The listener, with the composers' help, has learned something new about the world. (Levitin 2009: 50)

In all live performances of "Dazed and Confused" after 1971, Led Zeppelin only ever played the drum/riff alignment as notated in Figure 4.11 (Brackett 2008: 70–2). Anecdotal evidence suggests that the band had experimented with various ways of constructing the riff and drum part, both during the compositional process and over the ensuing years, as shown in the following two quotes by band members John Paul Jones and Robert Plant:

> "Dazed and Confused" came in 'cause Jimmy knew that. I could never get the sequence for years. It kept changing all the time with different parts and I was never used to that. (Furniss 2007; 1977 interview by Steven Rosen with John Paul Jones)

> Well, at the beginning it was the construction of things with different time patterns and with changes ... y'know like in "Dazed and Confused" and "How Many More Times?" which somehow or another came to

---

[29] A full rhythmic analysis of the song is found on pages 67–72; to my knowledge, this is the only academic treatment of this backbeat shift.
[30] While the "official" score does not notate the drum part, it does imply that the backbeats did not shift, but rather that the electric bass and guitar lines shifted over a beat; this is achieved by "cheating" a bar of one beat (12/8 to 9/8) between verse 2 and 3 so that everything aligns properly (Dick 2009: 22–3).

us like that [snaps his fingers]. (Brackett 2008: 54; transcribed bootleg conversation with Robert Plant)

And so while the band seemed to have settled into just one interpretation or perspective, their initial studio recording nevertheless revealed possibilities that continue to capture fans' and critics' imagination.

Coda

As both a rhythmic place keeper and an expressive device, the backbeat is a central element in audiences' understanding of all popular music, particularly groove- and/or dance-based genres. Its apparent simplicity masks the ways it has been used to support and transgress its common metrical positioning, and in combination with other musical elements such as bass, melodic, vocal, and harmonic rhythm creates rich avenues for understanding why certain artists and pieces of music grip us so tightly, driving us to dig deeper into what is so intriguing and/or makes us want to move. This research also hopes to provide further evidence of the connections made by music theorists and cognitive scientists between metrical prediction, entrainment, embodiment, listener participation, and meaning. The composers and performers of the works presented here clearly understood this potential to reinforce, thwart, and/or enhance listener's expectations, and thus bolster the expressive power of music.

In this chapter, I only looked at targeted examples of the snare backbeat in a largely quadruple meter context. Much more could be said about the realization of the backbeat in melodic instruments and vocal lines, as well as how it might be passed around the ensemble. But to close out this topic I want to briefly entertain the strategies taken by drummers in triple meters, as well as the potential combination of duple/quadruple and triple meters found in bars of 7/4.

Songs in 3/4 are surprisingly rare in rock and pop music. While a quick internet search will generate a number of websites claiming that the so-called waltz rhythm is quite common in popular music, some even posting their top choices, the problem is that often the work they're describing is really in a slow 12/8 or 12/4 groove. The key here is listening to the snare backbeat placement, which is something I've argued for throughout this chapter. Examples include the Beatles' "You've Got to Hide Your Love Away" (*Help!*, 1965), which starts off seemingly in waltz time, but then reveals itself as a long 12/8 or 12/4 when Ringo adds his tambourine backbeats. The same is true of Billy Joel's "Piano Man" (*Piano Man*, 1973), "Blackout" by Muse (*Absolution*, 2003), and the chorus of "Kiss From a Rose" by Seal (*Batman Forever: Music from the Motion Picture*, 1995). One of the only true samples of a 3/4 waltz song I could find was Kate Bush's

FIGURE 4.13 *Opening four bars of "Broken Toy."*

"Army Dreamers" (*Never for Ever*, 1980), which directly references the [boom-chick-chick] texture with guitar and strings, but with no backbeat in the drums. This raises an important issue: Can the accented or marked snare in triple meters be properly called a "backbeat"? And if so, must it play on all of the "weak" beats of the bar—beats 2 and 3 in conventional wisdom—or can/should it only play on beat 2 or 3, so as to avoid sounding like a waltz?[31]

This issue comes up again with compound triple meters of 9/8, which internet commentators often misunderstand as a waltz rhythm in their lists of 3/4 pop-rock songs. While there aren't that many songs in a true 9/8 (versus a long 12/8 or 12/4), a good example is found in Keane's "Broken Toy" (*Under the Iron Sea*, 2006). As Figure 4.13 illustrates, while the bass drum hits on every beat of every bar, the snare drum is careful not to play on any beat 2, and to almost always play on beat 3 (though note the syncopations in bar 4). A nearly identical approach is found in George Michael's "Cowboys and Angels" (*Listen Without Prejudice Vol. 1*, 1991), which leads me to the premature assumption that pop and rock drummers tend to avoid playing snare "backbeats" on every beat 2 and 3 in 9/8 and 3/4 bars, most likely as a way of distancing their sound from the older and "squarer" sound of the waltz.[32]

I finish with two examples of songs that can easily be notated as 7/4, but with a clear rationale for also considering them as paired bars of 7/8 (Hanenberg refers to the former as metric septuple time, the latter submetric septuple time; 2018: 141–2). The first is King Crimson's "Three of a Perfect Pair" (*Three of a Perfect Pair*, 1984), which features two broader sections that alternate between 3/4—Bill Bruford hits backbeats on every beat 2, unlike the earlier examples—and 7/4 (or 7/8). At roughly 1:00 into the song, we encounter the first 7/4 section, which features electric guitar and vocal lines that neatly bracket into groups of 7/8 (refer to Figure 4.14).

---

[31]While based on a fairly small sample size of my own choosing but over a number of decades, drummers within the subgenre of country waltz overwhelmingly choose to place the snare backbeat on beat 3.

[32]I would go a step further out over the edge and say that rock drummers, if having to choose beat 2 or 3, would choose beat 3 in most cases; though see the King Crimson "Three of a Perfect Pair" discussion that follows.

FIGURE 4.14 *"Three of a Perfect Pair," 7/4 (7/8) passage at 1:00.*

FIGURE 4.15 *First full bar of "St. Augustine in Hell," 7/4 realization.*

The drum part, however, even with its syncopated bass drum hits, exhibits the typical snare backbeat placement every other beat on beats 2, 4, and 6. It is as if Bruford is playing two bars of 4/4, but is "dropping" the last beat (later in the song at 3:22 he will briefly reconfigure his playing to match up with the 7/8 phrasing of the guitars). The same strategy in snare backbeat placement is found in Pink Floyd's "Money" (*Dark Side of the Moon*, 1973) and the choruses of Tegan and Sara's "Night Watch" (*Sainthood*, 2009),[33] in which all melodic lines align with the 7/4 meter.

The second example is less clear-cut in terms of what the drummer is trying to accomplish metrically, which adds to the ambiguity and also interest in this passage. The excerpt is taken from Sting's "St. Augustine in Hell" (*Ten Summoner's Tales*, 1993), featuring the drumming of studio legend Vinnie Colaiuta. Figure 4.15 reproduces the first full bar of the piece if we notate it as 7/4. The electric keyboard part plays in phrases that could match up with this interpretation, though a bass line (not notated) seems to be playing in bars of 7/8. Colaiuta has a number of choices, which include playing a pattern akin to what was used in the King Crimson example that would support the 7/4 feel, or to "reload" the bass and snare to start over in each 7/8 bar. A third choice would be to isolate (musically) one or more of his appendages from the rest, to create a sense of simultaneous meters being played.

---

[33]In the last extended (instrumental) chorus the drummer locks into 4/4, played against the 7/4 of the melodic lines.

FIGURE 4.16 *First two full bars of "St. Augustine in Hell," 7/8 realization.*

It is the last option that Colaiuta chose, and why so many amateur and professional drummers have weighed on this particular Sting track.[34] If you look at the ride cymbal part of Figure 4.15, you can see that he is maintaining a strict 7/4 pattern, marking each of the quarter-note beats. If you compare this with Figure 4.16, the same music realized as two bars of 7/8, however, one can see the familiar bass-snare drum alternation of the typical 4/4 bar, but with the "and" of beat 4 dropped and the same alternation restarting at the beginning of the next 7/8 bar (typical of the standard backbeat for most 7/8 grooves; Hanenberg 2018: 142–4). It is an extremely subtle manipulation of rhythmic textures, yet if you play the passage only thinking of 7/8, the ride cymbal becomes "syncopated" in the second bar against what the bass and snare drums are doing. It is as if Colaiuta is providing the listener with choices, with multiple interpretive possibilities, that allow us to make our way through this music on different paths.

This rhythm played an important part in my development as an arranger and composer of South Korean percussion music. In 2008–9, I received funding from the Korean Government to bring together Seoul and Vancouver musicians to UBC for a joint recording and performance project under the title "*Beopgo Changsin*: New Music for Samul Nori." Under the rubric of "creating the new while preserving the old" (*beopgo changsin*), I wrote or arranged three new pieces for the Korean percussion ensemble known as *samul nori*, exploring different ways of combining "East" and "West." The most hybrid work of them all, a piece titled "Han-Mi Karak" (Rhythms from Korea and the United States), featured as the penultimate rhythm my interpretation of Colaiuta's 7/4 structure for the four Korean percussion instruments under the name "Ilgop Mach'i," literally, "Seven Strokes" (Hesselink 2014b; see especially 40–3).

This project also introduced me to Factory Studios located at 201 W. 7th Avenue, where we recorded the base tracks for our collaboration. More readers will recognize this space by its original name, Little Mountain Sound Studios, the historic place where many of the leading hard rockers of the 1980s and early 1990s conducted their most successful work. We return to this space in Chapter 6.

---

[34]A small sampling includes Dave (2007), Sparlour (2011), and Sweetman (2016).

5

Entrainment and the Human-Technology Interface, Historical and Technological Considerations

Finding the Beat

Most if not all readers of this book are familiar with the cantankerous object of the metronome. Found in homes, practice rooms, and studios around the world, it might surprise many to know that such a time-keeping device was only developed in Western European classical music[1] and that no other world music tradition ever conceived of or felt the need for such an externalized, mechanized entraining agent.

In the early days of rock 'n' roll/rock—from the 1950s through the mid-1970s—audiences would have tapped or danced along with a beat that existed within a relatively flexible time frame. Music naturally and subtly sped up and slowed down; no place for metronomic playing here. This began to change, however, in the late 1970s. Unbeknownst to most fans and consumers, the metronome began to find its way through the back door into recordings and live concerts in the form of click tracks, sequencers, and electronic drum machines. In the process, our understanding of "playing in time" and "keeping the beat" would undergo a radical transformation, at the same time creating new challenges and opportunities for producing rock records.

---

[1] For the historical development of the metronome, see Martin (1988), Bonus (2010), Grant (2014), and Bingham and Turner (2017).

In this chapter "finding the beat" takes on the additional meaning of the need to capture and locate the beat for new and enhanced contexts for synchronization beyond the cognitive and artistic motivations outlined in Chapters 2–4. This requires a search for and understanding of the historical and technological settings for the transition from the metronome to the click track and a flexible to a metronomic beat. In the following companion chapter, I explore a significant outgrowth of such phenomena, the newly required skill for drummers to locate and manipulate their playing in relation to the unforgiving beat of the click, with a greater emphasis on sociological and aesthetic considerations.

Development of the Click Track

The standard definition of a click track is a series of audio cues provided by a machine or software program used to synchronize sound. There are many ways such technology can be employed: between humans (such as in a stadium rock concert), between humans and machines (such as in a studio recording combining live musicians with sequencers), between humans and moving images (such as an orchestra syncing up with a film), or between machines and moving images (such as pre-programmed sounds with a television commercial). I have yet to discover the first time the phrase "click track" was used in print; but for the purposes of this chapter, I will further delineate the term as a series of rhythmic cues that can include visual and/ or tactile stimuli. I will refer to these instances as a "visual click track" and "tactile click track," respectively.

Entrainment studies of the twentieth century have relied on metronome technology not only to explore our general ability to perceive and physically react to an externalized entraining agent[2] but also the effectiveness of our different sensory modalities in achieving these tasks. Recalling again Patel's six key features of beat perception and synchronization from Chapter 1, the third feature tells us that we get a stronger sense of the beat—including our ability to synchronize with it—with aural stimuli than we do with visual stimuli. The research is extensive and seems conclusive on this point, extending back to the 1950s.[3] While a 2015 study found that a moving, colliding visual stimulus created better results than a flashing light in hearing participants, deaf participants under the same conditions performed nearly identical to their hearing counterparts, suggesting that "cross-modal

---

[2] An example of such work is found in Iversen and Patel (2008).
[3] Representative examples include Fraisse (1952), Brittin (1993), and Iversen et al. (2015); I thank my colleague John Roeder for identifying the French source.

plasticity enhances the ability to synchronize with temporally discrete visual stimuli" (Iversen et al. 2015: 232).

Research on tactile metronomes—often referred to as "vibrotactile feedback and/or stimulation" in the literature—is more recent and less conclusive. As Giordano and Wanderly noted:

> [S]everal patents for tactile metronomes have been filed in the last decade, and commercial tactile-augmented devices have started to appear on the market claiming to be able to provide musicians with reliable tempo cues. Surprisingly though, no quantitative evaluation of the capability of the sense of touch to process such information, in the context of music performance, has been conducted so far. (Giordano and Wanderly 2015: 1)

While their research suggests that a tactile metronome sits somewhere between an auditory one and a visual one in synchronization exercises (discussed further in Giordano 2016: 11–12), there are still questions pertaining to the role and capacities of advanced musical training, the part of the body used to receive the vibrotactile stimulation, and any advantages that might accrue due to bimodal engagement with the source (Giordano 2016: 14; Ammirante et al. 2016).[4]

With the ubiquity of audio click tracks in the studio and live concert, and knowing the general uses of the metronome, it would seem logical to assume that a strictly musical-performative challenge provided the context for its genesis. This is not, interestingly, the case. The story of the click track began with a very different set of problems in need of solving; only decades later did musicians envision alternate uses, including interfaces with computer technology. And throughout this long and fascinating narrative, regardless of the task, actors continued to experiment with various modalities for synchronizing the human and nonhuman worlds.

Early Twentieth Century

The history of sound-on-film is the history of synchronization and where we will find the birth of the modern-day click track as we recognize it today.[5] While motion pictures with recorded sound exist from the mid-1890s, it is not until 1928 and the advent of animated cartoon films that artists, directors, and musicians were presented with the challenge of syncing moving images

---

[4]See further Kosonen and Raisamo (2006) and Jokiniemi et al. (2008).
[5]For an excellent social-cultural history of recorded sound, including music, in early films, see the section titled "Music and the Early Sound Film (1894–1933)" in Wierzbicki (2009: 69–130).

on the screen, frame-by-frame, with music, dialogue, and sound effects. It took a number of individuals, working with various mediums and using visual and/or aural cues, that eventually led to the first patented click track in 1933.[6]

It is not entirely clear who should be credited with inventing the click track—a term not in use then—between these two endpoints of 1928 and 1933, due to the number of individuals involved in creating the films, professional pride, terminological inconsistencies, and the vagaries of memory. What is known is that the first cartoon conceived for sound was created by the Walt Disney Studios, released in 1928 under the title *Steamboat Willie*. Featuring the adventures of Mickey Mouse and his girlfriend Minnie, its directors Walt Disney and Ubbe "Ub" Iwerks desired a level of synchronization that went beyond the usual rough mapping of an orchestral score on top of the "live" action on screen.

The studio had already figured out the speed of animated film (24 frames per second), and so it was just a matter of time for someone to translate the number of frames to a standard Maelzel metronome marking. This credit seems due to the animator Wilfred Jackson who began working for Disney in 1928:

> I knew what a metronome was. So I brought one to work and showed it to Walt. I set the metronome at 60 and it ticked sixty times in a minute—one tick every twenty-four frames. I set it at 120 and got a tick every twelve frames. I could make it tick any multiple of frames Walt wanted. Then I got out my harmonica and played "Turkey in the Straw" while the metronome ticked away, and Walt could tell how fast the music was going. (Jackson quoted in Care 1976–7: 41)

If we assign the audible portion of the cue and its connection to the metronome as the most important discovery of the fledgling click track system, then Jackson becomes our first candidate as its inventor.

Disney, however, did not initially seem drawn to the idea of an audible click or tick when trying to match the music and sounds to the cartoon films. William Garity, an inventor and audio engineer who also worked for Disney, remembered experiments using wavy lines and a bouncing ball superimposed on the film that the conductor and musicians would watch as they performed the music (Cohen 2009: 106; Barrier 1999: 53–4). Carl Stalling, a composer and arranger who worked at the studio from 1926 to 1933, recalled drawing "half-moon" lines on the prints that moved in time

---

[6] In 1925 a patent was granted for reproducing music in synchronism with moving pictures (Blum 1925). In many ways the technology for a click track system was in place here, but its potential was not explored.

FIGURE 5.1 *Streamers (left and middle) and punch (right) applied to* Mabel and Fatty *(public domain).*

from left to right across a number of frames, then back to the left again (Barrier 2002: 44). Ub Iwerks revamped this approach to work out a way of having horizontal lines move up and down according to the metronome setting (one complete cycle = a single rising and falling), while across town at Twentieth Century-Fox Alfred Newman and Charles Dunworth developed a similar technique known as "streamers and punches," a reference to diagonal lines that moved across the screen, followed by a flash of light created by a hole punched in the frame to help mark important events (Barrier 2002: 45; Cohen 2009: 106). Figure 5.1 is a composite still-shot from the 1915 comedy *Mabel and Fatty Viewing the World's Fair at San Francisco, Cal.*, in which I have added streamers and a punch to recreate the original technique (see also Waletzky 2007[7]); do any of these individuals deserve a share in the credit of invention?

According to Disney's daughter (as told to a third party), as well as others, the bouncing ball system was used for *Steamboat Willie* (Newsom 1985: 64; Barrier 1999: 53–4). From here, however, the details become muddied. It is clear that Disney decided to use some kind of aural click track for his next animated film, *The Skeleton Dance* (1929). A number of sources credit Carl Stalling with creating the first click track, which began with a pre-recorded beat (similar to an electronic metronome pulse) played through headphones that the conductor and musicians wore (Curtis 1992: 195; Garity 1933: 320–1). Stalling himself in a 1971 interview recalled his initial thought process that first created this process, followed soon thereafter by an even more direct approach in which holes were punched into a reel of unexposed film at the proper moments that created pops or ticks as they ran over an optical reader:

> The thought struck me that if each member of the orchestra had a steady beat in his ear, from a telephone receiver, this would solve the problem.

---

[7] I thank Michael Bushnell for providing me a copy of the Waletzky documentary.

I had exposure sheets for the films, with the picture broken down frame by frame, sort of like a script, and twelve of the film frames went through the projector in a half second. That gave us a beat. (Barrier 2002: 42–3)[8]

The problem with the above account is that other sources credit Disney sound effects man Jim Macdonald (who worked closely with Stalling) with devising the hole punch system creating the pops or ticks (Strauss 2002: 7; Thomas and Johnston 1981: 294). This proto-click track is certainly the direct progenitor of what we understand as a click track today, and yet when Disney filed for the first patent employing such technology only two years later in 1931 (granted in 1933)—under the title "Method and Apparatus for Synchronizing Photoplays"—his only co-authors were Wilfred Jackson, the man who introduced Disney to metronomic timing, and William Garity, who has an unclear connection to moving lines and bouncing balls. Stalling's input and design are certainly present, yet it is unclear why he was not included when the official credit came due.

Regardless of origins or contributors, the machinery and strategies documented in Disney's patent prefigured most developments in later twentieth-century click track technology. As the authors noted on the first page of the patent, there were two primary challenges that needed to be overcome: (1) the synchronization of sound with the stop motion technique used in animated cartoons, and (2) "to disclose and provide a method of imparting time signals to musicians, actors and other sound sources during the preparation of sound accompaniments without superimposing the time beats upon the sound record being prepared" (Disney et al. 1931–3: 1).

Figure 5.2 reproduces Figure 4 from the patent. The illustration shows a strip of film with the individual frames numbered (#173–183) in which synchronization is only required for a brief passage. At the beginning of frames 175 and 180 there are black marks painted directly on the film; when this specially prepared film is run through a projector, as shown in Figure 5.3 (Disney Figure 5), a pop or click sounds for the musicians to hear. The film runs through an aperture plate (#34 on Figure 5) through which light from an external source passes through the plate (#33). Whenever the light source is interrupted by the black painted dots, a sound is created and sent to the musicians via an amplifier (#35) and into their headphones (#37–39). As noted earlier, it is difficult to know whether to attribute this idea to Carl Stalling or to Jim Macdonald (though remember the original strategy was to punch holes out of the film, not paint black holes on it).

When the tempo is constant for the musicians over a longer period of time, then the options shown in Disney Figures 6 or 7 (Figure 5.3) can be used. In Figure 6, a metronome (#40) is placed before a microphone

---

[8] See also Curtis (1992: 195) and Jacobs (2015: 64).

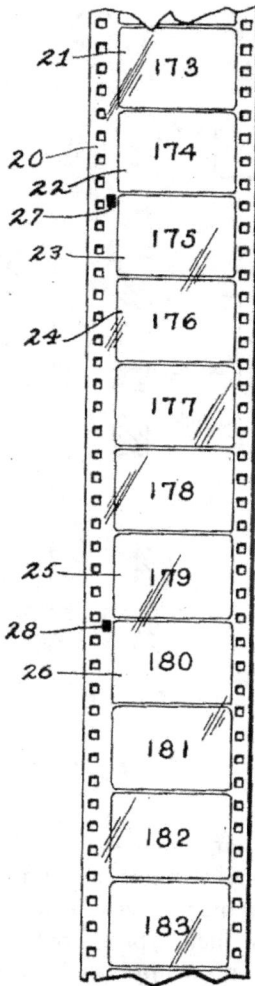

FIGURE 5.2 *Disney patent Figure 4 (public domain).*

(#41) and sent to the headphones of the musicians (#37–39). Figure 7 shows an alternate system in which a gear or gears (#46 and # 47) is mounted on a shaft (#45) that spins at the desired rate of speed for the musicians. This triggers a switch (#42) attached to a source of electrical energy (#43) that then creates a click or pop sent to the headphones of the musicians (#37–39). Over time, of course, the apparatuses depicted in Disney Figures 6 and 7 would be replaced by digital technology; but the impetus behind and outcome of these realizations remain the same.

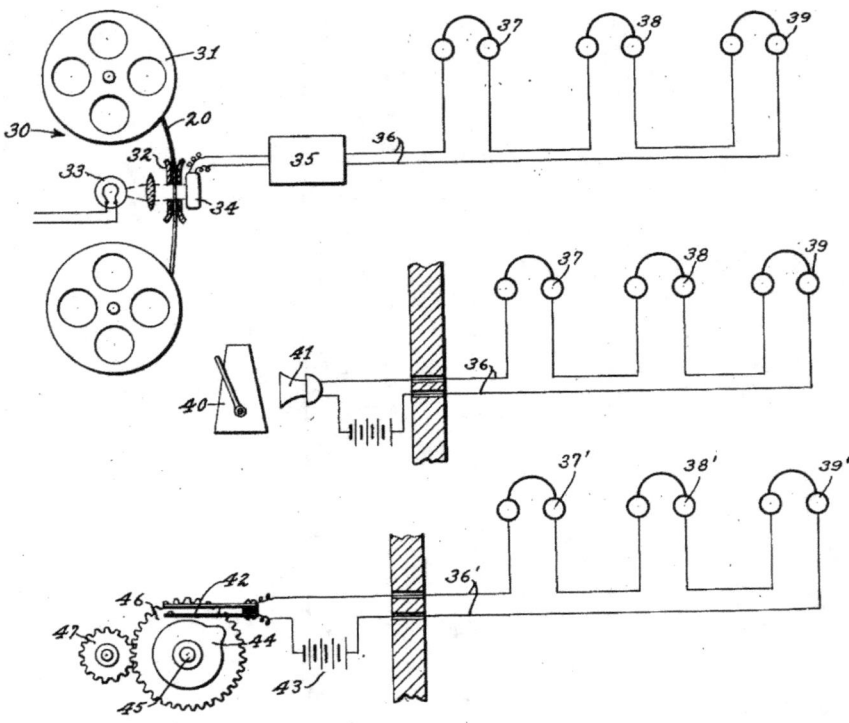

FIGURE 5.3 *Disney patent Figures 5–7 (public domain).*

It is already impressive what Disney and his fellow inventors accomplished with the aural click tracks. What made it even more remarkable is that they also imagined scenarios in which musicians might not want to be distracted by auditory cues, and so in their typical comprehensive manner, they also developed tactile and visual means by which to synchronize the movements of the musicians with the moving images on the screen. Even in the absence of research that would be carried out on these various modalities decades later, Disney knew that musicians of his time—and ostensibly in the future—would have various reasons for employing rhythmic cues and that such circumstances would or could require different senses. (We can surmise this as neither the visual or tactile click tracks were used in the films surrounding the granting of this patent.)

With Disney Figure 8 (Figure 5.4) we are presented with the idea for the world's first mechanized, tactile click track. Their motivation was to provide an alternative to an aural cue through a method that imparted the tempo silently through physical contact. A coil (#50) contains within it a solenoid (#51)—a type of electromagnet that generates a controlled

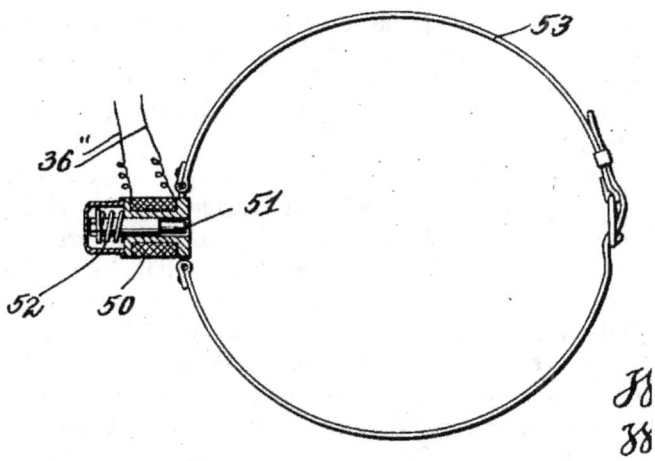

FIGURE 5.4 *Disney patent Figure 8 (public domain).*

magnetic field—that is held in place by a spring (#52). The coil is fastened to the performer via a strap or belt (#53) that may be attached to the arm, leg, or ankle. The coil is connected through electrical conductors (#36") to a current that is interrupted in some manner. The interruptions are timed to the desired tempo, causing the circuit to be closed and the solenoid to strike the musician. The electrical conductors can be connected to the leads in Figure 7 (#36') to achieve the same effect.

Last, but not least, Disney and his team developed a purely visual click track.[9] The appropriate passage from the patent is worth quoting at length:

> Instead of aurally imparting the tempo to the musicians and instead of imparting the tempo to the musicians by the application of physical contact, as by means of the solenoid described hereinabove, the tempo may be imparted to the musicians by flashing small lights fastened on the stands of the musicians. A make-and-break device of the character shown in Fig. 7 may be employed for this purpose, the leads [#]36' leading to lamps on the stands of the musicians instead of to the ear phones [#]37', 38', 39', etc. Such flashing lights may be mounted in close proximity to the music, therefore not detracting the musicians' attention from the music or from the conductor. (Disney et al. 1931–3: 4)

---

[9] A year later in 1914 an aural metronome combined with a visual indicator called the Rythmikon was released on the commercial market (Plummer 1914). The device was invented by the English violinist Bonarios Grimson; it would be logical to assume that he was unaware of what was going on at Disney Studios.

The abovementioned description is eerily close to the composer Hector Berlioz's conception of the "electric [visual] metronome" as set out in his novella *Euphonia* nearly 90 years previous (Berlioz 1969 [1854]: 286–7). If he were still alive in 1933, he would have been able to take credit for his prescient vision.

Film studios continued (and continue) to use click tracks for purposes of synchronization, with modifications that included the introduction of the SMPTE (Society of Motion Picture and Television Engineers) time code in 1967, and the integration of the time code with MIDI (Musical Instrument Digital Interface) technology in the 1980s. The SMPTE time code marks film, video, or audio location in terms of hours, minutes, seconds, and frames, providing a time reference for synchronization, editing, and identification (Cohen 2009: 108–9; Ratcliff 1999). Click tracks and synchronization also found a home in advertising, eventually finding their way into radio and television. The chronology of their usage is unclear, as the first commercials in radio broadcasting appeared in the late 1910s (before Disney's patent), and later in television in the 1940s. Nevertheless, by the 1950s radio and TV advertisements had to adhere to strict time guidelines—such as the 30-second or 60-second spot—with the musicians playing to a click.[10]

Though not nearly as widespread, click tracks also found their way intermittently into classical/academic concert-hall performances, including avant-garde electronic studio music (Taruskin 2010b: 300; Kimura 1995: 71), as well as into fusion jazz and "world beat" styles (Zagorski-Thomas 2014: 182). The metronome has even been treated as an instrument in its own right, as seen in György Ligeti's *Symphonic Poem* for 100 metronomes (1962), and Gordon Crosse's *Play Ground* for orchestra, expanded percussion, and metronome (1978). But where click tracks would eventually find their true home is in rock-pop music (including rap/hip-hop), to which I now turn.

The Rock Era

This section will necessarily be brief, as I will address in considerable detail the sociological and aesthetic transformations that took place as a result of click tracks being adopted by the rock industry, especially the time period encompassing the late 1970s to the early 1990s, in Chapter 6. Here I will focus on the basic technological accomplishments, providing important historical contexts for more recent developments (to be entertained at the end of this chapter) and the discussions that follow in the next chapter.

As we now know, click tracks in one format or another had been around since the 1930s, and by the time of the emergence and/or success of electric

---

[10]The topic of music and advertising is a gargantuan one, and beyond the scope of this chapter. For cultural-political primers on the history of music in advertising, see Klein (2009) and Taylor (2012).

FIGURE 5.5 *UREI 964 Digital Metronome (photo courtesy of Ron "Obvious" Vermeulen)*.

blues, jump bands, and early rock 'n' roll in the 1950s they had already become a norm in advertising for radio and television, in addition to their continued use in films. The first mass-produced digital metronome was released in 1959 by the Universal Audio Company under the product name UA 960 (Anonymous 1964: 4); by the mid-1970s the third-generation machine the UREI 964 Digital Metronome would become the industry standard for all forms of recorded music for the next two decades (Ron "Obvious" Vermeulen, personal communication, 2018).[11] What is most interesting from a historical point of view is the UREI 964's continued reliance on frames per beat as a temporal reference point (refer to Figure 5.5). With such a device the larger the number on the front of the machine, the *slower* the click (and, conversely, the fewer the frames per click, faster). Musicians and engineers of the period who needed to know the equivalent bpms (beats per minute) (standard metronome markings) had to make the corresponding calculations.[12]

During the 1970s other pre-digital, pre-MIDI recording technology included functions that frequently served the role of a click track. Many

---

[11]Engineer-producers Ron "Obvious" Vermeulen and Mike Fraser remember the UREI 964 being used at Little Mountain Sound Studios, the largest of the music studios active in Vancouver during this era (Ron "Obvious" Vermeulen and Mike Fraser, personal communication, 2018). UA or UREI digital metronomes were also used at Mushroom Studios in Vancouver (Charlie Richmond and Rolf Hennemann, personal communication, 2018), in all of the major LA studios (Keith Olsen, Mike Frondelli, Mike Shapiro, Ross Hogarth, and Neal Avron, personal communication, 2019), in Seattle (Brian Foraker, personal communication, 2019), and in New York City (Mike Frondelli, personal communication, 2019). After the release of the second generation of the UA 960, the UA 962, the company underwent a name change to United Recording Electronics Industries; in 1999 they switched back to the original Universal Audio.
[12]The first commercially successful electric metronome was patented in 1938 by Frederick Franz (Turner 2017: 54).

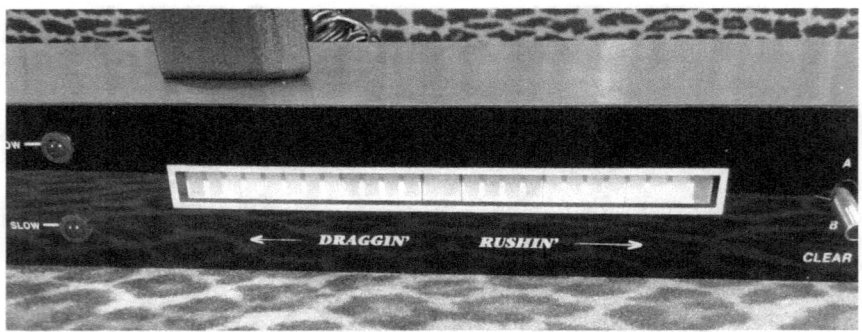

FIGURE 5.6 *Russian Dragon (photo courtesy of Peter Langston).*

analog modular synthesizers had a "clock out" (sometimes "sync out") jack that provided a pulse or click so that other modules could stay in time with each other (the line goes into the "clock in" jack on the paired device).[13] Modular, microprocessor-based sequencers also by nature included programming along set/consistent tempo parameters. Ralph Dyck's invention and later commercialization of the iconic sequencer the Roland MC-8 Microcomposer was used extensively in the studio and live by such bands as Toto, The Human League, Tangerine Dream, Yellow Magic Orchestra, and Kraftwerk, as well as projects by the composer and producer Giorgio Moroder (more on this below).[14]

A tangentially related device was the Russian Dragon, a studio tool invented by Marius Perron for Jeanius Electronics in San Antonio, Texas in the late 1980s. Frequently used in tandem with the UREI 964, the degree of its simplicity and usefulness was matched by the cleverness of its product name (refer to Figure 5.6):

> The Russian Dragon was an amazing piece of gear. It had two inputs in the back of it. One of them was your click, and then you could select the other input—either the kick drum or the snare drum, or any other thing you wanted to put in it. And I would usually put the snare drum in it. And I would look, and if the click drum was "tick, tick, tick," and the snare drum was every two and four, it would show on a row of LEDs if you were "rushin'" or "draggin'" on the beat. So they called it the Russian Dragon [laughs]. That was the product name! It was really clever, and

---

[13] Many thanks to Spencer Carson at GGRP (Griffiths, Gibson, and Ramsay Production) Audio House for his patience in explaining and demonstrating this technology live for me.
[14] Dyck developed his sequencer while working at the electronic music studio at the University of British Columbia (Gord Lord, personal communication, 2018).

most LA studios started using them all the time. Because you could tell right away if the drummer was off the click. (Keith Olsen, personal communication, 2019)[15]

According to Randy Raine-Reusch, a performing musician and composer active in the Vancouver popular and avant-garde scenes of the 1970s and 1980s, tape loops seem to have served the purpose of a poorer artist's click track, with proper clicks being the domain of the big studios. Repetitive rhythms and/or melodic ostinati formed the basis of loops that could be used for synchronization purposes, or as compositional elements in their own right (the same technology allowed for delay or echo in those early days as well). The use of tape loops goes back to electro-acoustic composing of the 1960s, though generally these "tracks" were not used as clicks (personal communication, 2018).

Examples of loops that acted as click tracks are sporadic pre-late 1970s, but they appear on high-profile songs by well-known artists. Ringo Starr created a one-bar loop that functioned as a click on the Beatles' "Tomorrow Never Knows" (*Revolver*, 1966), a cut-and-paste drum loop played underneath Fleetwood Mac's "Rhiannon" (*Fleetwood Mac*, 1975), and an arpeggiated synth loop on the Who's "Won't Get Fooled Again" (*Who's Next*, 1971) required Keith Moon to keep a relatively steady pulse for the entirety of the track.[16] One of the earliest documented commentaries on its use in rock music comes from the recollection of the musician and producer Alan Parsons, who worked on Pink Floyd's *Dark Side of the Moon* (1973):

> They were quite revolutionary at the time and had a very individual sound. On the heartbeats [opening of the album], you hear the noise being modulated by a noise gate which is an integral part of that sound. Nick Mason originally played the bass drum to a click track, then we just chose the best few bars and looped them. (quoted in Cunningham 1998: 205)

Most commentators from that period (and since), however, acknowledge that it was the mainstream, commercial success of disco in the mid- to late

---

[15]Further technical specifications can be found in Marans (1990); I thank Brian Foraker for introducing me to the Russian Dragon.
[16]I thank (again) Ron "Obvious" Vermeulen for identifying the Beatles and Who tracks, and give credit to Kent Hartman's writing for the information on Fleetwood Mac (2017: 68). I also can't pass up an extended (and colorful) comment made by Stan Lynch (original drummer for Tom Petty and the Heartbreakers) in an interview I conducted with him in 2019: "The perfect blend would be 'Won't Get Fooled Again' by the Who. There's a sequence, and Moon *torments* that sequence. You know what I mean? He doesn't cleave to it, he plays *with* it and stomps it to death. He doesn't give a shit about it. He's so irreverent. He comes and goes at his leisure, makes the sequence work for him. That was the perfect combination, a bar of precise musical steel up Moon's ass to make a brilliant record" (personal communication, 2019).

1970s that led to the widespread adoption of the click track in the recording studio.[17] As Simon Zagorski-Thomas notes in his chapter on the interaction of recording technology and rock drum kit performance beginning in the 1970s, from the middle of that decade it had become common for DJs to use the technique of "beat matching" when playing two records simultaneously, which required altering the speed of the two turntables so that the beats would align (2010: 196). This led to a heightened sense of steady (metronomic) time, synchronization, and the categorization of tracks according to bpms, since you couldn't have overlying tracks with instruments speeding up and slowing down in different places. While the general public most likely didn't perceive the subtle but very important shift toward the reliance on click tracks that was taking place, DJs, producers, and the studio musicians creating those albums ushered in a new era in which "playing in time" took on radically new meanings.

Many credit Donna Summer's breakthrough hit "I Feel Love" (*Remember Yesterday*, 1977) as the primary instigator of this new trend. Co-produced by Giorgio Moroder and Pete Bellotte, it is understood as the first disco piece to use only sequencers and synthesizers on the backing tracks—instead of the usual acoustic instruments/orchestras—as well as the first commercially successful song to align synthesizers to a click track.[18] The song became immortalized on Daft Punk's hugely successful *Random Access Memories* (2013) on track #3, titled "Giorgio by Moroder," in which we hear an excerpt of an interview with Moroder speaking about how he constructed "I Feel Love" by adding a click to the 24-track tape that was then synched to the Moog modular.[19] The song is often identified as the first EDM (electronic dance music) piece, simultaneously popularizing disco for a wide demographic. With a floating human voice over a mechanized, metronomic foundation, Brian Eno would comment: "This single is going to change the sound of club music for the next 15 years"; Moroder himself would go even further: "I knew that could be a sound of the future [synthesizers], but I didn't realize how much the impact would be."[20]

The final push of click tracks into the studio and rock world came about due to creations and adaptations in response to technological challenges. The aforementioned MIDI technology was created because of the rise and popularity of electronic musical instruments in the early 1980s. MIDI

---

[17] Anonymous (1977); Fish (1978: 14); Mattingly (1990: 64–5); Zagorski-Thomas (2010: 196); Danielsen (2010: 3).

[18] Two years previous Moroder and Summer had worked together on the hit "Love to Love You Baby" (1975), which was based rhythmically on a drum loop conceived and performed by Keith Forsey (Ross Hogarth, personal communication, 2019).

[19] "I Feel Love" is only identified by name on the longer interview that is included on the *RAM* Deluxe Edition, 10' vinyl.

[20] The significance of this track as outlined in this paragraph, as well as the Brian Eno quote, is found in Buskin (2009) and Cheal (2016); Moroder's observation is from track #3 of *RAM*.

helped standardize and synchronize the vast array of electronic devices that were coming out, including drum machines (most significantly in a rock music context) and computers. As composers and bands began to record background tracks and drum parts with these newly discovered sounds, there arose the need to coordinate with these nonhuman agents, and the click track served this purpose perfectly.[21] The click track was liberated from the studio soon thereafter, as musicians began playing along with this pre-recorded material in concert; it was only a matter of time before clicks were found to be equally helpful in coordinating music with stage lighting and other dramatic effects in live performances.

The arrival of MIDI and click tracks also had important and enduring structural and financial ramifications in the studio. Producers and engineers realized that recordings could be made cheaper with less musicians (but not always) and that you could engage in non-linear performances and recordings—a bit at a time, out of order, and/or single musicians by themselves—because the click would ensure that later sessions would all line up. Digital recording technology existed since the late 1960s, though its convergence with computers, MIDI interfaces, and compact discs in the 1980s gave industry professionals powerful new tools of further control and distribution. Tape degradation from multitracking was no longer an issue, richer bass frequencies became possible, and individual instruments and the voice could now be moved temporally and manipulated timbrally in ways only dreamed about by the cut-and-splice engineers of the previous generation. The drummer extraordinaire Bill Bruford who was active during this technological transition noted with a touch of pathos the increased power it afforded record producers and engineers over drummers and other musicians in the studio (Bruford 2018: 100–1).

Numerous sources are easily found in print and on the internet that addresses the nuts-and-bolts of creating and manipulating a click track, including historical approaches. This is not of interest to me or most of my readers at this point in the story, I'm assuming. But for the basic details, and by way of conclusion, a click track is generally provided by a sequencer, synthesizer, or software program (unless one wants to record the sound of an actual metronome). A tremendous amount of choice can be used for the audio signal, everything from something that sounds like a "click" to isolated parts of the drum, such as just a cowbell or a floor tom. The rationale for these choices will be discussed in more detail in Chapter 6; but a number

---

[21]Samplers and drum machines were used during this same era with similar rhythmic/metronomic effects in rap/hip-hop (Schloss 2004: 25–62; Bell 2018: 58–62). While there is not as much written about country music studio production during this decade, Hughes (2015: 167–88) suggests that soul and "discobeats" began to pull country in the same direction (in terms of rhythmic-synchronization) as rock and hip-hop. The first #1 hit to feature an electronic drum machine is credited to "It's a Family Affair" (1971) by Sly and the Family Stone.

of drummers in the 1980s also chose to program a quantized percussion part on a drum machine, which would then play in the headphones in lieu of the traditional "click" of the metronome.

The earlier observations are only strategies for a quantized, aural rhythmic cue, however (understanding that blinking lights had become standard on metronomes, and some studio musicians experimented with purely visual click tracks). I finish this chapter with more recent explorations into visual and tactile feedback, including new approaches to the manipulation of time that rely on click tracks but are nevertheless not consistent or regularized as dictated by a metronomic pulse.

Recent Developments

Every decade of the twentieth century saw patents filed in the United States for "new" and "improved" metronomes and their design, with the numbers increasing dramatically from mid-century onwards (mostly aural devices, but also a few visual and tactile ones).[22] Electronic, digital, and micro-processing technologies opened many new avenues of exploration, though at the core of each new patent was a vision already anticipated by Disney and his colleagues.[23] It is worth noting what may be overlooked here: many patents, even if granted, never saw the light of commercial production; and many applications for grants were also not successful. Nevertheless, a number of patents and available products are fascinating from the perspective of history and the possibilities they afford for new ways of interfacing with externalized entraining agents.

Visual metronome/synchronizing device patents are the next most numerous after aural metronomes, and most of them were conceived as a way of freeing musicians from headphones and the "tyranny" of the click, as well as potential hearing loss. Two of the more creative designs are reproduced in Figure 5.7, Juan del Castillo's "Optical Metronome" and Gary Duke's "Digital Pulsing Visual Metronome." Filed roughly 30 years apart, they both provide new strategies for synchronization with music that do not rely on an aural cue.

Beginning with del Castillo's "Optical Metronome" (image on the left in Figure 5.7), we see an approach that joins the visual light or blip of the

---

[22]A number of interesting patents were also submitted by French and Chinese inventors, though the numbers are much fewer, and my lack of language ability did not allow for their translation.
[23]Once slight exception to this rule is a metronome ("Time-Measuring Device") developed by William Duncan in 1952 that was capable of beating out non-isochronous beats—such as 2+3+3+2—to help performers with "modern" compositions (Duncan 1952). While I'm not aware of its use outside of Western music contexts, such a device could potentially aid South Korean drumming students who must learn a number of such metrical types.

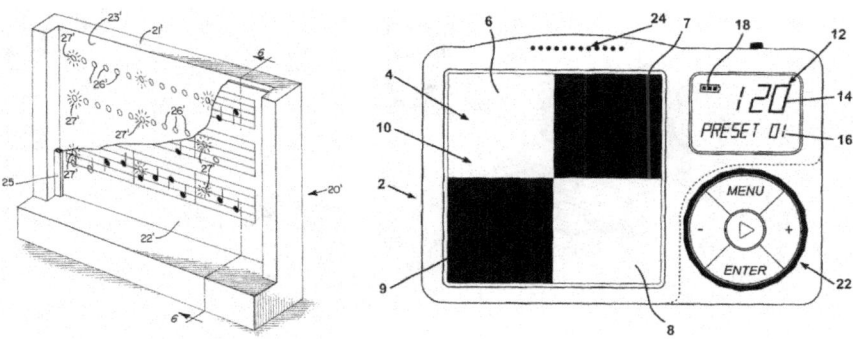

FIGURE 5.7 *"Optical Metronome" (del Castillo 1976), left; and "Digital Pulsing Visual Metronome" (Duke 2008), right (public domain).*

electric metronome with traditional staff notation. One begins by inserting sheet music into the front of the device (it's not clear if one uses a "real" piece of music, or something prepared to fit within the interface). A decision is then made whether or not visual cues will follow single staves of music or a number of staves in coordination simultaneously. From here a final choice is made whether or not only the beginnings of the measures will be cued (such as what we see in Figure 5.7), or any number of divisions of the bar. Once ready, the device then shines light through the score at a steady speed according to a pre-set metronome marking.

The second metronome depicted in Figure 5.7 (right) is a variation on technology conceived by both Berlioz and Disney, a visual synchronization device that is kept close to the performer but just out of his/her direct vision. Realizing what researchers in entrainment studies have documented, movement combined with a visual cue increases the accuracy/speed of synchronization, in this particular case a four-region checkerboard pattern that alternates the dark and light spaces in metronomic time. Duke goes further in providing a rationale for a visual metronome that resonates with the experience of many performers (he includes in a previous passage the danger of hearing loss with traditional click tracks):

> A predominantly visual metronome offers some key advantages. Firstly, the musician can concentrate on the music being produced without audible interference from the metronome. Secondly, there is no decrease in perception of the tempo when a musician is playing along in perfect synchronicity (unlike the audible click track which can "disappear" when the musician is playing in perfect time). Lastly, the musician has greater flexibility in that he or she can effectively receive tempo information only when desired. For example, the musician can look away from or wilfully

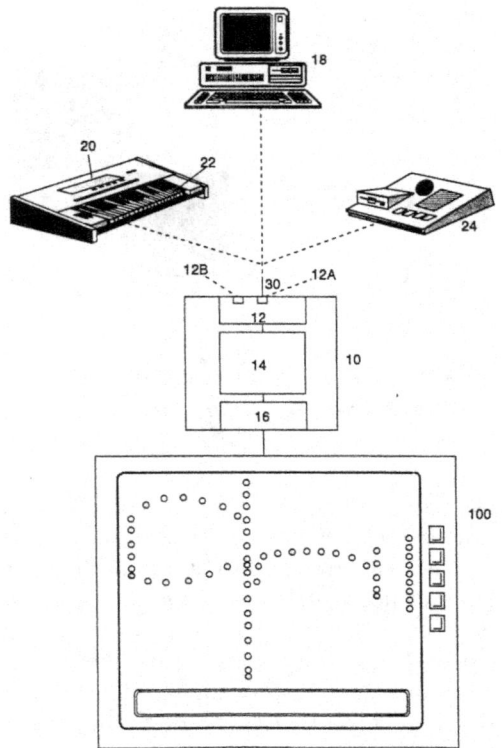

FIGURE 5.8 *"Visual Music Conducting Device" (Kestner-Clifton and Vogel 1994; public domain).*

ignore the visual signal, effectively using it on as-needed basis. In contrast it is extremely difficult, if not impossible, to wilfully ignore an audio based metronome. (Duke 2008: 1)

Duke's "Digital Pulsing Visual Metronome" was eventually released commercially as the "Viziklik."[24]

The last patent I want to highlight here brings together computers, electronic instruments, MIDI interfaces, and a visual cueing system in one complete package (refer to Figure 5.8). From the origin of the signals employing MIDI technology we know we are located no earlier than the 1980s; but with the nature of the visual output—a display that mimics the

---

[24]http://www.viziklik.com

motion of a conductor's baton—we move back in time to the seventeenth or eighteenth centuries:

> An electronic visual music conducting device is provided which is adapted to receive electronic timing signals representative of the tempo of a piece of music, and to use these timing signals to control a visual display which indicates tempo and rhythm by simulating the movement of a conductor's baton, including the acceleration normally present as the baton approaches the point of a beat, and the deceleration normally present as the baton moves away from the point of a beat. The electronic timing signals are preferably MIDI System Exclusive Real Time Message Timing Clock signals (F8H). (Kestner-Clifton and Vogel 1994)

Where the "Visual Music Conducting Device" improves on earlier visual metronomes or click tracks is the manner in which it allows performers to anticipate when the next beat or pulse is to sound.[25] This patent was also released commercially as "The Visual Conductor."[26]

Visual click tracks were mentioned in interviews I conducted with Vancouver- and LA-based engineer-producers and drummers and in trade magazines. Vancouver and LA engineer-producer Mike Flicker saw a few drummers in the studio using blinking lights in place of an auditory click (personal communication, 2019), and Michael Hanson, the drummer for the Canadian band Glass Tiger, mentions using one for touring (Budofsky 1988: 8). Randy-Raine-Reusch recalls seeing musicians going into the mixing room and getting their cues from the lights on the board (personal communication, 2018). While engineer-producers Ross Hogarth (LA) and Ron Obvious (Vancouver) both saw attempts at using visual clicks in the studio, both reported that the musicians they observed could not work with them, due to the extra few milliseconds it required in reaction time. This makes sense with what we know about sensory modalities and entrainment, in addition to the fact that many people I spoke with reminded me that drummers often like to play with their eyes closed.

As noted earlier in this chapter, Giordano and Wanderly (2015) found that while there was a rise in the number of tactile metronomes that were appearing on the market, most (if not all) of them had not engaged in empirical research and had based their assumptions on anecdotal evidence from practitioners. Nevertheless, in addition to synchronization, a secondary but equally important advantage arose from the use of tactile cueing

---

[25]While not tracing the path of a typical baton, the "Visual Metronome" patented by Burrell George also uses a block or stream of moving light to help users visualize and anticipate the placement of the next sound (George 1987).
[26]http://www.bartal.com/vc.htm

devices, which was the physical feedback and sense of touch it provided the musician—what people in the industry often refer to as haptic perception or communication: "Increasing interest has also been dedicated to the role of haptic feedback and stimulation in the context of musical interaction. Haptic perception plays an important part in the process of embodiment of a musical instrument, in shaping the perceived qualities of an acoustic musical instrument and, in expert performance, for tasks such as articulation and timing" (Giordano and Wanderly 2015: 1).

One of the earliest patents for a tactile metronome appears right at the turn of the century in Scott Fulford's "Tactile Tempo Indicating Device" (1999). This "invention" is really just Disney et al.'s solenoid configuration found in Figure 5.4. Fulford's patent in fact relies specifically on solenoids—electrical impulses, springs, and all—and is conveyed to the user through a belt clip, neck strap, or through the wall of the solenoid-containing case itself. It is difficult to see how this patent improves on or further develops the work done at Disney Studios; but Fulford does provide commentary that shows very real benefits to users of "his" device, such as mitigating eye strain from visual metronomes, and by helping hearing-impaired musicians coordinate within large ensembles such as choirs or orchestras. Five years later a patent by Parsons (2004) would expand Fulford's work by introducing different kinds of tactile inducers in what he called simply a "Tactile Metronome."

A further development on this basic design is found in Manuel Diaz's "Pulsating Metronome," which was granted a patent the same year as Parsons (2004). The beauty of Diaz's vision lies in his marriage of very old chronometer technology with modern tactile-haptic feedback. In a nutshell, Diaz packaged his pulsating stimuli within the body of a timepiece worn on the wrist. Designed to look like a digital watch, it promises portability that was not possible with its predecessors. Diaz's approach and design found commercial production in the Soundbrenner Pulse, a digital "wristwatch" that can be worn on the wrist, ankle, arm, or chest (with a body strap). Purely tactile in conception, a user can twist the outer wheel of the device to set tempo or can tap in a speed manually. The Soundbrenner Pulse has the additional advantage of syncing with any number of musicians wearing the same device[27] (see Figure 5.9).[28]

The last of the portable, body-affixed tactile metronomes I will discuss here is the Peterson Body Beat Sync™, which the company claims is "the world's most versatile metronome."[29] More clunky in its design than its

---

[27]http://www.soundbrenner.com
[28]In 1814 "watch-for-metronomes" appeared, roughly the same period as Maelzel's metronome, so the idea of joining chronometers with (stop) watches occurred centuries ago (see Turner 2017b: 43–5).
[29]https://www.petersontuners.com/products/bodybeatsync/

FIGURE 5.9 *Soundbrenner Pulse on guitarist (photo courtesy of Soundbrenner).*

relative the Soundbrenner Pulse, it surpasses in function where it loses in overall look. The Body Beat Sync™ is a fully programmable unit that can accommodate tempo, meter, subdivisions, and accent pattern, and it can even be programmed to include "tempo maps" (variable click track patterns; more below) from a computer via a MIDI interface. The pulse is delivered to the musician's body via a clamp that is attached to the wearer's clothing, and like the Soundbrenner Pulse, a number of musicians can sync with each other remotely. The Body Beat Sync™ goes one step further, however, in that it can produce aural, visual, and tactile cues.

The remaining tactile-driven devices were developed primarily for the use of drum set players, though all of the products I will discuss are advertised as being of use to other rhythm section members, especially electric bass players. This category or family of devices—with some of the most colorful and evocative product titles out there—includes the ButtKicker,[30] the Throne Thumper,[31] and the Porter & Davies BC2.[32] In all cases, the device represents a small box that is attached to the stool that the musician sits on, which sends reinforced low frequencies triggered by the bass drum (or other low-pitched instruments) through the thighs of the performer. In the case of the ButtKicker, the website openly advertises its possible use as a tactile click track; for the other two products, it seems that they can also be used for this purpose,

---

[30] http://www.thebuttkicker.com/pro-audio
[31] http://pearldrum.com/news-events/drumset-news/pearls-throne-thumper...-a-real-world-review
[32] https://www.porteranddavies.co.uk/products/bc2/

though they're more effective for returning a sense of feel and feedback from the drum kit (or bass or keyboard) that is often lost when having to play with headphones and/or through amplification systems that frequently separate the performer significantly from the where the sound eventually is heard.[33]

For performers and composers of the twenty-first century, the full gamut of modal interfaces is now available, either at a distance or attached to the body. Visual and tactile cues brought back a sense of embodiment once part and parcel of live, face-to-face music-making, even if today we have the additional contexts of musicians only "coming together" in a final recording, or participating together simultaneously but at great distances from each other online. The last remaining component of pre-metronome time-keeping—human volition separate from external mechanisms that may or may not strive for metronomic synchronization—would appear only in the past few decades, with its full ramifications yet to be fully appreciated or understood.

Composer-Performer Directed Click Tracks

With the advent of MIDI files in the early 1980s, it became possible for a musician-programmer to create a click track that could vary in speed, even down to the individual beat level. One of the earliest sequencers on the market for computers, the Mark of the Unicorn Performer developed for Apple Macintosh in 1985, had a Metronome window that allowed the programmer to fine-tune note lengths and change the lengths of the individual clicks.[34] There didn't seem to be much use for it in the 1980s, at least in the popular music world and its focus on metronomic time, but it has become the norm in film composition and is currently used by some bands in live performances (usually by the drummer) to allow a song to speed up, even just minutely, for heightened dramatic effect. The earliest reference to a "variable click" that I found in my survey of *Modern Drummer* articles appeared in April of 1985 in an interview with the TV and film studio drummer Steve Schaeffer (Flans 1985: 53).

Today such a variable click track is known as a "tempo map," where it can be used proactively—such as in a film score—when you want the music

---

[33]In an email message from the artistic director of Porter & Davies, Dil Davies, he indicated that their systems were more often used for tactile feedback, and that audible clicks were still used, but at a lower level: "P&D systems work at their very best as monitor systems: not only do most people call them 'Game changers,' but they drastically help reduce on-stage volume and also allow the musician to have a much more simple and quieter in-ear or wedge mix. This in turn allows you to have a click much quieter, as it would not be fighting other sounds volume-wise in the traditional monitoring" (personal communication, 2018). The only drummer I met that used the Throne Thumper, LA session great Denny Fongheiser, told me he only used it for the tactile feedback (personal communication, 2019).

[34]I thank my UBC composition colleagues Keith Hamel and Bob Pritchard for helping me locate this information (personal communication, 2018).

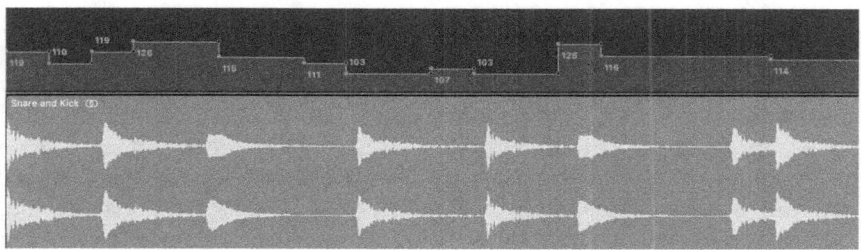

FIGURE 5.10 *A tempo map using Logic Pro (change in bpm indicated by numbers and horizontal lines on top of screen; image courtesy of Holly Winter).*

to breathe a bit (slow down, speed up), but still desire tight synchronization from your musicians (with each other, and also with visual cues in the film). This capability is now ubiquitous in industry-standard programs such as Pro Tools or Logic Pro. Tempo maps can also be used after the fact, such as trying to document the tempo of a recorded performance that wasn't initially set to a click track or metronome, so that one can later add MIDI tracks, production effects, etc. (see Figure 5.10). Tempo maps can become quite sophisticated, including sudden changes in tempi and/or meter changes, with each new layer of manipulation requiring additional rehearsal time by the musicians, as well as an enhanced sense of timing related to, but also distinct from, metronomic performance. One such anecdote was related to me by LA studio drummer and UCLA professor Mike Shapiro:

> When Natalie Cole did the *Unforgettable* album and she did the duet with her father, when in the short time that I played with her when you play that song, you're playing with Nat's vocal with the band. Because there was no click on that original recording, a drummer had come and had clicked his sticks to the original track to try to create a click. But that thing is *all over the place*. It's worse than when a click is programmed to slow down or speed up. This thing is like—if you measured it on a grid, it wasn't close. You had to really learn where the hiccups were, and then adjust accordingly. That was a challenge. And then after a while, once I got more in tune with what was happening with the track I stopped listening to that click, because it was a hassle. I was just sort of reading with the strings and his voice. (personal communication, 2019)

The greatest change in the evolution of the click track, however, comes in the product known as BeatSeeker,[35] a Max for Live responsive click

---

[35] The original program was called "Beat-Keeper," or "B-Keeper" for short; Robertson and his colleague Mark Plumbley published heir initial findings in 2007 (Robertson and Plumbley 2007).

track software program developed by Dr. Andrew Robertson at Queen Mary, the University of London in 2011. The technology completely turns the traditional click track system on its head, so that the drummer is now able to dictate the speed and flow of a performance, even with pre-recorded tracks, up to a 5 percent differential. With BeatSeeker the drummer mics up the snare and bass/kick drums, with the live signals fed into the software program. By using a sequencer that incorporates a pitch-tracking algorithm, the software is able to automatically adjust the speed of any pre-recorded track.[36]

There are a number of applications for this program. The immediate benefit comes to bands in live performance settings, where the drummer can now speed up or slow down—within the 5 percent range—in response to the mood of the audience, fellow band members, and/or the way she/he/they is feeling in the moment. BeatSeeker also allows for the drummer through a MIDI controller to switch back and forth on the fly between a metronomic click and the responsive click track setting. The same approach can also be used in the studio, for bands or artists who wish for a studio recording with a little more space or flexibility in the timing of the tracks. While the program currently relies on drum set playing with the relatively conventional placement of the hits—backbeat snare and bass drum strokes that don't syncopate or deviate too far from their "normal" positions—it seems that over time the program will be able to further adapt to more complex patterns.[37]

It's too early to say what this all means about the desire for or standard of metronomic time-keeping and performance in current rock music settings. What it does signal is the return of human input and control as instigator into rhythmic cueing technology, especially by live musicians in real time (whether in the studio or a concert). How it will be used in the future will depend on ever-changing ideas about what it means to "play in time," and how our relationships with machinery as well as finding the beat continue to evolve. At the core of this issue is how we come to define "human feel" in the timing process, and whether or not that can include playing in strict metronomic time. The next chapter will address all of these concerns as I move to the related sociological and aesthetic considerations of entrainment and the human-technology interface.

---

[36] An earlier product known as the Human Clock by the company Kahler was used sporadically during the 1980s with the same claims of musician-driven synchronization. According to one of the top studio drummers of that era, however, it was not effective because of its slow reaction time and its overall inaccuracy (Denny Fongheiser, personal communication, 2019).
[37] A similar function has been integrated into James Holden's Group Humanizer patch, though Holden's work has more to do with microtiming and interpersonal reactions within an ensemble. I thank Justin Devries for introducing these products to me.

6

Entrainment and the Human-Technology Interface, Sociological and Aesthetic Considerations

Finding the Beat, Redux

From 2004 until 2010 an extended research project was carried out at the University of Oslo called Rhythm in the Age of Digital Reproduction (RADR).[1] Under the project manager Professor Anne Danielsen the team worked on a single question: "What happened to the sound and rhythm of African-American-derived, groove-directed popular music styles when these grooves began to be produced and played by machines?" (Danielsen 2010: 1). The central assumptions they tackled are worth reproducing in full:

> The question is a challenge to the view shared by many researchers up to the present that a groove depends on human performativity to be aesthetically satisfying: "feel" is something that musicians add to an otherwise stiff rhythmic structure through their performance of it. It has further been assumed that the groove qualities of rhythmic music arise specifically from microtemporal deviations from a presumed norm. It therefore also follows that machine-generated music must be necessarily devoid of groove qualities, because it typically lacks the microtemporal variation added by people in performance. (Danielsen 2010: 1)[2]

---

[1] This title is a play on Walter Benjamin's classic *The Work of Art in the Age of Mechanical Reproduction* (2008 [1936]).
[2] A representative sample of such continued thinking is found in Hennig et al. (2011).

The project was aimed at computer-based, groove-oriented musics, but the conclusions drawn are directly pertinent to the material of this chapter, which has to do with sociological and aesthetic responses to human interfaces with externalized entraining agents. The first trend they noted was how, since the 1990s, digital technology has actually led to significant experimentation with and the manipulation of rhythms on the microtiming level, even to extremes beyond older human approaches.[3] The second trend is a counterargument to the entire discourse on groove requiring a human, microtemporal-reflected performance that finds strictly metrical, quantized rhythmic musics as an ideal. Both of these trends are only possible with the advent and use of the click track.

In this chapter, I want to explore the "conventional wisdom" held by many of us—including drummers, producers, and musicians in general—that playing with a "human" touch means playing without the aid of a synchronization device, and/or periodically deviating from a metronomical norm. To play devil's advocate, perhaps click tracks have moved us closer to a kind of rhythmic perfection we could only imagine before. Technological advances in instrument construction and software development have already led to normalized behavior regarding the in tune-ness of equal temperament on our keyboards and the timbre and intonation of voices modified by autotuning.[4] What about a kind of "perfect rhythm" analogous to "perfect pitch," one in which a performer can maintain a strict tempo without rhythmic deviation but with no recourse to a metronome or other externalized entraining technologies?[5] What if drummers in the past *couldn't* play in such perfect time, and that click tracks both exposed this weakness and helped usher in a new era of human capabilities?

Regardless of one's views on this topic, as computers, electronic drum machines, and click tracks became the new standard in studios and concerts of the rock and pop worlds from the 1980s onward, the resultant sound and feel became part of the overall performance aesthetic. As the sound

---

[3] Andrew Goodwin noticed the same tendency more than twenty-five years ago with regard to the multitracking process: "Similarly, where the multitracking process [with its reliance on click tracks] can be seen as one that rationalizes temporality in music production, the new technologies achieve precisely the reverse. Now, parts can be programmed out of sync with each other and the tempo itself can be programmed to vary. In other words, the tendency toward rhythmic one-dimensionality that is identified as an effect of multitracking is in fact reversed by machines and samplers" (1992: 90–1).

[4] In addition to an excellent discussion of autotune technology and the cyborg voice, Prior (2009) addresses relationships between humans and machines, analog and digital, live and mediated, and the real and the simulated (see further Prior 2018).

[5] One author has made a claim that all humans possess a perfect rhythm inherent to human biology—he even links it to the mutual phase-locking understanding of the term entrainment—though what he has in mind is much more metaphysical, even cosmic, in conception (Leonard 2006).

engineer and academic Simon Zagorski-Thomas acutely noted, this situation "situates the click track in the realm of a non-human agent in actor-network theory (ANT) or as a technology whose design and use configures its human user" (2014: 183). As many of the drummers documented in this chapter will express in the section that follows, it was their personal negotiation with the click track that led to significant and even unexpected discoveries about not only their capabilities as a musician and timekeeper but also about what it meant to "find the beat" and "play in time" with interest and in an emotionally captivating manner. These discoveries were as varied as the men who embodied them.[6]

Technological changes frequently usher in interpersonal changes, and the use of click tracks in the studio and concert altered in profound ways the skills and strategies employed by professional musicians, especially drum set players, who were often isolated in the recording booth away from their bandmates, both physically and/or temporally. For all of the benefits of multitrack and non-linear recording practices, the socialization of learning through music-making with others face-to-face nevertheless suffered a deep blow, potentially robbing beginning players—those too young to have worked and lived in the "analog" world—of an important outlet for musical instruction. As Rock & Roll Hall of Famer Bill Bruford (Yes, Genesis, King Crimson, Gong) reflected on in the context of the transition to computers and digital recording in the world of drumming:

> Furthermore, [the digitization of drumming] is held responsible in part for a diminution of collaborative interaction in performance, lamented by some of our experts. Technology is seen as disconnecting the younger player from the cultural ways of learning that transfer skills and deliver a cultural context for their appropriate use. It is thus a principal agent underlying the decline of cultural connectedness identified earlier. (2018: 75)

If there is a privileged vantage point to this chapter, it is that culture— or, more precisely, cultural practice—tends to trump everything else. If we have learned anything from anthropology and/or ethnomusicology, it is that claims of the "natural," "normal," "correct," or even "biological" are almost always culturally constructed. It is like trying to hit an elusive and ever-moving target. While a number of practitioners in the passages that follow were distrustful of the new technologies of time-keeping and synchronization, many more embraced the challenges and possibilities they

---

[6]In my research on the 1980s and early 1990s in rock music, including numerous live interviews, I encountered no female drummers or engineer-producers. One perspective on such gendering of technological and creative control is found in Wolfe (2019).

afforded, though never to the point of sacrificing their humanity. It is with this sense of curiosity and open-mindedness that I now turn to the voices of our musical mentors.

Setting the Scene: Studios, Crews, and *Modern Drummer*

It was evident early on in my research that I would need to travel to Los Angeles if I was interested in meeting the musicians (engineers, producers, and drummers) and visiting the studios that were at the heart of this human-technology interface that began in the late 1970s and swelled to prominence in the 1980s and early 1990s. By the 1960s the center of recording influence and power in the United States had already shifted from New York City to LA; according to Chris Stone (co-founder of the renowned Record Plant) there were six primary reasons for this transformation: (1) the number and quality of studios; (2) the number and quality of producers and engineers; (3) the number and quality of artists who resided and/or moved to LA; (4) technological advances (companies and inventors in LA); (5) the early use of digital machines and studios; and (6) the many contributions to acoustic technology (2005: 49–53). Stone provided one underlying motive for these changes, as expressed through the words of the producer extraordinaire Bill Szymczyk: "Producer Bill Szymczyk (Joe Walsh, Eagles, B.B. King) says it well: 'It was really those damn Beatles and the whole London scene. Those guys were always ahead, whether it was George Martin doing something different with 4-track, tape doubling techniques, phasing, wrapping masking tape around the capstan motor, whatever. We could not keep up'" (2005: 51).

During this period of growth from the 1950s to the 1960s in LA, the major studios such as RCA, Warner Brothers, A&M, and Capitol did not grasp the full artistic and commercial significance of rock 'n' roll/rock (though they would later jump on the bandwagon), as noted by British music critic Barney Hoskyns: "Capitol were slow to recognize the true impact of rock'n'roll. Reflecting the taste of its original owners, the company remained cool towards a youth phenomenon it regarded as faddish and ephemeral . . . leaving the way open for a multitude of smaller independents to scoop up neglected Los Angeles talent" (2009: 46; see further Hartman 2017 and Cogan and Clark 2003 [first three chapters]).

And scoop up they did. Five of the most successful and iconic rock studios of all time—all independent—were opened in LA in the 1960s, in the following chronological order (refer also to Figure 6.1): (1) United Western Recorders (6000 and 6050 Sunset Blvd, 1961; its founder, Bill Putnam, was the inventor of the UREI click track and the Universal console); (2) Sunset Sound (6650 Sunset Blvd, 1962); (3) Village Recorder (1616 Butler Ave,

FIGURE 6.1 *LA's great independent recording studios of the 1960s (all still active), clockwise from top left: United Western Recorders, Sunset Sound, Sound City, Village Recorder, and Record Plant Recording Studios (photos by author).*

1968); (4) Record Plant Recording Studios (originally 8456 W. 3rd Street, now 1032 N. Sycamore Ave, 1969); and (5) Sound City (15456 Cabrito Road, 1969) (see Figure 6.1). By the 1970s these institutions were joined by the equally impressive Kendun Recorders (619 South Glenwood Place, 1971), Cherokee Studios (5241 Melrose Ave, 1972 [no longer exists]), and Westlake Recording Studios (7265 Santa Monica Blvd, early 1970s), to be followed in 1981 by The Sound Factory (6357 Selma Ave), a subsidiary of Sunset Sound. While some of the studios have undergone changes in name and management, with the exception of Cherokee, all locations continue to produce top-notch recordings.[7]

While by most accounts LA seemed to have a stranglehold on the rock music scene of the 1980s and early 1990s—certainly in North America—there has been surprisingly little written or acknowledged about a small but influential studio located in "Hollywood North," namely Vancouver, British

---

[7] LA industry insider David Leaf also pointed out the higher cost of recording at the majors, as well as the fact that pressure was often compounded by having the record company executives just an elevator ride away, or a few steps across the lot (personal communication, 2019).

Columbia (Canada). Little Mountain Sound Studios began in 1972 as the joint venture of Western Broadcasting (radio) and Griffiths, Gibson, and Ramsay Productions, a jingles company that went on to become the largest music production house in Canada in the 1980s. Built in a non-descript warehouse (like so many of the independents) in the Fairview neighborhood at 201 W. 7th Ave, the British audio engineer Geoff Turner was brought in to build and manage a space that had the same floor space as Abbey Road Studios in London.[8]

In the first few years, Little Mountain was able to bring in an international roster of artists, though without much international recognition. The tides turned, however, in 1977 when a local Vancouver trumpet player named Bruce Fairbairn brought in his band Prism to record their debut album. In addition to the hit "Spaceship Superstar," it was Fairbairn's production skills that began to draw attention to himself and the studio. By 1980 he had brought in the guitarist Bob Rock of the Payolas fame ("Eyes of a Stranger") as an engineer, and in combination with in-house assistant engineer Mike Fraser (nephew of Bob Brooks, early manager of Little Mountain) the trio produced Loverboy's self-titled debut *Loverboy* (1980), the studio's first multi-million-dollar seller. Word about Little Mountain Sound Studios began to spread.

Over the next fifteen years this production "power trio"—alongside a tremendous support staff of talented engineers—would go on to release some of the most commercially and critically successful rock albums of all time, as shown in Figure 6.2. Many of my colleagues, as well as a number of LA engineers and producers, were frankly astounded by the range and depth of the talent that came through this single studio in Vancouver during this period. Rock and Fraser went on to establish themselves as internationally sought-after producers, and the staff that worked under them fuelled a large and talented base of professionals who kept their vision going in the now numerous studios that dot the map in current-day Vancouver and throughout the province.[9]

Figure 6.3 provides the "crews" I interviewed or queried in both Vancouver and LA, with more details about their specific professional endeavors listed in the Appendix.[10] For both Chapter 5 and this chapter,

---

[8]Turner trained at Manchester Tech and worked for EMI before moving to New York City, then finally Vancouver. He was responsible for bringing in and installing the Neve Consoles that became such a large part of the studio's sound (Sharman King, personal communication, 2018).
[9]A fuller account of Little Mountain Sound and the Vancouver commercial music scene is found in Hesselink (2021).
[10]I am also including individuals interviewed by phone who now live outside of LA or Vancouver, but who spent the majority or entirety of their career during the studied period in one of these two locales. The only exception to this rule is Bob Ezrin, the legendary Canadian engineer-producer, who did work on a few projects in LA during the 1980s (Rod Stewart's *Every Beat of My Heart* [1986] and Pink Floyd's *A Momentary Lapse of Reason* [1987]), but

ENTRAINMENT AND THE HUMAN-TECHNOLOGY INTERFACE

Aerosmith: *Permanent Vacation* (1987; Fairbairn P, Fraser E/M, Rock E), *Pump* (1989; Fairbairn P, Fraser E/M), *Get a Grip* (1993; Fairbairn P)
Bon Jovi: *Slippery When Wet* (1986; Fairbairn P, Rock E/M), *New Jersey* (1988; Fairbairn P, Rock E/M), *Keep the Faith* (1992; Rock P/M)
Bryan Adams: *Cuts Like a Knife* (1983; Fraser E), *Reckless* (1984; Fraser E/M)
Mötley Crüe: *Dr. Feelgood* (1989; Rock P/E/M), *Decade of Decadence* (1991; Rock P/E/M, Fraser E/M), *Mötley Crüe* (1994; Rock P/M)
Loverboy: *Loverboy* (1980; Fairbairn P, Rock E, Fraser AE), *Get Lucky* (1981; Fairbairn P, Rock M), *Lovin' Every Minute Of It* (1985)
The Cult: *Sonic Temple* (1989; Rock P, Fraser E/M)
Poison: *Flesh and Blood* (1990; Fairbairn P, Fraser P)
Van Halen: *Balance* (1995; Fairbairn P, Fraser M) [vocals only]
AC/DC: *The Razor's Edge* (1990; Fairbairn P, Fraser E); *Live* (1992; Fairbairn P)
David Lee Roth: *A Little Ain't Enough* (1991; Rock P)
Metallica: *Metallica/The Black Album* (1991; Rock P)
Scorpions: *Face the Heat* (1993; Fairbairn P)
Whitesnake: *Whitesnake* (1987)
David Coverdale and Jimmy Page: *Coverdale • Page* (1993; Fraser Co-P/M/E)

FIGURE 6.2 *Albums released by Little Mountain Sound Studios from 1980 to 1995 (P = producer, E = engineering, AE = assistant engineer, M = mixing).*

Los Angeles
engineer-producers: Neal Avron, Bob Ezrin, Mike Flicker, Brian Foraker, Mike Frondelli, Ross Hogarth, Mark Linett, Keith Olsen, Jim Scott
drummers: Gregg Bissonette, Denny Fongheiser, Stan Lynch, Mike Shapiro
industry professionals: David Leaf

Vancouver
engineer-producers: Spencer Carson, Mike Fraser, Rolf Hennemann, Ron "Obvious" Vermeulen, Charlie Richmond
studio musicians: Randy Raine-Reusch, Sharman King
composers: Keith Hamel, Robert Pritchard
industry professionals: Gord Lord

FIGURE 6.3 *Los Angeles and Vancouver crews.*

my starting point was talking with engineer-producers who represented all of the studios noted above, both major and independent (including Mushroom Studios in Vancouver); this I was able to accomplish. These were the individuals who often made the executive decisions about what timing technology to use if any (though I also met with some composers, drummers, studio musicians, and industry professionals). Live, directed interviews with acknowledged masters of the craft gave me special insights into the human-technology interface gleaned from the life experiences of those who lived (or survived!) during the period and could now look back with some

---

is really known for his work in Chicago, New York, and London. I included him here for his overview of 1970s' rock recording and production culture, as well as his many contributions to the Canadian music scene.

perspective. The kindness and generosity of this group were already noted in the Acknowledgments to this book.

As the project grew, however, I also desired to have the immediate perspectives and reflections of those who were experiencing these changes as they happened through interviews conducted in the target time range, especially the drummers. I was able to find an ideal source in *Modern Drummer* magazine, for three central reasons: (1) it provided conversations with nearly all of the leading studio and band drummers of the mid-to-late twentieth century, as well as producers and engineers; (2) the first issue coincided with my desired date range = January, 1977 (I read all issues up through December 1992); and (3) most of these musicians were based in LA, which provided a valuable grounding for the interviews I conducted live. A nice balance was thus achieved between personal and print sources.

A last note before diving into the interviews. The purpose of this chapter is to explore critically and with interest the sociological and aesthetic transformations that occurred as engineer-producers and performing musicians (primarily drummers) interacted with new timing technologies in the studio and in live performance. It most certainly is *not* to "expose" which bands or songs used click tracks or unacknowledged electronic drums, which has become an interest of a small but robust community on the internet. While the issue is intimately tied up with notions of competency and professional pride—concerns that will appear in the interviews below—the fact is that a lot of "house cleaning" in the form of tape splicing and insertion on the micro and macro level was done on many tracks after the recording session was over which may or may not have used a click to begin with (a complex, scrappy, and frequently mind-numbing operation beyond the scope of this chapter). And so in many cases, even the session musicians themselves are unaware of such manipulation of their otherwise "unassisted" recordings.

The Interviews

> The drums gave me everything, provided for me spiritually, financially, physically, and socially. The groove, love, and passion are my guiding stars. I was lost when they were no longer the coin of the realm. (Stan Lynch)[11]

As was outlined in Chapter 5, a confluence of interests, trends, and technological advances contributed to the prominence of the click track

---

[11] Personal communication, 2019.

in rock and pop recording and performance beginning in the early 1980s. While the influence of disco, other dance musics, and the rise of pre-recorded material (sequencers, samples, etc.) was felt throughout the music industry as a whole, it was the electronic drum machine that ushered in the greatest changes in the rock music world. Most of the machines of legend and lore—many that are still coveted today—appeared during this decade: (1) the Linn LM-1 (1980), the LinnDrum (1982), and the Linn 9000 (1984); (2) the Roland 808 (1980), alongside its predecessor the Roland Rhythm Ace (1964); (3) the Oberheim DMX (1981); (4) the Yamaha RX11 (1984); and (5) the Akai MPC60 (1988). The various Linn drums, however, became the industry standard, as they distinguished themselves from the day's competitors in their realistic sound achieved through live drum samples recorded by digital sampling (the Oberheim also used digital sampling).[12] As Stan Lynch, drummer for Tom Petty and the Heartbreakers, noted:

> Roger Linn came into the studio to show us his original steam-powered Linn Machine and said to me, "Your life is fixin' to change, man." I poo pooed him, and then went, "Oh, he's right, it's never gonna be the same again." Because they have a machine that does it. They really do! Oh, crap. Roger Linn is one of the most influential drummers of the twentieth century. (personal communication, 2019)

At the very beginning it was producers and engineers like Mike Flicker and Rolf Hennemann—a team that initially worked together in Vancouver on Heart's first album (*Dreamboat Annie*, 1975) but continued on projects in LA in the 1980s—who helped Roger Linn develop those early drum sounds:

> I guess the biggest change was when the Linn drum machine came in—that was the real big one for me for rhythm because it was the first thing that actually sounded like the real thing. And you could use it and integrate it. And that was the first problem—finding synchronization.
> I was producing an artist named Marcy [Marcy Levy; actual name: Marcella Detroit] who sang "Lay Down Sally" with Eric Clapton. Her boyfriend was Roger Linn's roommate! So I just started working with him on things like, beginning with the LM-1, the first drum machine that used samples. But that's what I think really changed everything, the fact that people really wanted to synchronize with rhythmic samples and then also actually being able to overdub playing. (Mike Flicker, personal communication, 2018)

---

[12]The LinnDrum (1982) was the most successful of its product line, outselling the other two versions combined.

And whenever Linn had a new sample for his snare drum, because as you well know, there are umpteen different ways to tune a snare drum: how thick is it, is it metal, is it wood, what kind of heads do you have on it. We used to tape wallets on it to give it a nice big thud, or paper towels. How much thud do you want? Do you want the Fleetwood Mac sound that sounds like it has no snare, just so wet and thick? So you could play with all of those things.

So when Linn had a different sample, he'd give us a chip! And in our drum machine at that time, and it wasn't a normal thing, he did it so you could open it and put in a different chip to get a different sound. We were basically experimenting for him and how that worked, which was fun. It was about '82, I think, that's when the LinnDrum machine came out. (Rolf Hennemann, personal communication, 2018)[13]

The benefits of the Linn were initially widely trumpeted, especially by composers and producers who saw a new creative tool to play with. The response by drummers, however, was mixed for aesthetic and financial reasons. For many the idea of a nonhuman agent producing a fairly "live" sound (due to sampling) had a Frankenstein effect; for many more, it signaled the potential end of the need for live drummers, at least in the studio. Charlie Watts' (Rolling Stones) perspective most likely captured the sentiment of many of his peers:

> The click track wasn't Charlie's only run-in with technology during the sessions for *Steel Wheels* [1989]. At one point, producer Chris Kimsey showed him how his drum sounds could be sampled and loaded into a drum machine. "He can actually play me," Charlie says, incredulously. "At least, he can play what he thinks I'd play, but it's my sound, the drums that I play. I mean, I would probably play them totally different, and I doubt if it would sound the same. But he could play his version of me playing with my drumkit sound. That's incredible, isn't it? That makes a mockery of all that I love, in a way." Charlie gives a grim chuckle. "He'll be the first one to get lynched, come the revolution." (Mattingly 1990: 21)

In the early 1980s, this became a reality as drummers were replaced in some cases on rock and pop tracks (and on even more jingles). By the end of the decade, however, the situation began to change as the above concerns were alleviated, as identified by two of LA's greatest studio drummers,

---

[13] LA studio drummer Art Wood is credited with providing most of the drum samples for the LM-1 (http://www.rogerlinndesign.com/past-products-museum.html).

Jim Keltner (Bob Dylan, John Lennon, Carly Simon, Steely Dan) and Jeff Porcaro (Toto, Steely Dan, Rickie Lee Jones, Pink Floyd):

> To me, what is happening with electronics right now is exactly what I thought was going to happen back in '83. A lot of people were panicking, but the very thing that did happen, which we all knew was going to happen, was that people were going to lose out on gigs. The players who did a lot of demos lost their gigs to machines, that's for sure. But the electronics took over for a long time because that was the trend. What's happening now is that electronics are just another piece of gear. The acoustic drums are as big and important as they ever were. Because everybody got to the point where, when they listen to a record and it's a machine, there's just something in your body that tells you there's nobody home, and that's not good for the average music listener when he can feel that. (Jim Keltner in Flans 1990: 84)

> I've gotten a lot of calls in the past two years where people wanted me to replace drum machines. Then they went back to just using clicks. Then they would say, "Let's get a rhythm section." Studio owners have been tearing down the walls of their 200-square-foot rooms for synthesizers to build 1,500-square-foot rooms for live drums again. At least around here I've been seeing that a lot. It's not cost efficient, either. They thought, "I don't have to pay a lousy drummer no more; I can program stuff." But it takes people hours and hours to do that, when a capable drummer can record as many songs in a day and a half as it would take a week to program. And it'll feel better and won't sound like every other record on the radio. (Jeff Porcaro in Flans 1988: 21)

More importantly from a timing/click track perspective, however, was the parallel trend that began in the early 1980s that featured human-drum machine hybrid performances. Many credit Billy Idol's *Rebel Yell* (1983) as providing the impetus and template for this process. What began as a stopgap measure turned into an album that balanced live drumming tracks, part drum machine and part live drumming tracks, and tracks that only featured the Linn. Mike Frondelli, lead engineer for the session at Electric Lady Studios in New York City, recalled:

> Billy came over with Gen X and they were in the midst of trying to find a new drummer. But in order not to delay the creative process, they were creating all of these songs with just the LinnDrum. And somehow or another, unless it's an intentional sound, it can fall very flat unless it's part of the character of the tune. Because of Gen X and his punk roots, it still had to have that edge, so they brought in the drummer Thommy Price.

So in some cases we had pre-records, and in some cases we just recorded straight, all brand new tracks and built it from the bottom up. It was all based on using that Linn pattern concept. So build the pattern—kick, snare, hat—around the creative syncopated percussion groove, and then take out the kick, snare, hat and put the real drums in. Let the drummer swing inside of that. Though some songs just stayed with the original drum machine track, like "Eyes Without a Face." (personal communication, 2019)

The "humanizing" element was at times applied to the sound of the LinnDrum itself, even in the absence of a live drummer. As the engineer-producer Brian Foraker (ELP, Stevie Nicks, Yes, KISS, Lynyrd Skynyrd) noted, producers often went to great lengths to create the illusion of a live drummer:

I was working at the Record Plant and across the hall Billy Idol was doing a record. And they would set up different speakers for the different instrument [sounds]. So the snare drum would be a speaker that was facing up, but they would get a speaker that maybe didn't have as much bottom end in it, and they would face that up like the snare drum would be, and they'd put a 57 [Shure SM57] on it. And then they would use a speaker that had mainly bottom end for the kick drum and they would put a microphone on that. Kind of crazy, but it's like you have this perfect technology for this perfect sound and some of us were trying to make it a little less than perfect. (personal communication, 2019)

More often than not, however, the kick and snare would be retained from the Linn and then the drummer would provide the "swing" on the hi-hat and/or toms, creating microtiming variations. This process has continued up to the present day, as observed by engineer-producer Neal Avron (Everclear, Fall Out Boy, Weezer, Linkin Park):

A lot of what's going on in music today is the main kick drum and snare drum might be very close to on the grid, or there may even be samples, but all of the other subdivisions are being taken by a live musician. So you get the interplay, say between beat 1 and beat 2, you've got a hi-hat that may not be perfect. So you get the perfection of that with the imperfection of the human drummer. Right now we're kind of in a place where we're hybriding, I think. At least a lot of the stuff I'm working on these days. (personal communication, 2019)

In all of these scenarios, the increased reliance on playing with machines, as well as synchronizing pre-recorded electronic drum tracks, forced live drummers to rely more and more on the click to match what was happening in the studio.

A number of the top session drummers of the decade did embrace the various drum machines as creative tools to control, not be controlled by. Arguably two of the top three studios drummers of the 1980s, Vinnie Colaiuta (Frank Zappa, Joni Mitchell, Jeff Beck, Sting) and Denny Fongheiser (Seal, Tracy Chapman, Pat Benatar, John Paul Jones), spoke positively about the new technology:

> [It] serves a purpose and as a matter of fact, I think it serves a wonderful purpose. But I don't think it serves a purpose of replacing drummers or the purpose of creating new jokes about drummers, like, "What happens if your drummer doesn't show up or if he shows up an hour late . . ." Come on! You gotta program the machine and if the thing messes up and fries a chip or something, then you're out of luck. And it only plays what you programmed into it; it doesn't have a mind and it can't jam. But it's a wonderful addendum and something that's an addition. I've played around with the Linn Machine and I've dug it. (Vinnie Colaiuta in Flans 1982: 56–7)

> When I came to LA in 1980, I really wanted to become a session musician and play on records and films. At that time, the Linn Drum, DMX, Yamaha, and 808 drum machines were becoming popular. A lot of the session drummers before me weren't into it. I embraced and enjoyed these machines. I really got into the feel of the internal clocking in each drum machine, which were all slightly different. I would use a different machine for a click track depending on the feel we wanted to play to. (Denny Fongheiser, personal communication, 2019)

Even for bands and producers not attracted to the sound of the Linn or its rivals in recordings, the drum machine provided a convenient tool during the compositional process. Drum machines could play patterns that live drummers couldn't, or could play for hours on end beyond the capabilities of their live counterparts. As the metronomic orientation began to creep into the sound worlds of these creators, consciously or not many began to demand a greater rhythmic "accuracy" from their drummers when sitting down to record. The engineer-producer Jim Scott (Tom Petty and the Heartbreakers, Rolling Stones, Sting, Wilco) captured this evolution in one of our conversations together:

> But I think the thing that's made the biggest difference in this kind of technology in click tracks and drum machines and everything has been the home songwriter/studio person. And from my personal experience, one of my best friends that I'm still making records with, we made records

back in the day—he had a record deal in the '80s and we were working with everybody and we thought we were going to be big stars.

So to write his own song, he'd just get his guitar, and sit down on the couch, and he'd just strum a few chords, and sometimes he'd have some excitement, and sometimes he wouldn't. So we got these old drum machines—I have some in here, like that 70s' Roland Rhythm Ace, things that had samba, rumba, tango, bossa nova, Rock 1, Rock 2—and you push a beat, and you could slow it down. So that guy [drum machine] over there is playing some [he imitates a funky groove], all night, just sitting there, waiting for him to find a thing. And it's great! And you practice, with a [drum machine] click, and then that becomes the groove. And then you can't do without it. (personal communication, 2019)

And it wasn't just the rhythmic "feel" of the drum machine that some composers and/or producers were looking for. For many, it was important that the live drummer sounds like an electronic drum, including upping their technical capabilities. We hear again from Denny Fongheiser, as well as Mike Shapiro (Herb Alpert, Sergio Mendes, Caetano Veloso, Earth, Wind & Fire):

When these drum machines came, producers wanted drummers to be able to play either tightly with them or as consistent as the machines were. Not only time-wise but attack as well. Hitting the drum to sound exactly the same pitch and velocity each time. With some purposeful variation on velocity.

In order to achieve this, I practiced with VU meters on a cassette machine with a microphone on a drum and practiced going soft and loud perfectly while making sure the stick hit the exact same spot of the drum for a consistent pitch. Then we had what they called "bury the click" where you had to nail it. If you didn't hear it, then you were on it. You inevitably got off it a little bit sometimes to make sure it's on, but you had to nail it or bury it. (Denny Fongheiser, personal communication, 2019)

So with us, we go into this thing where, I mean, we were playing things on the bass drum with a single pedal that guys were programming. And so we were like, "Oh, you're going to go 'doo doo doo doo gat, du-doo doo doo doo gat'"—like really quantized. No problem! So we were practicing licks like that [sings it again]—there were times where you couldn't tell the difference between the machine quantization and what the live guys were doing. (Mike Shapiro, personal communication, 2019)

Ironically, most of these early electronic drum machines did *not* actually produce strictly metronomic outputs. As was already alluded to by Denny Fongheiser ("I really got into the feel of the internal clocking in each drum machine, which were all slightly different"), it was the limits of the technology that gave each drum their rhythmic character, as outlined by engineer-producer Ross Hogarth (Van Halen, Mötley Crüe, REM, Roger Waters):

> And the really funny thing is, to circle back on the Linn 9000, the reason the Linn 9000 actually felt good is that the processor in it was not perfectly stable. So it was never, it was like a human, it almost had a human feel.
>
> The thing about those drum machines is that they *did not* have absolutely relentless time. There was this like weird, like if you chop a tape loop, it's still a human playing the tape loop, so there's going to be a certain amount of fluctuation. And so the same thing with these drum machines, because of those processors, depending on whether you just turned them on, or whether they'd been on all day, the warmth of the chips, and the voltage into the power supply, and how the power supply was regulated with its Mil Spec of a capacitor and a resistor, because there's a way to regulate the supply as it comes off the wall. How's the power? Is the power sagging? Is it spiking?
>
> But in the Linn 9000, since that processor was a really basic 8-bit processor and the sounds were 8-bit, it was not a fast processor. So it could only hold on to just so much. So what they've done is actually analyze the Linn 9000 groove, and now they have that as a template inside of Beat Detective. So you can take your real drums and make them feel like a Linn 9000, which is insane to me! There's something so wrong about that. (personal communication, 2019)

⌘

Feel sells, groove sells, performance sells. (Keith Olsen)[14]

With all of the focus on the electronic drum machine and the click track in this chapter, I must step back for just a moment and acknowledge the elephant in the room: many rock producers and drummers did not like the mechanization of time that occurred during the 1980s and 1990s. While everyone I spoke with either openly or grudgingly extolled its benefits, and also admitted its central place in music production and performance, it's still worth providing a counter perspective by two of that era's great engineer-producers, Keith Olsen (Fleetwood Mac, Rick Springfield, Ozzy Osbourne, Foreigner) and Ted Templeman (Van Halen, David Lee Roth Band, The Doobie Brothers, Aerosmith), via the drummer Gregg Bissonette (David Lee Roth Band, Santana, Ringo Starr, Toto):

---

[14]Personal communication, 2019.

I have kind of a love-hate relationship with that era [the 1980s and early '90s]. Because for me it was all about feel. I used to hire drummers that could play in time. So when a certain artist would say, "Aren't you going to use a click track?," I would introduce them to *the drummer*. This guy is a *really* good click track. [laughter] People played in time or they didn't get record deals. People played with feel or they didn't get record deals. (Keith Olsen, personal communication, 2019)

I went in [to Ted] and said, "How would you like to cut this tune? Shall we play with a click, or do you want a drum machine shaker underneath?" And he said, "No, I don't record that way. I record totally human. We're not going to use a click track. We're not going to sync up with any other kind of track. You're not going to trigger any electronics on this album. You're going to play real drums with your real feel. If you speed up or slow down, I'll tell you, and we'll do another take. I like the way you play, and it's going to be great. We're just going to capture the moment." (Gregg Bissonette in Flans 1987: 53)

It took at least a decade for drummers to achieve this level of proficiency, however. As Canadian legend Bob Ezrin (Pink Floyd, Peter Gabriel, Alice Cooper, KISS) noted in regard to the 1970s:

I can't even remember when I just went "click-less" with those early '70's rock bands. Because most of them were not that proficient, and they would speed up massively and it would kind of kill the feel. On *Love It to Death* by Alice Cooper, Jack Richardson [co-producer] would stand in a booth with a cowbell keeping the beat, and he had really good time. So he would be our click track, and the band would have to try and play with him. But also he could adjust to what they were doing to help it sound human. And then we came up with this idea of putting a microphone inside of a box that was stuffed with foam and wrapped in lots of gaffer tape all around it and instead of a cowbell in the booth we could just hit the box in the control room. Jack was really good at it, but I turned out to be even better! So I used to use it pretty much on every record I did in those days.

But later on as musicians got better and better, I would often just take the click away and have the band play. I would give them the click for a while, get them started at the right tempo, then just let them play.

Another technique I used in lieu of a sterile click track was to ask the drummer to play a few bars to the click, pick the best bar of the lot and then make a physical tape loop out of it and use that as a more human version of the click. I found that drummers in particular were much more comfortable playing with the loops. (personal communication, 2019)

This latter process seemed to have been adopted by a number of bands and producers, so that the song would be close to the agreed-upon tempo, but could then breathe as the performance evolved:

That's how a lot of the AC/DC records were made. They never played with a click. Sometimes, just to kind of keep them in the ballpark of where the tempo was, they would sometimes play a chorus or something with the click, we'd cut the click, and they'd count off, then away they went. (Mike Fraser, personal communication, 2018)

Nowadays what I do is that I have a TAMA Rhythm Watch [RW200; an electronic drum metronome], and that's a programmable click. And I have these songs that the band agrees are the right tempo. It's not always the record tempo, but I'll ask each guy before we do the song, "Where do you want to do the song?" And I'll get that tempo they like, and I'll click off and get the tempo going, and once it's there, it's really great.

Even Ringo said, "What is that little box?" And I tell him, "It's a song starter." And he said, "I thought you were going to start the song!" I said, "I am." But I get the click for the tempo, and put that in one of my in-ears, the other from the monitor of the band playing. And I'll just get that tempo, I'll start it off, and then I'll turn it off and we can go from there. And at least we have a starting place. And with that tempo then—I did the same thing with David Lee Roth—I had a good starting point where I could keep the click going for a little while so I'd be where I wanted it. (Gregg Bissonette, personal communication, 2019)

But for all session and pop drummers, and even a large number of rock drummers (many who were session musicians), however, playing with a click track became a required part of the professional percussionist's toolbox. An article about the challenges of the click even appeared in the first issue of *Modern Drummer* magazine in January of 1977 (Anonymous 1977: 19). Playing to the click immediately exposed common rhythmic weaknesses, the two most common being the tendency for a drummer to speed up into the chorus (thus arriving at the "1" early), and then to slow down on the back side of the chorus re-entering the verse. Mark Linett (Beach Boys, Paul Simon, Frank Zappa, Red Hot Chili Peppers), an engineer-producer who worked during the transition from the 1970s into the early 1980s, recalled:

I don't think anybody recorded with me with a click track until the '80s, maybe later than that. Generally speaking, it had much more to do with the inability of the players to play as good as people used to play. So you'd try to keep the drummer in line by stabbing him with a click track. It was never tremendously satisfying, and even then was rarely used except on a film or TV date where the precise timing was needed to match the cue. (personal communication, 2019)

In the drummer's defense, however, it was also noted that the click could serve as a neutral umpire for bands that accused him or her (rightfully or not) of speeding up and/or slowing down.

For many drummers, those first few experiences with the click track were a trial by fire. The literature is ripe with perspectives by almost every session drummer who went on to become a superstar within the field; here I reproduce just two of them by drummers we haven't heard from yet, Andy Newmark (Sly and the Family Stone, Carly Simon, Ronnie Wood, David Bowie) and Jonathan Moffett (The Jacksons, Elton John, Madonna, Kenny Loggins):

> The first time I had to play with a click track, I was a nervous wreck. I mean, I really had problems. I was hung up on listening to the click, and if I couldn't hear it, I inevitably went out of time with it. You just have to get over the nervousness of it because this machine is going. You know it's perfect and you know you're not, because you're human. I make believe in my mind that the machine is Ralph MacDonald, and he has a cowbell, and everyone accepts that "Ralph" has perfect time, so I will follow him. (Andy Newmark in Mattingly 1984: 48)

> First you're nervous and go into shock. It was really a scary experience, but I had to pull myself together and say, "It's either now or never. I have to get my feet wet, and find out just where I stand and how much improvement I have to make." I was thrust into it, but that was the time for me to start. I wasn't used to that harsh sound in my ear, and it affected the flow of my playing. But in time, I got used to it, although I have found that I work better now with a click, a drum machine or just the hi-hat from the drum machine. I had no problems with it right off because it wasn't such a harsh, piercing sound. I can do either now, though. I enjoy it, because in the time I've been working, I feel that I've improved a great deal. (Jonathan Moffett in Flans 1984: 101)

The first task for the fledgling drummer was being able to play perfectly with the click in strict metronomic time in a process referred to in the business as "burying the click":

> We had to learn how to bury the click. My personal opinion is, if you want to play with the groove you have to know what perfection in timing is. If you don't know where that is, and you're just moving all around it [the click], then it's just being loose. Good or bad. But if you know what that more perfect spot is, and you can feel where that is and

play around it purposefully, then you are making things feel the way you want in a far more purposeful way. (Denny Fongheiser, personal communication, 2019)

The next step—one that took many drummers years to achieve—was to be able to move around the click expressively (something Brain Foraker called playing *with* a click, not *to* a click), a mastery of what Anne Danielsen referred to at the beginning of this chapter as "microtemporal deviations from a presumed norm":

Playing with a click track is a bit of an art; you think it's really easy, but it's not. Because you need to figure out where in the click you're going to play—are you playing right on top of it, a hair before it, right in the middle, just at the end, or slightly after? And so you need to know what that space is. And if you're playing too mechanically, it sounds like you're just some kind of automaton, so you needed to make that alive, to always play with that click and not rush it, or sit slightly back.

And so in the studio they would say, "You're on top of the click, lean back a little bit, relax a bit"; the engineers would listen intently to this. And we would become very fussy with a click, like "That click is too sharp," or "I'm hearing the attack, but the bloom of the note is slightly behind the attack," or "I want to hear a click that has more attack," or if I'm sitting back on the click I might play to the bloom. (Randy Raine-Reusch, personal communication, 2018)

The most common such manipulation was to play just before the beats on the chorus (often just the snare), while "relaxing" the placement (just after the beats) for the verses:

At times, especially in the chorus, I would just get way out on the edge of it. Then bring it on the back side of the click for the verse, and then maybe up again on the second verse (or down), and then at the ride out you're *really* on top of it. This would make it feel like it's picking up a little energy. At least that was how many of the song arrangements were back then. Those were our natural instincts. (Denny Fongheiser, personal communication, 2019)

Very early on drummers began to experiment with alternatives to the relentless sound of "click, click, click" that was provided by industry standards such as the UREI digital metronome. For all of the negative feelings that were often harbored against electronics, especially drum machines, a surprising number of musicians programmed such devices to give them a feeling closer to playing with another human:

We don't normally use click tracks, but we did do something similar to that for the first time on "Strike Zone [1981]," which was quite a challenge. It wasn't actually a click track. It was a Fairlight keyboard—a computer keyboard that plays perfect time. We set up a drum program on it that was playing almost the same pattern as I was, and we pumped that through my headphones. It was like playing to double drums. (Matt Frenette [Loverboy] in Fish 1984: 42)

D&D: How did you become comfortable playing to a click?
Vinnie: Well, I learned it on the job. I mean, practicing with a metronome was great with a practice pad, but not that cool with the full kit; I couldn't hear it. So, these days, the drum machine is the way to go for that situation. I never use a straight click at home, I play to a pattern on my Linn machine and set up a cross stick and shaker groove or something. (Vinnie Colaiuta in Rule 1991: 28)

For a click, I use the hi-hat and/or cabasa sounds on the [Akai] MPC60, which are played back to me through the monitors via a separate volume control that is close at hand so I can reach it in case I have to adjust the volume. The whole mess is started and stopped by a footswitch near my hi-hat pedal, and I get my tempos from a little Boss metronome. (Ian Wallace [King Crimson, Bob Dylan, Jon Anderson, Stevie Nicks] 1990: 12)

Others chose to isolate a different part of the drum kit:

Working with a click track in the studio, as I have done for the last several years, I learned to play games with it, too. I don't use a conventional click, by the way. I use a quarter-note bass drum sound. So if I'm playing along with it and I can't hear it, I know I'm in time. That's great because then I don't have to listen to the stupid thing. It's almost become a subliminal relationship with this bass drum pounding away, and I just sit in with it. (Neil Peart [Rush] in Miller 1989: 23)

At the top of this chapter, I had asked if an ability such as "perfect rhythm" (or "perfect time") existed such that a performer could maintain a strict tempo without recourse to any kind of metronomic device. In a number of my interviews the topic came up without prompting, and when it did appear it was always acknowledged as a special, even mysterious, skill:

There are people that are gifted in the world with perfect pitch. There are also people that are gifted in the world with perfect tempo. One of them is Mickey Curry, Bryan Adams' drummer. Mickey Curry used to be with Hall and Oates in the early '70s; he was brought in to be the session drummer when Bryan did his second album in New York with Bob Clearmountain producing.

Mickey Curry is one of these people in the world that has perfect tempo. You can give him the tempo—dum, dum, dum, dum—and he'll lock it in his brain, and probably three minutes later he's still absolutely on it. And the simple analogy is, like we've talked about, there are people that have perfect pitch, and there are also people that have perfect rhythm—they do exist. It's just this mental capability that they have, this gift that they were given, that most of us in this world are not. When they find them, that's that. (Ron "Obvious" Vermeulen, personal communication, 2018)

I remember we'd do this very strange thing. I think it was back in 1972. I was recording a Ringo solo album up in Vancouver and Jim Gordon, the drummer—and his time was so amazing that we used to do things afterwards as engineers and stuff. We'd set a metronome to him, turn him off, and let the metronome play, and then unmute him. And *unbelievable*, he'd just be "boom, click, click, click" [clapped and snapped his fingers in time]. How some people have got that, who knows. Just locked in. (Mike Flicker, personal communication, 2019)

I was doing a band from Florida. And this band was great, except their drummer was just all over the place. And so I told the drummer, "Well, I'm gonna bring in Denny Fongheiser." And at the time Denny was like the #3 studio drummer in LA. This guy was so depressed! I said, "Oh no! He's not gonna play drums. You're gonna play the drums. He's just gonna be here. He's gonna help."

So I set up a mic for Denny to play a groove on a shaker or a cabasa, something just to keep the groove there. And it was like magic, totally magic! This drummer all of a sudden—there was no click track, because Denny's time is perfect, all of the time. It was perfect. He would count it off, "That's it!" Amazing—he's one of those guys. Like with [Jeff] Porcaro, it was the same thing. Just amazing. (Keith Olsen, personal communication, 2019)

A final note about expressive playing with the click track. While the overwhelming number of drummers I met with and read about in the literature manipulated their playing—albeit on an extremely subtle, millisecond level—to not match up perfectly with the click, I was provided an alternative perspective by studio great Gregg Bissonette and engineer-producer Neal Avron who felt that one should play right on the beat, all the time, and if you wanted the chorus (for example) to feel faster, then actually play it faster:

I don't buy into that whole mentality of "Let's put your snare drum behind the beat, put your kick drum on the beat." That's impossible, I can't play like that! Then what do you do with your fills to regulate that? I like to play right in the middle of the click, that's what I've always felt. If someone wants it to be more edgy or on top, I can't (I'm not sure who really can) play *everything*—fills, kick, snares, circles, all of that. And then drum fills, in that same exact percentage? You wannit on top, I speed it up a couple of notches! It's really simple.

The bottom line is that if some producer is telling you, "Bro, this take has to be more in your face, on top," just go ahead, you don't even have to tell the producer, just go ahead and ask the engineer to bump up it up from 130 to 132. Chances are the producer will go "Yeah, man, thanks for doing that! That's more on top!" I wasn't playing on top, I'm playing in a different tempo! (Gregg Bissonette, personal communication, 2019)

But I was very interested in the idea that different sections didn't have to be in the same tempo. Because bands naturally want to speed up going into the chorus. So I would program the click, if the song called for it, to speed up or whatever. Especially doing some of the punk rock records where there would be these breakdowns which would come into these half-time sections. Even though it was strictly half-time, it still *felt* slower than half-time. So I would speed up the click so the half-time still felt like it had just as much energy as the earlier parts of the song, like the verses, that were more full-time. (Neal Avron, personal communication, 2019)

⌘

Once the click showed up, it changed the whole face of record making. It had to loosen up. It couldn't have survived. (Ross Hogarth)[15]

The same month that Nirvana's *Nevermind* was released (September 1991) the studio musician and composer Peter Cohen opened his excellent article on time-keeping in *Modern Drummer* with the following words:

This is the Day of the Click. It has seeped through our defenses and infiltrated all of our consciousness. How could we have helped it? The click track has set the standard for meter and tempo in almost every recorded piece that we have heard for the last 15 years, at least in rock, pop, and commercials. Our ears have become accustomed to it. And as a result, whether we, as musicians, actually use an external reference or not, all of us today seem to have lower thresholds of tolerance for uneven time than we did in the past. The Click reigns supreme, in our minds and in our cells. (1991: 56)

---

[15]Personal communication, 2019.

There was no way Cohen could have known how everything was about to change in the industry around the release of Nirvana's masterpiece, and about the lasting impact that record and grunge would have on altering previous standards of "playing in time":

> When the Nirvana record came out in the '90s and did so well, it made all of the record labels go more that way. The whole thing shifted at that point from tight. From the drum machine to a looser feel. It kind of came full circle for a while. And then with hip-hop—I credit hip-hop a lot with great modern grooves. It's a combination of that locking things in but also making some things loose on purpose to get that right groove. If you go back to the '50s when rock 'n' roll was coming about, it was a mixture of jazz and blues and other things. The drummer might be more of a jazz player, and the guitar player might be more of a rock player. It was those combinations that made those grooves what they were. Kind of a swing feel mixed with more of a straight feel. To me hip-hop was a completely new version of that concept. (Denny Fongheiser, personal communication, 2019)

Almost everyone I spoke with looked back on the 1980s and early 1990s as something that had to be survived, though almost always with an admittance (grudgingly) that overall the timing of drummers and the engineer-producers who worked with them improved to the point that decisions could now be made about how a record was made from a position of understanding *exactly* where the beat was or could be placed. Less positive changes in the realm of social-performance qualities due to clicks, electronics, and multitracking, however, loomed over many of these same individuals.

Earlier in the chapter, I had noted how Bill Bruford, when looking back on his life, lamented the loss of learning and sharing contexts for younger drummers who entered the field during the age of the digitization of instrument reproduction and record production. In the thick of it all in the late 1980s he also expressed alarm about the ways that the physicality of playing the drum was being taken away from the performers and the audiences, as well as the straight-jacketing effect of the click:

> I remember going to a Peter Gabriel concert in the early '80s, and coming away with a big feeling of disappointment. There was the drummer, Jerry Marotta, obviously doing a good job: [mimes] "boom-boom da, boom-boom da." You could see his hands moving and locate that sound; there was no problem with that. But meanwhile the rest of the rhythm was going "dugga-dugga-dugga-dugga," and it was all happening, but you couldn't see anybody actually playing it. So you think, "Is there a tribe of African drummers there, or isn't there? If they are there, I want to see

them, I want to *feel* them play. If they aren't there, why are we hearing them?"

I do feel very strongly that at concert level we must be very careful about letting sequencers run, about using huge sounds that are obviously generated by dropping a little stick from about four inches onto a pad. If it's a big sound, you *hit* it hard. You defy these basic perceptions at your peril, because if the audience can't relate what they see to what they hear, they won't be satisfied. So with my own electronic work I try to make damn sure that you know that it's flesh and blood playing the stuff. If it's loud, if it's soft, that's the way I'll play it. I want these electronic instruments to respond under the stick. Forget sequencers, forget clicks; we *need* live push and pull. (Bruford in Goodwin 1989: 70)

With the increase of non-linear recordings afforded by click tracks frequently came the separation of band members from each other in time and space. For those who experienced recording before the advent of this technology, or who worked with producers who valorized older ways of making a record, there was a tangible sense of losing the practice of *recording as live performance* and the excitement that it often evoked:

These days, we make records in our own studio quite often. It's great in many ways, but I actually mourn the loss of being able to go to a studio as much as we used to. Like walking into Capitol, A&M, or East West studios—we were at those places all the time—amazing places, where you really felt like you were doing something special. The pressure was on, money was being spent, there was a certain amount of time allotted with a room full of amazing musicians, artists, engineers, and producers. We all played together and reacted off of each other. I could start playing something and tell by looking at the musicians' faces or the way they were moving—the engineer, artist, or producer—and immediately know what they thought. (Whether or not it was hitting them or if I needed to try something else.) We were able to shift into many different ideas until we landed on something that made the song shine. (Denny Fongheiser, personal communication, 2019)

You used to hear band awareness in their tracks. At the beginning of the song you'd hear, "Oh shit, hope we nail a good intro." You'd hear the music and go, "That's a live take, they're not even *settled* yet." And then the drummer would do the tighten up on the first verse, and he'd get settled, and everybody would be cool. First chorus, getting better, second chorus, even better. Bridge, great. And by the tag, you'd hear drummers taking victory laps. You'd hear 'em take fills that you knew they would *never* have ventured to take earlier in that song. You could feel the fear, commitment, and desire and then the absolute "Nailed it!" in the fade.

You'd catch amazing drum fills and you knew, he was absolutely riding this thing, couldn't fall off if he tried! Jeff Porcaro's tracks always spoke to me that way.

It's very interesting, the idea of performing, it's pretty well gone. People don't perform much in the studio anymore. (Stan Lynch, personal communication, 2019)

It would be impossible to describe all the strategies now employed by rock bands and their engineers and producers in the studio, including the kind of gear they use and the extent to which analog and/or digital technology is used from beginning to end (including the means by which the music is disseminated). And while I'm certainly not in a place to advocate for one approach over another, as a performing musician on acoustic instruments and a lover of the old rock albums I do empathize with the sentiments of the engineer-producer Jim Scott:

I work with humans everyday. And I don't send files all around the country—I don't get a drummer sending me a beat, and then I straighten it out. And then I send it to a bass player, and he sends it to a guitar player. I don't do that. They all come over here. And we listen to the song, and we chart it out on music paper—old school, manuscript music paper!—and everybody goes in and sits down with their music chart, if they need it. And they play the song. And the singer sings, and the drummer drums, and we talk about it. What are you going to play? Is that the right tempo? What if I played an electric guitar? (personal communication, 2019)

"Playing in Time"

The underlying theme of this entire chapter has been the tension and interplay between notions of what it means to play with "human feel"—most often understood as microtemporal deviations from a metronomic norm, as described by Danielsen—versus adhering strictly to the beat or click with "machine feel." Within this broad playing field, I did encounter examples of drummers and producers who felt that a satisfying, "groovy" rhythm could be achieved by "burying the click," and that "perfect rhythm" as the ability to maintain a consistent, metronomic tempo without recourse to technology was also a very real and desired entity.

Having said this—and I must stress that I can only make this claim within the parameters of a rock music context set up by this chapter's criteria—moving around the placement of the click with purpose and for expressive reasons was seen as essential by the vast majority of those I spoke with and read about. Even at the height of electronic drum machines, the example provided by Billy Idol is indicative of how such technology was frequently used: as one part of a composite, hybrid sound that featured some part of the drum kit being played by a human agent that deviated in some way from the quantized grid. Even with tracks that omitted the human drummer, there was the interesting phenomenon of how the first few generations of electronic drums did not actually reproduce a strictly metronomic output—a kind of (human) ghost in the machine. The overall message of this chapter has been that human variation and volition will always be part of what it means to "play in time."

At the beginning of this chapter, I suggested that perhaps click tracks had moved us closer to a kind of rhythmic perfection we could only imagine before the advent of such technology. Even with the rhythmic "loosening up" that was (re)introduced by grunge in the early 1990s, timing in general has become much more exact, metronomically speaking. Audiences—and thus the industry—demand a much "tighter" rhythmic organization, at least at the percussive and/or metric level, from their music. As producer Bob Ezrin noted, however, the metronome has been a part of music-making in the West for hundreds of years. His grand perspective on this all provides a fitting conclusion to this chapter:

> The technology of the metronome has been around for hundreds of years. We've been sort of chasing perfection on so many different levels, including the sense of time, since the beginning of performing music. There is a certain regularity to the cycles of the world that we experience one way or another, from our mother's heartbeat when we're in the womb, until we get outside on a summer night and hear the cicadas in a certain rhythm and it's always the same.
>
> Music became more organized and less just a random expression of someone's feelings on something they could make a nice noise on. It evolved into something that was actually an act of intention and an act of invention. We started to think in terms of the shapes and sizes of it. The shape of music would be like the shape of any work of art you were making. You would think it through, it would have a beginning, a middle, an ending. It would have a pulse to it that would be of a certain tempo. And then you wanted to try and realize it as close to that tempo as possible. The goal always was creating a certain kind of perfection in the shape of the music that would then allow for there to be more expression and interpretation within the actual content of that shape.
>
> And so when programmable clicks came into the studio, to me that was nothing new. (personal communication, 2019)

7

Radiohead, Oxford, and a Rhythmic Holy Grail

June 21, 2012, Oxford, England

My sabbatical year at St John's College, Oxford, was coming to a close. Although my stated research project was rhythmic play in the music of Radiohead, the Police, and Led Zeppelin, unofficially and on the sly I also pursued what seemed like every avenue available to me to get at the underlying meter of Radiohead's enigmatic "Pyramid Song" (the subject of Chapter 2). This meant reaching out to band members, management, the producer of the album, the conductor of the string orchestra session, studio musicians, and former faculty members and associates of the band. I also attempted to contact the transcriber of the official score, and even the artist (Stanley Donwood) who had created the cover art. Most of these meetings never transpired; and those that did—including brief encounters with Phil Selway (Radiohead's drummer) and Ed O'Brien (one of Radiohead's guitarists)—were frequently rushed and left me with more questions than answers.

Crucially, I never met Thom Yorke, the primary composer of the work and certainly the magic key to opening up this box of mysteries. My inability to hold council with him weighed on me nearly the entire year, and I didn't anticipate any change in this status as I made my way to college late morning on the longest day of the year.

I had plans to have lunch at St John's early afternoon, then go to the Faculty of Music to pick up some library books. Walking north up Turl Street (my favorite side alley) to Broad Street, then turning left (west) and making my way past Balliol College, I passed by a swiftly moving individual in a long raincoat sporting a gray-haired ponytail. Without realizing why,

I immediately turned around and took in the fellow's gait, the excitement palpably rising in my throat. That's Thom Yorke, by god!—I thought to myself—and with only a moment to spare, I began running toward the unsuspecting target.

As I approached I yelled out, "Thom!" "Thom!" No response. This was quickly followed by, "Mr. Yorke!" This successfully stopped him in his tracks, and he turned around slowly with what can only be interpreted as trepidation. With the same clumsiness that I met Phil and later Ed, I extended my hand and choked out that I'm looking forward to seeing him in Switzerland at Radiohead's upcoming show. His manner then softened as he told me there's been some kind of accident and that most likely the shows (including the one in Switzerland) will be canceled. It seems like someone has been hurt (fatally?),[1] and he tells me about the lighting and instruments that have been destroyed. He also tells me the road crew is freaked out, and he's not sure if the shows will be rescheduled.

As I sense this topic of conversation coming to a close, it suddenly dawns on me, it's now or never to ask him about "Pyramid Song." Quickly I sputtered out, "Hey, I have a question I've been dying to ask you. Is that alright?" He looked at me again with the fear that first greeted me—who knows what fans have asked him over the years—and then I popped the million-dollar question: "I have a huge interest in meter and time signatures, and I've been tracking what fans have thought about 'Pyramid Song.' If you don't mind telling me, what is the meter?"

After what seemed like an interminable pause, followed by a fleeting mischievous smile, Thom said, "You mean you don't know?" Completely unaware of how far I had come, and how much I had thought about it— how could he have possibly guessed?—I say, "Well, some people think it's just 4/4, and many others think it's some kind of asymmetrical complicated time signature." "Yeah, I kind of knew that fans had all kinds of theories," he continued, "but I've always thought of it as just straight 4/4, though you swing the eighths hard." He then explained that he had been listening a lot to a jazz song by Charles Mingus while he was writing "Pyramid Song," something I already knew from interviews. He finished by saying, "The asymmetrical groupings only sound that way because of the way the band plays it."

⌘

Like the protagonist in *Indiana Jones and the Last Crusade*, I expected to find a silver and jewel-encrusted chalice (a complex metrical structure)

---

[1] I eventually learn that it is Scott Johnson, a drum tech working their show in Toronto, who has been killed. Radiohead later released information on the inquiry (https://www.radiohead.com/deadairspace/20191105).

but rather stumbled upon a plain wooden cup (just ordinary 4/4). In the end, however, the enjoyment resided in the search and in my heightened imagination, not in finding the "real" thing. The song was actually mine all along, the way I feel it and immerse myself in it with my own rhythmic interpretation (and, as I discovered, band members, too, might understand it differently). Music is always personal, always "ours," regardless of what the composer or performer tells us. And with the beautiful and haunting metrical ambiguity of "Pyramid Song," Radiohead opened it up so that many different listeners with differing opinions could make it their own.

APPENDIX

Los Angeles and Vancouver Crews

The following individuals were interviewed or queried in 2018 (Vancouver) and 2019 (Los Angeles) for information contained in Chapters 5 and 6. Associated bands, artists, and/or institutions are listed with the appropriate personnel; it should be noted that this is only a brief sampling of their full abilities and projects, here focused on rock and/or popular music activity. Nearly everyone listed has also worked extensively in film, television, and jingles, as well as other genres. Geographical affiliation is based on place of work during the era documented in Chapter 6.

Los Angeles

Engineer-producers

Neal Avron—Everclear; Fall Out Boy; Weezer; Linkin Park; Yellowcard; Twentyone Pilots; The Wallfowers; Blink 182

Bob Ezrin—Pink Floyd; Lou Reed; Peter Gabriel; Deep Purple; Alice Cooper; KISS; Rod Stewart; Kansas; Phish

Mike Flicker—Heart; Poco; Al Stewart; TKO; Chilliwack; Ann Wilson; built and designed Mushroom Studios

Brian Foraker—Heart; .38 Special; Jefferson Airplane; Emerson, Lake & Palmer; Stevie Nicks; Yes; KISS; Lynyrd Skynyrd

Mike Frondelli—KISS; Rolling Stones; Led Zeppelin; Chic; Billy Idol; Pat Benatar; Poison; Eddie Money; Oingo Boingo; April Wine; previous VP of Capitol Records; founding partner of Coolsville/Interscope label

Ross Hogarth—Van Halen; Doobie Brothers; Mötley Crüe; REM; Roger Waters; John Mellencamp; John Fogerty; Bob Seger; Hall and Oates

Mark Linett—Beach Boys; Paul Simon; Frank Zappa; Red Hot Chili Peppers; Michael McDonald; Rickie Lee Jones; Brian Wilson

Keith Olsen—Fleetwood Mac; Stevie Nicks; Rick Springfield; Ozzy Osbourne; Foreigner; Pat Benatar; Whitesnake; Scorpions; Santana; Grateful Dead; Jethro Tull

Jim Scott—Tom Petty and the Heartbreakers; Rolling Stones; Sting; Wilco; Red Hot Chili Peppers; Styx; The Doobie Brothers; Rage Against the Machine; Barenaked Ladies

Drummers

Gregg Bissonette—David Lee Roth Band; Steve Vai; Santana; Ringo Starr; Toto; Electric Light Orchestra; Bee Gees; Spinal Tap; Don Henley; Duran Duran

Denny Fongheiser—Seal; Tracy Chapman; Pat Benatar; John Paul Jones; Counting Crows; Tom Cochrane and Red Rider; Roger Waters; Peter Frampton

Stan Lynch—original drummer, Tom Petty and the Heartbreakers

Mike Shapiro—University of California-Los Angeles faculty member; Herb Alpert; Sergio Mendes; Caetano Veloso; Earth, Wind & Fire; will.i.am; Macy Gray; Justin Timberlake

Industry Professionals

David Leaf—University of California-Los Angeles faculty member; author-biographer of A&M Records, Capitol Records, Bee Gees, Beach Boys

Vancouver

Engineer-producers

Spencer Carson—head audio engineer at Griffiths, Gibson, and Ramsay Productions

Mike Fraser—Aerosmith; Bryan Adams; Mötley Crüe; Loverboy; The Cult; Poison; AC/DC; David Coverdale and Jimmy Page; Dio; Metallica; Rush

Rolf Hennemann—Heart; Prism; Randy Meisner; Chilliwack; B.T.O.

Ron "Obvious" Vermeulen—Loverboy; Bryan Adams; D.O.A.; built and designed studios for The Warehouse Studio, Armoury Studios, Bob Rock, k.d. lang, Bob Buckley, Mutt Lange

Charlie Richmond—head technical adviser and later owner of Mushroom Studios; software and sound designer

Studio Musicians

Randy Raine-Reusch (world music multi-instrumentalist)—Aerosmith; Yes; The Cranberries; David Amram; Jon Gibson

Sharman King (trombone)—University of British Columbia faculty member; Buddy Rich Orchestra; Tony Bennett; Frank Sinatra; Tom Jones; Ray Charles; Sarah Vaughn

Composers

Keith Hamel—University of British Columbia faculty member; Institute for Computing, Information, and Cognitive Systems (UBC); IRCAM

Robert Pritchard—University of British Columbia faculty member; Institute for Computing, Information, and Cognitive Systems (UBC); Canadian Broadcasting Company (CBC)

Industry Professionals

Gord Lord—partner at Griffiths, Gibson, and Ramsay Productions

BIBLIOGRAPHY

Abel, Mark. (2014). *Groove: An Aesthetic of Measured Time*. Leiden: Brill.
Agawu, Kofi. (1994). "Ambiguity in Tonal Music: A Preliminary Study." In Anthony Pople (ed.), *Theory, Analysis and Meaning in Music*, 86–107. Cambridge: Cambridge University Press.
Agawu, Kofi. (2003). *Representing African Music: Postcolonial Notes, Queries, Positions*. New York: Routledge.
AlanTubeViewer (2011). "YouTube Comments to 'Bring On the Night.'" http://www.youtube.com/all_comments?v=Bz1mEMiNPHQ (accessed July 1, 2013).
Altman, Billy. (1978). "Review of The Cars." *Creem*, 10 (4): 61.
Ammirante, Paolo, Aniruddh D. Patel, and Frank A. Russo. (2016). "Synchronizing to Auditory and Tactile Metronomes: A Test of the Auditory-Motor Enhancement Hypothesis." *Psychonomic Bulletin and Review*, 23: 1882–90.
Anonymous. (1955). "A Question of Questionable Meanings." *Life*, April 18, 168.
Anonymous. (1956). "White Council vs. Rock and Roll." *Newsweek*, April 23, 32.
Anonymous. (1964). "New Digital Metronome Displayed at 11th Annual Audio Engineering Society Convention." *United and Affiliates Newsletter*, 1 (2): 1–4.
Anonymous. (1977). "Show and Studio." *Modern Drummer*, 1 (1): 19.
Anonymous. (1982). "Evangelist Warns of Devil Messages." *The Daily Record* (Ellensburg, Washington), September 24, 10.
Anonymous. (2001). "Radiohead: Avant Contrarians Consider Selling Out. Or At Least a Video." *Spin*, 17 (4): 79–80.
Anonymous. (2007). Album notes to *Malik* (1975) by The Lafayette Afro Rock Band. America Records AM 6137 (LP).
Anonymous. (2011). "Radiohead." https://web.archive.org/web/20111031083801/http://www.rollingstone.com/music/artists/radiohead/albumguide (accessed November 13, 2011).
Aquila, Richard. (2000). *That Old-Time Rock & Roll: A Chronicle of an Era, 1954-63*. Urbana: University of Illinois Press.
Arom, Simha. (2004). *African Polyphony and Polyrhythm: Musical Structure and Methodology*. New York: Cambridge University Press.
Artemis Music Ltd, arranger. (2008). *Radiohead: Amnesiac*. Guitar Tablature Vocal Score. London: Faber Music.
Asbury, Edith Evans. (1957). "Rock 'n' Roll Teen-Agers Tie Up the Times Square Area." *New York Times*, February 23, page 1, column 2, page 12, column 2.
Attas, Robin. (2011). "Meter as Process in Groove-Based Popular Music." Ph.D. dissertation, University of British Columbia.
Attas, Robin. (2015). "Form as Process: The Buildup Introduction in Popular Music." *Music Theory Spectrum*, 37 (2): 275–96.

Ball, Philip. (2010). *The Music Instinct: How Music Works and Why We Can't Do Without It*. Oxford: Oxford University Press.

Barrier, Michael. (1999). *Hollywood Cartoons: American Animation in Its Golden Age*. New York: Oxford University Press.

Barrier, Michael. (2002). "An Interview with Carl Stalling." In Daniel Goldmark and Yuval Taylor (eds.), *The Cartoon Music Book*, 37–60. Chicago: A Cappella Books.

Baur, Steven. (2021). "Towards a Cultural History of the Backbeat." In Matt Brennan, Joseph Michael Pignato, and Daniel Akira Stadnicki (eds.), *The Cambridge Companion to the Drum Kit*, 34–51. Cambridge: Cambridge University Press.

Becker, Judith. (2010). "Exploring the Habitus of Listening: Anthropological Perspectives." In Patrik N. Juslin and John A. Sloboda (eds.), *Handbook of Music and Emotion: Theory, Research, Applications*, 127–57. Oxford: Oxford University Press.

Bell, Adam Patrick. (2018). *Dawn of the DAW: The Studio as Musical Instrument*. New York: Oxford University Press.

Belz, Carl (1972). *The Story of Rock*. 2nd ed. New York: Oxford University Press.

Bennett, Joe. (2013). "Review of 'Tyranny of the Snare: The Changing Status of the Drum Kit in Record Production.'" https://joebennett.net/2013/07/13/tyranny-of-the-snare-the-changing-status-of-the-drum-kit-in-record-production-matt-brennan-arp13/ (accessed July 29, 2016).

Benjamin, Walter. (2008[1936]). *The Work of Art in the Age of Mechanical Reproduction*. Trans. J. A. Underwood. New York: Penguin Books.

Benjamin, William. (2006). "Mozart: Piano Concerto No.17 in G Major, K. 453, Movement I." In Michael Tenzer (ed.), *Analytical Studies in World Music*, 332–76. New York: Oxford University Press.

Bergamanini, Joe. (2005). *Drum Techniques of Led Zeppelin: Note for Note Transcriptions of 23 Classic John Bonham Drum Tracks*. Van Nuys: Alfred.

Berlioz, Hector. (1969[1854]). *Evenings with the Orchestra*. Trans. and Ed. with an Introduction and Notes by Jacques Barzun. New York: Alfred A Knopf.

Bernstein, Leonard. (1976). *The Unanswered Question*. Cambridge: Harvard University Press.

Biamonte, Nicole. (2014). "Formal Functions of Metric Dissonance in Rock Music." *Music Theory Online*, 20 (2). https://www.mtosmt.org/issues/mto.14.20.2/mto.14.20.2.biamonte.html

Bingham, Tony and Anthony Turner. (2017). *Metronomes and Musical Time: Catalogue of the Tony Bingham Collection at the Exhibition AUK TAKT!, Museum für Musik, Basel, 20 January to 20 August 2017*. London: Tony Bingham.

Bird, S. Charles. (1976). "Poetry in Mande: Its Form and Meaning." *Poetics*, 5: 89–100.

Bjørkvold, Jon Roar. (1989). *The Muse Within: Creativity and Communication, Song and Play from Childhood through Maturity*. New York: Harper Collins.

Black Rock Coalition. (2021). "BRC Manifesto." http://blackrockcoalition.org/mission/manifesto/ (accessed July 15, 2021).

Blackburn, Simon. (2006). *Dictionary of Philosophy: A Guide to All Aspects of Philosophy, from Aristotle to Zen*. 2nd ed. Oxford: Oxford University Press.

Blacking, John. (1973). *How Musical is Man?* Seattle and London: University of Washington Press.

Blom, Jan-Petter. (1981). "The Dancing Fiddle." In Jan-Petter Blom, Sven Nyhus, and Reidar Sevåg (eds.), *Slåttar for the Harding Fiddle*, 305–12. Oslo: Universitetsforlaget.
Bloom, Allan. (1987). "Is Rock Music Rotting Our Kids' Minds." *The Washington Post* [digital edition], June 7.
Blum, Carl Robert. Patent # 1,544,427, "Reproduction of Music in Synchronism with Moving Pictures." Filed January 6, 1923; granted June 30, 1925.
Bonus, Alexander Evan. (2010). "The Metronomic Performance Practice: A History of Rhythm, Metronomes, and the Mechanization of Musicality." Ph.D. dissertation, Case Western Reserve University.
Bosso, Joe. (2013). "Stewart Copeland Picks 16 Fun Drum Albums." Musicradar: The #1 Website for Musicians. https://www.musicradar.com/news/drums/stewart-copeland-picks-16-fun-drum-albums-578893 (accessed July 21, 2021).
Bowman, Rob and Andy Schwartz. (2019). "Rock & Roll Hall of Fame Singles." In Holly George-Warren (ed.), *Rock & Roll Hall of Fame 34th Annual Induction Ceremony: March 29, 2019*, 78–89. Cleveland: Rock & Roll Hall of Fame.
Brackett, John. (2008). "Examining Rhythmic and Metric Practices in Led Zeppelin's Musical Style." *Popular Music*, 27 (1): 53–76.
Bradley, Lloyd. (2001). *This is Reggae Music: The Story of Jamaica's Music*. New York: Grove Press.
Bramwell, Murray. (2005). "Getting the Band Back Together. Review of 'Cream at the Royal Albert Hall, London.'" *The Adelaide Review*, 269: 13.
Brittin, Ruth V. (1993). "Discrimination of Aural and Visual Tempo Modulation." *Bulletin of the Council for Research in Music Education*, 116: 23–32.
Brochard, Renaud, Donna Abecasis, Doug Potter, Richard Ragot, and Carolyn Drake. (2003). "The 'Ticktock' of Our Internal Clock: Direct Brain Evidence of Subjective Accents in Isochronous Sequences." *Psychological Science*, 14 (4): 362–6.
Brown, Steven, Björn Merker, and Nils L. Wallin. (2000). "An Introduction to Evolutionary Musicology." In Nils L. Wallin, Björn Merker, and Steven Brown (eds.), *The Origins of Music*, 3–24. Cambridge, MA: The MIT Press.
Brown, Theodore. (1976). "A History and Analysis of Jazz Drumming to 1942." Ph.D. dissertation, University of Michigan.
Bruford, Bill. (2018). *Uncharted: Creativity and the Expert Drummer*. Foreword by Mark Doffman. Ann Arbor: University of Michigan Press.
Budofsky, Adam. (1988). "Michael Hanson." *Modern Drummer*, 12 (8): 8.
Buskin, Richard. (2009). "Donna Summer 'I Feel Love': Classic Tracks." *Sound on Sound*, October, 2009. https://www.soundonsound.com/people/donna-summer-i-feel-love-classic-tracks (accessed September 30, 2018).
Butler, Mark. (2001). "Turning the Beat Around: Reinterpretation, Metrical Dissonance, and Asymmetry in Electronic Dance Music." *Music Theory Online*, 7 (6). https://www.mtosmt.org/issues/mto.01.7.6/mto.01.7.6.butler.html
Butler, Mark. (2006). *Unlocking the Groove: Rhythm, Meter, and Musical Design in Electronic Dance Music*. Bloomington: Indiana University Press.
Butterfield, Matthew W. (2006). "The Power of Anacrusis: Engendered Feeling in Groove-Based Musics." *Music Theory Online*, 12 (4). https://mtosmt.org/issues/mto.06.12.4/mto.06.12.4.butterfield.html
Butterfield, Matthew W. (2010). "Participatory Discrepancies and the Perception of Beats in Jazz." *Music Perception*, 27 (3): 157–76.

Cage, John. (1973). *Silence: Lectures and Writings by John Cage*. Middletown: Wesleyan University Press.
Campbell, Michael and James Brody. (1999). *Rock and Roll: An Introduction*. Belmont: Schirmer.
Care, Ross. (1976–77). "Cinesymphony: Music and Animation at the Disney Studio 1928–1942." *Sight and Sound*, 46 (1): 40–4.
Cateforis, Theodore. (2011). *Are We Not New Wave? Modern Pop at the Turn of the 1980s*. Ann Arbor: University of Michigan Press.
Charlton, Katherine. (2003). *Rock Music Styles: A History*. 4th ed. New York: McGraw-Hill.
Cheal, David. (2016). "The Life of a Song: 'I Feel Love.'" *Financial Times*, June 3, 2016. https://www.ft.com/content/147b4da8-27e3-11e6-8ba3-cdd781d02d89 (accessed September 30, 2018).
Chernoff, John Miller. (1979). *African Rhythm and African Sensibility: Aesthetics and Social Action in African Musical Idioms*. Chicago: University of Chicago Press.
Chiang, Ted. (2019). "The Great Silence." In *Exhalation*, 231–6. New York: Alfred A. Knopf.
Clark, Dick. (1985). *History of American Bandstand: It's Got a Great Beat and You Can Dance to It*. New York: Ballantine Books.
Clarke, Eric F. (2005). *Ways of Listening: An Ecological Approach to the Perception of Musical Meaning*. New York: Oxford University Press.
Clarke, Martin. (2010). *Radiohead: Hysterical and Useless*. Revised and updated. London: Plexus.
Clayton, Martin. (2013). "Entrainment, Ethnography and Musical Interaction." In Martin Clayton, Byron Dueck, and Laura Leante (eds.), *Experience and Meaning in Music Performance*, 17–39. Oxford: Oxford University Press.
Cogan, Jim and William Clark. (2003). *Temples of Sound: Inside the Great Recording Studios*. Foreword by Quincy Jones. San Francisco: Chronicle Books.
Cohen, Debra Rae. (1979). "Reggatta de Blanc, The Police." *Rolling Stone*, 306: 84, 86.
Cohen, Debra Rae. (1981). "The Police Investigate Themselves: Ghost in the Machine, The Police." *Rolling Stone*, 358: 81, 83.
Cohen, Peter. (1991). "Getting Serious About Timekeeping." *Modern Drummer*, 15 (9): 56–7, 106.
Cohen, Thomas F. (2009). "The Click Track / The Business of Time: Metronomes, Movie Scores and Mickey Mousing." In Graeme Harper, Ruth Doughty, and Jochen Eisentraut (eds.), *Sound and Music in Film and Visual Media: An Overview*, 100–13. New York: Bloomsbury.
Collins, Nick. (2004). "Review of Radiohead: Kid A, Radiohead: Amnesiac, and Radiohead: Hail to the Thief." *Computer Music Journal*, 28 (1): 73–7.
Cook, Nicholas. (1990). *Music, Imagination and Culture*. Oxford: Oxford University Press.
Cook, Peter, Andrew Rouse, Margaret Wilson, and Colleen Reichmuth. (2013). "A California Sea Lion (Zalophus californianus) Can Keep the Beat: Motor Entrainment to Rhythmic Auditory Stimuli in a Non Vocal Mimic." *Journal of Comparative Psychology*, 127 (4): 412–27.

Copeland, Stewart. (2009). *Strange Things Happen: A Life with the Police, Polo and Pygmies*. London: Friday Books.
Copland, Aaron. (1980). *Music and Imagination*. Cambridge: Harvard University Press.
Covach, John. (2003). "Pangs of History in Late 1970s New-wave Rock." In Allan F. Moore (ed.), *Analyzing Popular Music*, 173–95. Cambridge: Cambridge University Press.
Covach, John and Andrew Flory. (2012). *What's That Sound: An Introduction to Rock and Its History*. 3rd ed. New York: W.W. Norton & Company.
Crafts, Susan D., Daniel Cavicchi, Charles Keil and the Music in Daily Life Project. (1993). *My Music*. Hanover: Wesleyan University Press.
Crazy Horse, Kandia, ed. (2004). *Rip It Up: The Black Experience in Rock 'N' Roll*. New York: Palgrave Macmillan.
Cross, Ian and Iain Morley. (2009). "The Evolution of Music: Theories, Definitions and the Nature of the Evidence." In Stephen Malloch and Colwyn Trevarthen (eds.), *Communicative Musicality: Exploring the Basis of Human Companionship*, 61–81. New York: Oxford University Press.
Cruikshank, Julie. (2014). "Tegan and Sara Close Worldpride." *Xtra! Toronto's Gay and Lesbian News*, 775: 11.
Cunningham, Mark. (1998). *Good Vibrations: A History of Record Production*. London: Sanctuary.
Curtis, Scott. (1992). "The Sound of Early Warner Bros. Cartoons." In Rick Altman (ed.), *Sound Theory, Sound Practice*, 191–203. New York: Routledge.
Danielsen, Anne. (2006). *Presence and Pleasure: The Funk Grooves of James Brown and Parliament*. Middletown: Wesleyan University Press.
Danielsen, Anne. (2010). "Introduction: Rhythm in the Age of Digital Reproduction." In Anne Danielsen (ed.), *Musical Rhythm in the Age of Digital Reproduction*, 1–16. New York: Routledge.
Dave. (2007). "7/8 Groove, Vinnie Colaiuta's Saint Augustine in Hell." *Online Drummer*. http://www.onlinedrummer.com/forum/index.php?/topic/10884-78-groove-vinnie-colaiutas-saint-augustine-in-hell/ (accessed April 11, 2018).
Davies, Mollie. (2003). *Movement and Dance in Early Childhood*. London: Paul Chapman Publishing.
Davies, Stephen. (2010). "Emotions Expressed and Aroused by Music: Philosophical Perspectives." In Patrik N. Juslin and John A. Sloboda (eds.), *Handbook of Music and Emotion: Theory, Research, Applications*, 15–43. Oxford: Oxford University Press.
de Clercq, Trevor. (2016). "Measuring a Measure: Absolute Time as a Factor for Determining Bar Lengths and Meter in Pop/Rock Music." *Music Theory Online*, 22 (3). https://mtosmt.org/issues/mto.16.22.3/mto.16.22.3.declercq.html
de Clercq, Trevor. (2017). "Swing, Shuffle, Half Time, Double: Beyond Traditional Time Signatures in the Classification of Meter in Pop/Rock Music." In Carlos Xavier Rodriguez (ed.), *Coming of Age: Teaching and Learning Popular Music in in Academia*. Ann Arbor: University of Michigan Press. DOI:10.3998/mpub.9470277
del Castillo, Juan M. Patent # 3,996,833, "Optical Metronome." Filed July 8, 1975; granted December 14, 1976.
DeNora, Tia. (2000). *Music in Everyday Life*. Cambridge: Cambridge University Press.

Diaz, Manuel. Patent # 6,727,419, "Pulsating Metronome." Filed December 3, 2002; granted April 27, 2004.
Dick, Arthur. (2009). *Led Zeppelin • Mothership: Guitar Tab Edition*. London: Wise Publications.
Dimery, Robert, ed. (2006). *1001 Albums You Must Hear Before You Die*. New York: Universe.
Disney, Walter E., Wilfred E. Jackson, and William E. Garity. Patent # 1,941,341, "Method and Apparatus for Synchronizing Photoplays." Filed April 2, 1931; granted December 26, 1933.
Doctor of Rock. (2015). "When One Melody Isn't Enough." http://doctorofrock.com/blog/when-one-melody-isnt-enough/#more-882 (accessed August 4, 2016).
Donald, Merlin. (1991). *Origins of the Modern Mind: Three Stages in the Evolution of Culture and Cognition*. Cambridge: Harvard University Press.
Donwood, Stanley and Dr. Tchok. (2007). *Dead Children Playing*. London: Verso.
Douridas, Chris, host. (2001). "Radiohead at Ground Zero." Interview with Ed O'Brien and Colin Greenwood, Sundance Festival (Park City, Utah).
Duke, Gary. Patent # 7,368,651, "Digital Pulsing Visual Metronome." Filed June 30, 2005; granted May 6, 2008.
Duncan, William Earl. Patent # 2,582,196, "Time-Measuring Device." Filed April 5, 1948; granted January 8, 1952.
Eidsheim, Nina Sun. (2019). *The Race of Sound: Listening, Timbre, and Vocality in African American Music*. Durham: Duke University Press.
Ejiri, Keiko. (1998). "Rhythmic Behavior and the Onset of Canonical Babbling in Early Infancy." *Japanese Journal of Developmental Psychology*, 9: 232–41.
Everett, Walter. (2009). *The Foundations of Rock: From "Blue Suede Shoes" to "Suite: Judy Blue Eyes."* New York: Oxford University Press.
Farncombe, Tom, ed. (2007). *The Police: Guitar Tab Edition*. London: Wise Publications.
Fast, Susan. (2001). *In the Houses of the Holy: Led Zeppelin and the Power of Rock Music*. Oxford: Oxford University Press.
Feld, Steven. (1990). *Sound and Sentiment: Birds, Weeping, Poetics, and Song in Kaluli Expression*. 2nd ed. Philadelphia: University of Pennsylvania Press.
Feldman, Heidi C. (2006). *Black Rhythms of Peru: Reviving African Musical Heritage in the Black Pacific*. Middletown: Wesleyan University Press.
Fish, Scott Kevin. (1978). "Mel Lewis: Straight Ahead." *Modern Drummer*, 2 (2): 14–15, 31–3.
Fish, Scott Kevin. (1984). "Matt Frenette: Keep It Up." *Modern Drummer*, 8 (3): 8–13, 38, 40–2, 44.
Flans, Robyn. (1982). "Vinnie Colaiuta." *Modern Drummer*, 6 (8): 8–11, 46, 48, 50, 52, 54, 56–8.
Flans, Robyn. (1984). "Jonathan Moffett: Have Drums Will Travel." *Modern Drummer*, 8 (9): 26–9, 100–2, 104, 106.
Flans, Robyn. (1985). "Steve Schaeffer: Heard But Not Seen." *Modern Drummer*, 9 (4): 14–17, 53–4, 56, 60, 62–3.
Flans, Robyn. (1988). "Jeff Porcaro: The Feel of the Music." *Modern Drummer*, 12 (11): 18–23, 54, 56–7, 59, 61.
Flans, Robyn. (1990). "L.A. Studio Round Table." *Modern Drummer*, 14 (11): 18–25, 82, 84, 86–8, 90–2, 94, 96–7, 99–100.

Floyd, Samuel A., Jr. and Marsha J. Reisser. (1984). "The Sources and Resources of Classic Ragtime Music." *Black Music Research Journal*, 4: 22–59.
Forbes, Brandon W. and George A. Reisch, eds. (2009). *Radiohead and Philosophy: Fitter Happier More Deductive*. Chicago: Open Court.
Fraisse, Paul. (1952). "La perception de la durée comme organisation du successif: Mise en évidence expérimentale." *L'année psychologique*, 52 (1): 39–46.
Fricke, David. (1980). "Zenyatta Mondatta, The Police." *Rolling Stone*, 333/334: 104.
Fricke, David. (1988). "The Rolling Stone Interview: Sting." *Rolling Stone*, 519: 50–3, 115, 117.
Fricke, David. (1990). "Living Colour's Time Is Now." *Rolling Stone*, November 1. https://www.rollingstone.com/music/music-news/living-colours-time-is-now-192320/ (accessed June 15, 2021).
Fricke, David. (2001a). "Radiohead: Making Music that Matters." *Rolling Stone*, 874: 42–8, 73.
Fricke, David. (2001b). "Radiohead Warm Up." *Rolling Stone*, 869: 21, 25.
Friedland, Ed. (2000). "Every Space You Make." *Bass Player*, 11 (3): 52–3.
Frühauf, Jan, Reinhard Kopiez, and Friedrich Platz. (2013). "Music on the Timing Grid: The Influence of Microtiming on the Perceived Groove Quality of a Simple Drum Pattern Performance." *Musicae Scientiae*, 17 (2): 246–60.
Fulford, Scott L. Patent # 5,959,230, "Tactile Tempo Indicating Device." Filed November 20, 1998; granted September 28, 1999.
Furniss, Matters. (2007). *Led Zeppelin: Up Close and Personal*. DVD and book set. London: Edgehill Publishing.
Garity, William. (1933). "The Production of Animated Cartoons." *Journal of the Society of Motion Picture Engineers*, 20 (4): 309–22.
Gaunt, Kyra. (2006). *The Games Black Girls Play: Learning the Ropes from Double-Dutch to Hip-Hop*. New York: New York University Press.
Geissman, Thomas. (2000). "Gibbon Songs and Human Music from an Evolutionary Perspective." In Nils L. Wallin, Björn Merker, and Steven Brown (eds.), *The Origins of Music*, 103–23. Cambridge, MA: The MIT Press.
George, Burrell F. Patent # 4,649,794A, "Visual Metronome." Filed December 23, 1985; granted March 17, 1987.
Giordano, Marcello. (2016). "Vibrotactile Feedback and Stimulation in Music Performance." Ph.D. dissertation, McGill University.
Giordano, Marcello and Marcelo M. Wanderley. (2015). "Follow the Tactile Metronome: Vibrotactile Stimulation for Tempo Synchronization in Music Performance." *Proceedings of the SMS Conference*, Maynooth, Ireland, 1–6.
Goldsmith, Lynn. (2007). *The Police: 1978–1983*. Introduction by Phil Sutcliffe. New York: Little, Brown and Company.
Goodwin, Andrew. (1992). "Rationalization and Democratization in the New Technologies of Popular Music." In James Lull (ed.), *Popular Music and Communication*, 75–100. Newbury Park: Sage.
Goodwin, Simon. (1989). "Bill Bruford." *Modern Drummer*, 13 (2): 18–22, 70, 72–4, 76–9.
Gracyk, Theodore. (1996). *Rhythm and Noise: An Aesthetic of Rock*. London: Tauris.
Grahn, Jessica A. and James B. Rowe. (2009). "Feeling the Beat: Premotor and Striatal Interactions in Musicians and Nonmusicians during Beat Perception." *Journal of Neuroscience*, 29 (23): 7540–8.

Grant, Roger. (2014). *Beating Time and Measuring Music in the Early Modern Era.* New York: Oxford University Press.

Greenacre, Phyllis. (1959). "Play in Relation to Creative Imagination." *The Psychoanalytic Study of the Child*, 14: 61–80.

Gress, Jesse. (2010). "10 Things You Gotta Do to Play Like Andy Summers (the Police Years)." http://www.guitarplayer.com/article/10-things-you-gotta-do-to-play-like-andy-summers-the-police-years/819 (accessed December 6, 2012).

Griffiths, Dai. (2005). "Public Schoolboy Music: Debating Radiohead." In Joseph Tate (ed.), *The Music and Art of Radiohead*, 159–67. Aldershot: Ashgate.

Guarisco, Donald A. (n.d.) "The Cars, *Just What I Needed*: Song Review." *AllMusic*. http://www.allmusic.com/song/just-what-i-needed-mt0028188672 (accessed August 4, 2016).

Gudino, Mariana. (2009). "Tegan and Sara: Sainthood." *PopMatters*. https://www.popmatters.com/114592-tegan-and-sara-sainthood-2496110273.html (accessed July 8, 2021).

Guralnick, Peter. (2015). *Sam Phillips: The Man Who Invented Rock 'n' Roll*. New York: Little, Brown and Company.

Hainge, Greg. (2005). "To(rt)uring the Minotaur: Radiohead, Pop, Unnatural Couplings, and Mainstream Subversion." In Joseph Tate (ed.), *The Music and Art of Radiohead*, 62–84. Aldershot: Ashgate.

Hale, Jonathan. (1999). *Radiohead: From a Great Height*. Toronto: ECW Press.

Hanenberg, Scott James. (2018). "Unpopular Meters: Irregular Grooves and Drumbeats in the Songs of Tori Amos, Radiohead, and Tool." Ph.D. dissertation, University of Toronto.

Harrison, Gavin. (1996). *Rhythmic Illusions*. Harlow: Alfred Publishing Company.

Hartman, Kent. (2017). *Goodnight, L.A.: The Rise and Fall of Classic Rock—The Untold Story from Inside the Legendary Recording Studios*. New York: Da Capo Press.

Hasty, Christopher F. (1997). *Meter as Rhythm*. Oxford: Oxford University Press.

Headlam, Dave. (1995). "Does the Song Remain the Same? Questions of Authorship and Identification in the Music of Led Zeppelin.' In Elizabeth West Marvin and Richard Hermann (eds.), *Concert Music, Rock, and Jazz since 1945: Essays and Analytical Studies*, 313–63. Rochester: University of Rochester Press.

Hein, Ethan. (2013). "Friends Don't Let Friends Clap on One and Three." http://www.ethanhein.com/wp/2013/friends-dont-let-friends-clap-on-one-and-three/ (accessed March 5, 2018).

Hennig, Holger, Ragnar Fleischmann, Anneke Fredebohm, York Hagmayer, Jan Nagler, Annette Witt, Fabian J. Theis, and Theo Geisel. (2011). "The Nature and Perception of Fluctuations in Human Musical Rhythms." *PLoS ONE*, 6 (10): 1–7 (e26457).

Hennion, Antoine. (1983). "The Production of Success: An Anti-Musicology of the Pop Song." *Popular Music*, 3: 159–93.

Hesselink, Nathan. (2006). *P'ungmul: South Korean Drumming and Dance*. Chicago: University of Chicago Press.

Hesselink, Nathan. (2013). "Radiohead's 'Pyramid Song': Ambiguity, Rhythm, and Participation." *Music Theory Online*, 19 (1). https://mtosmt.org/issues/mto.13.19.1/mto.13.19.1.hesselink.html.

Hesselink, Nathan. (2014a). "Rhythmic Play, Compositional Intent, and Communication in Rock Music." *Popular Music*, 33 (1): 69–90.
Hesselink, Nathan. (2014b). "The Ethnomusicologist as Composer." *Music and Culture*, 31: 31–44.
Hesselink, Nathan. (2021). "From Point Grey to Little Mountain: Connections and Intersections between UBC Music and Little Mountain Sound." *MUSICultures*, 48: 205–33.
Hills, Matt. (2002). *Fan Cultures*. New York: Routledge.
Hine, Christine. (2000). *Virtual Ethnography*. London: SAGE Publications.
Hoskyns, Barney. (2009). *Waiting for the Sun: A Rock 'n' Roll History of Los Angeles*. New York: Backbeat Books.
Howe, Jeff. (2008). *Crowdsourcing: Why the Power of the Crowd is Driving the Future of Business*. New York: Crown Business.
Hubbs, Nadine. (2008). "The Imagination of Pop-Rock Criticism." In Walter Everett (ed.), *Expression in Pop-Rock Music: Critical and Analytical Essays*, 215–37. New York: Routledge.
Hughes, Charles L. (2015). *Country Soul: Making Music and Making Race in the American South*. Chapel Hill: The University of North Carolina Press.
Huron, David. (2006). *Sweet Anticipation: Music and the Psychology of Expectation*. Cambridge, MA: The MIT Press.
Huron, David and Elizabeth Hellmuth Margulis. (2010). "Musical Expectancy and Thrills." In Patrik N. Juslin and John A. Sloboda (eds.), *Handbook of Music and Emotion: Theory, Research, Applications*, 575–604. Oxford: Oxford University Press.
Huron, David and Ann Ommen. (2006). "An Empirical Study of Syncopation in American Popular Music, 1890–1939." *Music Theory Spectrum*, 28 (2): 211–31.
Irwin, Theodore. (1957). "Rock'n Roll'n Alan Freed." *Pageant*, July, 56–63.
Iversen, John R. and Aniruddh D. Patel. (2008). "The Beat Alignment Test (BAT): Surveying Beat Processing Abilities in the General Population." *Proceedings of the 10th International Conference on Music Perception and Cognition*, 465–8.
Iversen, John R., Aniruddh D. Patel, Brenda Nicodemus, and Karen Emmorey. (2015). "Synchronization to Auditory and Visual Rhythms in Hearing and Deaf Individuals." *Cognition*, 134: 232–44.
Iyer, Vijay. (2002). "Embodied Mind, Situated Cognition, and Expressive Microtiming in African-American Music." *Music Perception*, 19 (3): 387–414.
Jacobs, Lea. (2015). *Film Rhythm after Sound*. Berkeley: University of California Press.
Jackson, John A. (1991). *Big Beat Heat: Alan Freed and the Early Years of Rock & Roll*. New York: Schirmer Books.
Jaffe, Joseph, Beatrice Beebe, Stanley Feldstein, Cynthia L. Crown, Michael D. Jasnow, Philippe Rochat, and Daniel N. Stern. (2001). "Rhythms of Dialogue in Infancy: Coordinated Timing in Development." *Monographs of the Society for Research in Child Development*, 66 (2): i–viii, 1–149.
Jasen, David A. and Trebor Jay Tichenor. (1978). *Rags and Ragtime: A Musical History*. New York: Dover.
Johansson, Mats. (2017). "Non-Isochronous Musical Meters: Towards a Multidimensional Model." *Ethnomusicology*, 61 (1): 31–51.

Jokiniemi, Maria, Roope Raisamo, Jani Lylykangas, and Veikko Surakka. (2008). "Crossmodal Rhythm Perception." In *International Workshop on Haptic and Audio Interaction Design*, 111–19.

Jung, Carl Gustav. (1997[1950]). "Symbols and the Interpretation of Dreams." In Robert Cole (ed.), *Selected Writings*, 203–84. New York: Book-of-the-Month Club.

Juslin, Patrik N., Simon Liljeström, Daniel Västfjäll, and Lars-Olov Lundqvist. (2010). "How Does Music Evoke Emotions?: Exploring the Underlying Mechanisms." In Patrik N. Juslin and John A. Sloboda (eds.), *Handbook of Music and Emotion: Theory, Research, Applications*, 605–42. Oxford: Oxford University Press.

Kent, Nick. (2001). "Happy Now?" *Mojo*, 91: 56–72.

Kestner-Clifton, John N. and Phillip M. Vogel. Patent # 5,275,082, "Visual Music Conducting Device." Filed September 9, 1991; granted January 4, 1994.

Kid Charlemagne. (2011). "Review of *The Police: Reggatta de Blanc*." *RateYourMusic*, February 24. http://rateyourmusic.com/release/album/the_police/reggatta_de_blanc/reviews/1 (accessed December 6, 2012).

Kimura, Mari. (1995). "Performance Practice in Computer Music." *Computer Music Journal*, 19 (1): 64–75.

Klein, Bethany. (2009). *As Heard on TV: Popular Music in Advertising*. New York: Routledge.

Kosonen, Katri and Roope Raisamo. (2006). "Rhythm Perception through Different Modalities." In *Proceedings of EuroHaptics 2006*, 365–70.

Kot, Greg. (2009). *Ripped: How the Wired Generation Revolutionized Music*. New York: Scribner.

Kozinets, Robert V. (2015). *Netnography: Redefined*. 2nd ed. London: SAGE Publications.

Kvifte, Tellef. (2007). "Categories and Timing: On the Perception of Meter." *Ethnomusicology*, 51 (1): 64–84.

Kwasniewski, Peter. (2013). "The Sexual Rhythm of Rock Music (1 of 2)." *Views From the Choir Loft*, September 13. http://www.ccwatershed.org/blog/2013/sep/12/sexual-rhythm-rock-music-1-2/ (accessed July 1, 2021).

Laing, Dave. (2015). *One Chord Wonders: Power and Meaning in Punk Rock*. Oakland: PM Press.

Larner, Jeremy. (1964). "What Do They Get from Rock'n'Roll?" *Atlantic*, 214 (2): 44–9.

Lawson, Selena Michelle. (2009). "Radiohead: The Guitar Wielding, Dancing, Singing Commodity." *Communication Theses*, 47. http://digitalarchive.gsu.edu/communication_theses/47

Leblanc, Lisa. (2005). "'Ice Age Coming': Apocalypse, the Sublime, and the Paintings of Stanley Donwood." In Joseph Tate (ed.), *The Music and Art of Radiohead*, 85–102. Aldershot: Ashgate.

Leonard, George. (2006). *The Silent Pulse: A Search for the Perfect Rhythm That Exists in Each of Us*. Layton: Gibbs Smith.

Lerdahl, Fred and Ray Jackendoff. (1996[1983]). *A Generative Theory of Tonal Music*. Cambridge, MA: The MIT Press.

Letts, Marianne Tatom. (2005). "'How to Disappear Completely': Radiohead and the Resistant Concept Album." Ph.D. dissertation, University of Texas-Austin.

Letts, Marianne Tatom. (2010a). "'I'm Not Here, This Isn't Happening': The Vanishing Subject in Radiohead's *Kid A*." In Mark Spicer and John Covach (eds.), *Sounding Out Pop: Analytical Essays in Popular Music*, 214-44. Ann Arbor: University of Michigan Press.

Letts, Marianne Tatom. (2010b). *Radiohead and the Resistant Concept Album: How to Disappear Completely*. Bloomington: Indiana University Press.

Levitin, Daniel J. (2006). *This Is Your Brain on Music: The Science of a Human Obsession*. New York: Dutton.

Levitin, Daniel J. (2009). *The World in Six Songs: How the Musical Brain Created Human Nature*. New York: Plume.

Lewis, Justin. (1994). "The Meaning of Things: Audiences, Ambiguity, and Power. In Jon Cruz and Justin Lewis" (eds.), *Viewing, Reading, Listening: Audiences and Cultural Reception*, 19-32. Boulder: Westview Press.

Lewis, Lisa A., ed. (1992). *The Adoring Audience: Fan Culture and Popular Media*. London: Routledge.

Linder, Brian. (2009). "Online *IGN* Review of Radiohead's work (March 24)." http://music.ign.com/articles/965/965634p1.html (accessed January 11, 2011).

Locke, David. (1998). *Drum Gahu*. Tempe: White Cliffs Media.

London, Justin. (n.d.a). "Cognitive and Aesthetic Aspects of Metrical Ambiguity." Unpublished manuscript.

London, Justin. (n.d.b). "Metric Fake Outs." (Excel spreadsheet). http://www.people.carleton.edu/~jlondon/

London, Justin. (2012). *Hearing in Time: Psychological Aspects of Musical Meter*. 2nd ed. New York: Oxford University Press.

Longuet-Higgins, Hugh Christopher and Christopher S. Lee. (1984). "The Rhythmic Interpretation of Monophonic Music." *Music Perception*, 1 (4): 424-41.

Lourie, Reginald. (1949). "The Role of Rhythmic Patterns in Childhood." *The American Journal of Psychiatry*, 105: 653-60.

Lull, James. (1992). "Popular Music and Communication: An Introduction." In James Lull (ed.), *Popular Music and Communication*, 2nd ed., 1-32. Newbury Park: Sage.

Luttjeboer, Hemme, transcriber. (1996). *Message in a Box: The Complete Transcriptions, The Police*. London: Wise Publications.

MacDonald, Ian. (2005). *Revolution in the Head: The Beatles' Records and the Sixties*. 2nd rev. ed. London: Pimlico.

Macneal, Christina. (2010). "Sara of Tegan and Sara Spells It Out." *Gay and Lesbian Times*, 1181: 38.

Mahon, Maureen. (2004). *Right to Rock: The Black Rock Coalition and the Cultural Politics of Race*. Durham: Duke University Press.

Mahon, Maureen. (2011). "Listening for Willie Mae 'Big Mama' Thornton's Voice: The Sound of Race and Gender Transgressions in Rock and Roll." *Women and Music*, 15 (1): 1-17.

Manuel, Peter. (2006). "Flamenco in Focus: An Analysis of a Performance of Soleares." In Michael Tenzer (ed.), *Analytical Studies in World Music*, 92-199. New York: Oxford University Press.

Marans, Michael. (1990). "Review of Jeanius Electronics Russian Dragon." *Keyboard*, 16 (11): 152.

Martens, Peter. (2011). "The Ambiguous Tactus: Tempo, Subdivision Benefit, and Three Listener Strategies." *Music Perception*, 28 (5): 433-48.

Martin, David. (1988). "An Early Metronome." *Early Music*, 16 (1): 90–2.
Mattingly, Rick. (1984). "Andy Newmark." *Modern Drummer*, 8 (2): 8–14, 44, 46, 48–50, 54–6, 58, 62–4.
Mattingly, Rick. (1990). "Charlie Watts." *Modern Drummer*, 14 (2): 18–21, 58–62, 64–6, 68, 70, 72.
Mazokopaki, Katerina and Giannis Kugiumutzakis. (2009). "Infant Rhythms: Expressions of Musical Companionship." In Stephen Malloch and Colwyn Trevarthen (eds.), *Communicative Musicality: Exploring the Basis of Human Companionship*, 185–208. New York: Oxford University Press.
Merker, Bjorn H., Guy S. Madison, and Patricia Eckerdal. (2008). "On the Role and Origin of Isochrony in Human Rhythmic Entrainment.' *Cortex*, 45: 4–17.
Meyer, Leonard B. (1956). *Emotion and Meaning in Music*. Chicago: The University of Chicago Press.
Micallef, Ken. (2006). "Stewart Copeland: Staring Down the Future." *Modern Drummer*, 30 (8): 44–50, 52–4, 56, 58, 60.
Micallef, Ken and Donnie Marshall. (2007). *Classic Rock Drummers*. New York: Backbeat Books.
Miller, Donovan. (2020). "Reggae School Episode 3: Reggae Drums, Part 1." *Reggae in the Ruff*. https://www.youtube.com/watch?v=NrzhQvSKpYo (accessed July 4, 2021).
Miller, William F. (1989). "Neil Peart." *Modern Drummer*, 13 (12): 18–23, 52–60.
Moore, Allan F. (2001). *Rock: The Primary Text / Developing a Musicology of Rock*. 2nd ed. Aldershot: Ashgate.
Mulholland, Garry. (2006). *Fear of Music: The 261 Greatest Albums Since Punk and Disco*. London: Orion.
Newsom, Jon. (1985). "'A Sound Idea': Music for Animated Films." In Iris Newsom (ed.), *Wonderful Inventions: Motion Pictures, Broadcasting, and Recorded Sound at the Library of Congress*, 59–79. Washington: Library of Congress.
Niaah, Sonjah Stanley. (2010). *Dancehall: From Slave Ship to Ghetto*. Ottawa: University of Ottawa Press.
Osborn, Brad. (2017). *Everything in its Right Place: Analyzing Radiohead*. New York: Oxford University Press.
Osborne, Nigel. (2009). "Towards a Chronobiology of Musical Rhythm." In Stephen Malloch and Colwyn Trevarthen (eds.), *Communicative Musicality: Exploring the Basis of Human Companionship*, 545–64. New York: Oxford University Press.
Palmer, Robert. (1978). "Pop: Cars Merge Styles." *The New York Times* (August 9): C17.
Pareles, Jon. (2001). "Radiohead Forget Melody and Save Progressive Rock on *Amnesiac*." *Rolling Stone*, 871: 74–5.
Papoušek, Hanuš. (1996). "Musicality in Infancy Research: Biological and Cultural Origins of Early Musicality." In Irene Deliège and John Sloboda (eds.), *Musical Beginnings: Origins and Development of Musical Competence*, 37–55. New York: Oxford University Press.
Papoušek, Mechthild. (1996). "Intuitive Parenting: A Hidden Source of Musical Stimulation in Infancy." In Irene Deliège and John Sloboda (eds.), *Musical Beginnings: Origins and Development of Musical Competence*, 88–112. New York: Oxford University Press.

Parsons, Christopher V. Patent # 2004/0099132, "Tactile Metronome." Filed November 27, 2002; granted May 27, 2004.
Patel, Aniruddh D. (2006). "Musical Rhythm, Linguistic Rhythm, and Human Evolution." *Music Perception*, 24 (1): 99–104.
Patel, Aniruddh D. (2008). *Music, Language, and the Brain*. New York: Oxford University Press.
Patel, Aniruddh D. (2015). *Music and the Brain: Course Guidebook*. Chantilly: The Great Courses.
Patel, Aniruddh D., John R. Iversen, Micah R. Bregman, and Irena Schulz. (2009). "Experimental Evidence for Synchronization to a Musical Beat in a Nonhuman Animal." *Current Biology*, 19 (10): 827–30.
Paytress, Mark. (2005). *Radiohead: The Complete Guide to their Music*. New York: Omnibus Press.
Pellegrini, A. D. and Peter K Smith. (1998). "Physical Activity Play: The Nature and Function of a Neglected Aspect of Play." *Child Development*, 69 (3): 577–98.
Petridis, Alexis. (2007). "Radiohead's In Rainbows: A Five-Star Review." *The Guardian* online version, October 10, 2007. https://www.theguardian.com/music/musicblog/2007/oct/10/radioheadsinrainbowsisita (accessed February 20, 2018).
Pickering, Michael, ed. (2010). *Popular Culture. Volume 3, Cultural Formations and Social Relations*. London: Sage.
Pinker, Steven. (2008). *The Language Instinct: The New Science of Language and Mind*. London: The Folio Society.
Plummer, Harry Chapin. (1914). "The Rythmikon—a New Aid to the Study of Musical Rhythm." *Scientific American*, 111 (22): 436.
Polak, Rainer, Nori Jacoby, and Justin London. (2016). "Both Isochronous and Non-isochronous Metrical Subdivision Afford Precise and Stable Ensemble Entrainment: A Corpus Study of Malian Jembe Drumming." *Frontiers in Auditory Neuroscience*. DOI:10.3389/fnins.2016.00285
Police, the. (2003). "Police in Montserrat." 1981 documentary included as bonus material on *The Police: Every Breath You Take, The DVD* (A&M Records, 493 671-9).
Potter, Jeff. (2012). "Bob Marley's Carlton Barrett." *Modern Drummer*, 36 (8): 30–4.
Povel, Dirk-Jan. (1981). "Internal Representation of Simple Temporal Patterns." *Journal of Experimental Psychology: Human Perception and Performance*, 7 (1): 3–18.
Povel, Dirk-Jan and Peter Essens. (1985). "Perception of Temporal Patterns." *Music Perception*, 2 (4): 411–40.
Prasad, Anil. (2007). "Dancing with Desire: Living Colour's Vernon Reid on Pushing the Creative Envelope." *Guitar Player*, 41 (1): 64–8.
Prior, Nick. (2009). "Software Sequencers and Cyborg Singers: Popular Music in the Digital Hypermodern." *New Formations*, 66: 81–99.
Prior, Nick. (2018). *Popular Music, Digital Technology and Society*. London: Sage.
Quin, Sara and Tegan Quin. (2019). *High School*. New York: Picador.
Randall, Mac. (2011). *Exit Music: The Story of Radiohead*. London: Omnibus Press.

Ratcliff, John. (1999). *Timecode: A User's Guide*. 3rd ed. New York: Focal Press.
Raziel. (2013). "Ripping My Shirt Off: Tegan and Sara Bring New Sound to Ambleside." *Xtra! West: Vancouver's Gay and Lesbian News*, 523: 20.
Reynolds, Simon. (2001). "Dissent into the Mainstream." *The Wire*, 209: 25-33.
Robertson, Andrew and Mark Plumbley. (2007). "B-Keeper: A Beat-Tracker for Live Performance." *Proceedings of the 2007 Conference on New Interfaces for Musical Expression*, New York, 234-7.
Rolontz, Bob and Joel Friedman. (1954). "Teenagers Demand Music With a Beat, Spur Rhythm-Blues." *The Billboard*, April 24, 1.
Ross, Alex. (2010). *Listen to This*. New York: Farrar, Straus and Giroux.
Rule, Greg. (1991). "Vinnie Colaiuta: From Zappa to Sting." *Drums & Drumming*, 3 (1): 28.
Sacks, Oliver. (2007). *Musicophilia: Tales of Music and the Brain*. New York: Alfred A. Knopf.
Sargeant, Winthrop and Sarat Lahiri. (1931). "A Study in East Indian Rhythm." *Musical Quarterly*, 17: 427-38.
Schloss, Joseph G. (2004). *Making Beats: The Art of Sample-Based Hip-Hop*. Middletown: Wesleyan University Press.
Scoates, Christopher. (2011). *Bullet Proof... I Wish I Was: The Lighting and Stage Design of Andi Watson*. Foreword by Thom Yorke. San Francisco: Chronicle Books.
Schuller, Gunther. (1968). *Early Jazz: Its Roots and Musical Development*. New York: Oxford University Press.
Simons, David. (1999). "Waddy Wachtel." *Musician*, 245: 14.
Sontag, Susan. (2001). "A Photograph Is Not an Opinion. Or Is It?" In *Where the Stress Falls: Essays*, 238-51. New York: Farrar, Straus and Giroux.
Sorowiecki, James. (2004). *The Wisdom of Crowds: Why the Many are Smarter than the Few and How Collective Wisdom Shapes Business, Economics, Societies, and Nations*. New York: Doubleday.
Sparlour, Tim. (2011). "Saint Augustine in Hell — Vinnie Colaiuta." *Jazz Drumming Blog*. http://drumming.timsparlour.com/drummers/vinnie_colautia.php (accessed April 11, 2018).
Spicer, Mark. (2004). "(Ac)cumulative Form in Pop-Rock Music." *Twentieth-century Music*, 1 (1): 29-64.
Spicer, Mark. (2010). "'Reggatta de Blanc': Analyzing Style in the Music of the Police." In Mark Spicer and John Covach (eds.), *Sounding Out Pop: Analytical Essays in Popular Music*, 124-53. Ann Arbor: University of Michigan Press.
Starr, Eric. (2009). *The Everything Rock Drums Book*. Avon: Adam Media.
Stein, Deborah. (2004). "Introduction to Musical Ambiguity." In Deborah Stein (ed.), *Engaging Music: Essays in Music Analysis*, 77-88. New York: Oxford University Press.
Sting. (2003). *Broken Music: A Memoir*. London: Simon and Schuster.
Sting. (2007). *Lyrics by Sting*. New York: The Dial Press.
Stone, Chris. (2005[1996]). "The L.A. Gold (Record) Rush: A Quarter Century of Studio Excellence from La La land." In Anthony Savona (ed.), *Console Confessions: The Great Music Producers in Their Own Words*, 49-53. San Francisco: Backbeat Books.

Strauss, Neil. (2002). "Tunes for Toons: A Cartoon Music Primer." In Daniel Goldmark and Yuval Taylor (eds.), *The Cartoon Music Book*, 5–13. Chicago: A Cappella Books.
Sullivan, Robert. (1955). "Rock 'n' Roll Riot." *Daily News* (New York City), Sunday News section, September 18, 88–9.
Summers, Andy. (2006). *One Train Later: A Memoir.* Foreword by the Edge. London: Portrait.
Sweetman, Simon. (2016). "Drummers You Just Can't Beat: #14—Vinnie Colaiuta." *Off the Tracks.* https://offthetracks.co.nz/drummers-you-just-cant-beat-14-vinnie-colaiuta/ (accessed April 11, 2018).
Tal, Idan, Edward W. Large, Eshed Rabinovitch, Yi Wei, Charles E. Schroeder, David Poeppel, and Elana Zion Golumbic. (2017). "Neural Entrainment to the Beat: The 'Missing-Pulse' Phenomenon." *The Journal of Neuroscience*, 37 (26): 6331–41.
Tamlyn, Garry Neville. (1998). "The Big Beat: Origins and Development of Snare Backbeat and Other Accompanimental Rhythms in Rock 'n' Roll." Ph.D. dissertation, University of Liverpool.
Tapscott, Don and Anthony D. Williams. (2006). *Wikinomics: How Mass Collaboration Changes Everything.* New York: Portfolio.
Taruskin, Richard. (2010a). *Music in the Seventeenth and Eighteenth Centuries.* New York: Oxford University Press.
Taruskin, Richard. (2010b). *Music in the Late Twentieth Century.* New York: Oxford University Press.
Tate, Joseph. (2005a). "Introduction." In Joseph Tate (ed.), *The Music and Art of Radiohead*, 1–8. Aldershot: Ashgate.
Tate, Joseph. (2005b). "Radiohead's Antivideos: Works of Art in the Age of Electronic Reproduction." In Joseph Tate (ed.), *The Music and Art of Radiohead*, 101–17. Aldershot: Ashgate.
Taylor, Stephen. (2010). "Rhythm Necklace and Hemiola: Hidden Meter in Radiohead and Björk." Conference paper read in Bellairs, Barbados, February 6.
Taylor, Timothy D. (2012). *The Sounds of Capitalism: Advertising, Music, and the Conquest of Culture.* Chicago: University of Chicago Press.
Tegan. (2014). "Yet Another Tegan and Sara Fanblog ("Northshore")." Tegan and Sara Quin tumblr. https://teganandorsaraquin.tumblr.com/post/91198987530/northshore-was-actually-written-about-this (accessed July 3, 2021).
Tegan and Sara. (2009). "Tegan and Sara Biography." Archived from original. https://teganandsara.com (accessed July 6, 2021).
Tegan and Sara. (2021). "About Tegan and Sara." Tegan and Sara Foundation. https://www.teganandsarafoundation.org/about (accessed July 3, 2021).
Temperley, David. (1999). "Syncopation in Rock: A Perceptual Perspective." *Popular Music*, 18 (1): 19–40.
Temperley, David. (2001). *The Cognition of Basic Musical Structures.* Cambridge, MA: The MIT Press.
Temperley, David. (2018). *The Musical Language of Rock.* New York: Oxford University Press.
Tenzer, Michael. (2006). "Introduction: Analysis, Categorization, and Theory of Musics of the World." In Michael Tenzer (ed.), *Analytical Studies in World Music*, 3–38. New York: Oxford University Press.

Terhardt, Ernst. (1991). "Music Perception and Sensory Information Acquisition: Relationships and Low-Level Analogies." *Music Perception*, 8 (3): 217–40.
Thomas, Frank and Ollie Johnston. (1981). *Disney Animation: The Illusion of Life*. New York: Abbeville Press.
Thompson, Michael. (2009). "The Signature of Time in 'Pyramid Song.'" In Brandon W. Forbes and George A. Reisch (eds.), *Radiohead and Philosophy: Fitter Happier More Deductive*, 221–8. Chicago: Open Court.
Thomson, William. (1983). "Functional Ambiguity in Musical Structures." *Music Perception*, 1: 3–27.
Tomlinson, Gary. (2015). *A Million Years of Music: The Emergence of Human Modernity*. New York: Zone Books.
Trainor, Laurel J. and Robert J. Zatorre. (2016). "The Neurobiology of Musical Expectations from Perception to Emotion." In Susan Hallam, Ian Cross, and Michael Thaut (eds.), *The Oxford Handbook of Music Psychology*, 2nd ed., 285–306. New York: Oxford University Press.
Trost, Wiebke, Sascha Frühholz, Daniele Schön, Carolina Labbé, Swann Pichon, Didier Grandjean, and Patrik Vuilleumier. (2014). "Getting the Beat: Entrainment of Brain Activity by Musical Rhythm and Pleasantness." *NeuroImage*, 103: 55–64.
Turner, Anthony. (2017). "A New Age: Electric and Electronic Metronomes." In Tony Bingham and Anthony Turner (eds.), *Metronomes and Musical Time*, 52–5. London: Tony Bingham.
Turner, Victor. (1982). *From Ritual to Theatre: The Human Seriousness of Play*. New York: Performing Arts Journal Publications.
Underberg, Natalie M. and Elayne Zorn. (2013). *Digital Ethnography: Anthropology, Narrative, and New Media*. Austin: University of Texas Press.
Vazan, Peter and Michael F. Schober. (2004). "Detecting and Resolving Metrical Ambiguity in a Rock Song upon Multiple Rehearsals." In Scott Lipscomb, Richard Ashley, Robert Gjerdingen, and Peter Webster (eds.), *Proceedings of the 8th International Conference on Music Perception & Cognition, Evanston, IL*, 426–32. Adelaide: Causal Productions.
Vuust, Peter, Leif Ostergaard, Karen Johanne Pallesen, Christopher Bailey, and Andreas Roepstorff. (2009). "Predictive Coding of Music: Brain Responses to Rhythmic Incongruity." *Cortex*, 45: 80–92.
Wallace, Ian. (1990). "Ian Wallace." *Modern Drummer*, 14 (9): 12.
Waletzky, Joshua, director. (2007). *The Hollywood Sound: Music for the Movies*. DVD documentary, Kultur Video.
Wall, Mick. (2008). *When Giants Walked the Earth: A Biography of Led Zeppelin*. London: Orion Books.
Waterman, Richard Alan. (1952). "African Influence on the Music of the Americas." In Sol Tax (ed.), *Acculturation in the Americas (Proceedings of the Nineteenth International Congress of Americanists)*, 207–18. Chicago: University of Chicago Press.
Waters, Keith. (1996). "Blurring the Barline: Metric Displacement in the Piano Solos of Herbie Hancock." *Annual Review of Jazz Studies*, 8: 19–37.
Watson, Ian. (2001). "The Ballad of Thom Yorke." *Rolling Stone* (Australian edition), 589: 46.

Weeks, Olly and Alex Davis, arrangers. (2011). *Radiohead: The Piano Songbook*. Milwaukee: Hal Leonard.
Weiss, Jeff. (2018). "The Secret History of One of the Most Sampled Albums of All Time." *Vinyl Me Please*. https://magazine.vinylmeplease.com/magazine/classics-soul-makossa-july-18/ (accessed July 3, 2021).
Welch, Chris. (1996). *The Complete Guide to the Music of the Police and Sting*. London: Omnibus Press.
Wierzbicki, James. (2009). *Film Music: A History*. New York: Routledge.
Wolfe, Paula. (2019). *Women in the Studio: Creativity, Control and Gender in Popular Music Sound Production*. London: Routledge.
Wood, Abigail. (2008). "E-Fieldwork: A Paradigm for the Twenty-first Century?" In Henry Stobart (ed.), *The New (Ethno)musicologies*, 40–7. Lanham: The Scarecrow Press.
Yorke, Ritchie. (1999). *Led Zeppelin: From Early Days to Page and Plant*. London: Virgin Books.
Zagorski-Thomas, Simon. (2010). "Real and Unreal Performances: The Interaction of Recording Technology and Rock Drum Kit Performance." In Anne Danielsen (ed.), *Musical Rhythm in the Age of Digital Reproduction*, 195–212. New York: Routledge.
Zagorski-Thomas, Simon. (2014). *The Musicology of Record Production*. Cambridge: Cambridge University Press.
Zuckerkandl, Victor. (1973[1956]). *Sound and Symbol: Music and the External World*. Princeton: Princeton University Press.

Websites (Chapter 2)

8N (http://www.8notes.com/school/riffs/piano/radiohead_pyramid.asp), "Pyramid Song Piano Tab"
FB (http://www.facebook.com/topic.php?uid=6979332244&topic=5330), "Time Signature in Pyramid Song???"
FH (http://www.freehandmusic.com/sheet-music/pyramid-song-290128), "Pyramid Song (Digital Sheet Music)"
GPL (http://www.greenplastic.com/lyrics/pyramidsong.php), "Radiohead Song Lyrics and Info"
GPT (http://www.greenplastic.com/lyrics/tabs/pyramidsong.txt), "Radiohead Pyramid Song (Piano Tab)"
MG (http://mortigitempo.com/really_bored/index.php?/topic/78491-what-do-you-count-pyramid-song-in/page__st__40), "What Do You Count Pyramid Song In?"
PB (http://s53.photobucket.com/albums/g54/dreddnott/music/?action=view&current=02Piano_0001.png), "Pyramid Song"
PS (http://www.youtube.com/watch?v=Ydc2HYjhO20), "Pyramid Song 4/4 Explained"
PS2 (http://www.youtube.com/watch?v=zbKQPqs-cqc), "Pyramid Song"
RM (http://www.rockmagic.net/guitar-tabs/radiohead/pyramid_song.btab), "Pyramid Song Bass Tab"

SF (http://www.songfacts.com/detail.php?id=1524), "Pyramid Song by Radiohead"
WP (http://en.wikipedia.org/wiki/Pyramid_Song), "Pyramid Song"
WPS (http://en.wikipedia.org/wiki/File:Pyramid_Song_for_Wikipedia.jpg), "Pyramid Song for Wikipedia"
YT (http://www.youtube.com/comment_servlet?all_comments=1&v=cqP0WNpojFM), "Radiohead — Pyramid Song"

INDEX

Abbey Road Studios   126
Abel, Mark   71, 77
   Groove: An Aesthetic of Measured Time   73
Abingdon (Oxfordshire)   12, 54
accumulative form   43, 67, 80
AC/DC   127, 137
actor-network theory (ANT)   123
Adams, Bryan   127, 140
Aerosmith   127, 135
African
   cultural influences   71, 75, 77, 78
   drummers   24, 143
   rhythms   73, 83
   West and Central rhythms   42, 71
African American
   cultural influences   75, 77
   musical practice   72, 78
   popular music styles   121
Africanization of Western popular music   71, 76
Afrobeat   78
Agawu, Kofi   71
Akai MPC60   129, 140
Alan Parson's Project   109
   I Robot   51
Alpert, Herb   134
A&M   124, 144
ambiguity   5, 7–10, 12, 14, 20, 39
   of beginning   47
   and clothing   55
   and the commodified object   9
   and fan relationships   14–15, 21, 55
   and gender   9
   and lyrics   39, 82
   and photography   9
   and race and vocal timbre   9
   and rhythm   4, 8, 95
   and snare backbeat   92
   and species   9
   and symbolic imagery   9
   and videos   55
   and walking bass line   90
   and web sites   55
American Bandstand   75
American popular music   3, 72, 76
Amnesiac (Radiohead album)   8, 12–22, 55
Andalusian Phrygian tonality   20
Anderson, Jon   140
animated cartoon films   99–102
anthropology   11, 123
April Wine
   Harder...Faster   89
   "Say Hello"   89
Aquila, Richard   76
Arabic music   47
Arom, Simha   24, 73
Atoms for Peace   14
attunement   1
audience participation   4, 8, 10
avant-garde electronic studio music   13, 106
Avron, Neal   107, 127, 132, 141, 142

backbeat   71–4
   as Africanization of American popular music   71, 75, 77
   as a central element in audiences' understanding of all popular music   5, 69, 93
   as creating ambiguity and providing clarification   89–93

INDEX

as creating ambiguity and
  uncertainty 84–9
as creating a sense of play, fun, and/
  or deviance 80–4
drawing in listeners and/or dancers
  physically and cognitively 69
and embodied engagement 73
as expressive device 4, 5, 70
expressivity in the timekeeping role
  of 5, 70
and microtiming 70
as oscillation, "to-fro" or "away-
  back" 73
as providing clarification and
  resolution 78–80
as raw and primitive 76
reversed 82, 83, 89, 91–2
setting up perceptual anchors 69
in 7/4 and 7/8 bars 94–6
syncopated 64
in 3/4 and 9/8 bars 89, 93–4
as "unnatural" and morally
  corrupting 76
Baker, Ginger 82, 83
Barbès district (Paris) 78
Baroque lament 44
Barrett, Carlton "Carly" 46
BBC Radio 4 56
Beach Boys 137
beat
  backwards 83
  finding the 1–6, 97–8, 120–4, 149
  "hidden" 23, 24, 63
  keeping the 97, 136
  matching 1, 3, 110
Beat Detective 135
Beatles, The 9, 124
  Help! 93
  Revolver 109
  Sgt. Pepper 80
  "Tomorrow Never Knows" 109
  "You've Got to Hide Your Love
    Away" 93
beat perception and synchronization
  (BPS) 1, 98
  six key features 2
BeatSeeker 119–20
Beck, Jeff 133

Bee Gees
  "Jive Talkin" 89
  Main Course 89
Bellotte, Pete 110
Benatar, Pat 133
Benjamin, Walter
  *The Work of Art in the Age of
  Mechanical Reproduction*
  121
"*Beopgo Changsin*: New Music
  for Samul Nori" (Nathan
  Hesselink) 96
Bergamanini, Joe 91
Berlioz, Hector 113
  Euphonia 106
Berry, Chuck 9, 75
Biamonte, Nicole 72, 80, 89
Big Beat, The 74–8
biocultural coevolution 3
Bissonette, Gregg 127, 135–7,
  141, 142
Black artists/musicians 6, 76
  and music industry racism 86
  and rock music 79, 86–8
Blacking, John 24
Black Rock Coalition (BRC) 86–8
Blind Faith 83
blues 3, 44, 76
  electric 107
  urban 77
Bombay Bicycle Club
  A Different Kind of Fix 89
  "Leave It" 89
Bonham, John 89
Bon Jovi 127
Bonnaroo 61
Boss metronome 140
Bowie, David 9, 138
Boyd, Bobby 78
Brackett, John 92
Bramwell, Murray 83
Brenston, Jackie and His Delta Cats
  "Rocket '88" 74
"Bring On the Night" (The
  Police) 43, 65
  and rhythmic fakeout 44–54, 67
"Broken Toy" (Keane) 94
Brown, Theodore 77

Bruford, Bill 94–5, 111, 123, 143–4
Bush, Kate
  "Army Dreamers" 94
  Never for Ever 94
Butler, Mark 10–12, 20, 47, 80
ButtKicker, The 117
Byrne, David 62

cabasa 140, 141
Cage, John 7, 8
Capitol Records 82, 124, 144
Cars, The
  The Cars 80
  "Just What I Needed" 80–2
Carson, Spencer 108, 127
Chapman, Tracy 133
Cherokee Studios 125
Chiang, Ted
  "The Great Silence" (short story) 2
Chords, The
  "Sh-Boom" 74
Clapton, Eric
  "Lay Down Sally" 129
Clark, Dick 75
classical music 13, 97
  and beat hierarchies 70, 71, 73, 77
  and metrical ambiguity 67
  and the metronome 5, 97, 106
  and rhythmic play 41
click track 35, 97, 99, 100, 123
  bury(ing) the 134, 138, 145
  composer-performer directed 118–20
  in concert 99, 122
  definition of 98, 111
  and lack of drummer's skill 128, 137
  microtemporal deviations from 138, 139, 145
  patents 100, 102, 112–13, 115
  placement of snare within 139
  placement of with purpose and for expressive reasons 141, 145
  during the rock era 106–12
  in the studio 99, 107–11, 124, 128, 130–1, 133–4, 136–43

  tactile 98, 104, 117–18
  as trial by fire 138
  visual 98, 104, 105, 112
cognitive (neuro)science 1, 4–6, 11, 33, 93
Cohen, Peter 142–3
Colaiuta, Vinnie 95–6, 133, 140
Cole, Natalie
  Unforgettable 119
Cole, Nat King 75
collaborative interaction in performance 123
collective communal experience 42
commercials
  in radio broadcasting 106
communication
  and collaborative aesthetics 68
  between composers and listeners/audiences 5, 41, 54, 68
  as in-group/insider knowledge 5, 41, 68
  and shared identity 54
composition
  and play 41, 46, 68
  and rhythmic play 41, 46
  and space 9, 39, 45, 46, 80
computer-based, groove-oriented musics 122
Cooper, Alice 136
Copeland, Stewart 44, 46–7, 49, 53
cosmology 38
country music 3, 111
Covach, John 80
Coverdale, David and Jimmy Page 127
Cream 82, 83
  Disraeli Gears 82
  "Sunshine of Your Love" 82–3
Crosse, Gordon
  Play Ground for orchestra, expanded percussion, and metronome 106
crowdsourcing 39
Cult, The 127
"Cult of Personality" (Living Colour) 84, 87–9
cultural studies 8
Curry, Mickey 140–1

Daft Punk
  "Giorgio by Moroder" 110
  Random Access Memories 110
dance
  entrainment and 3, 74
  musics 3, 5, 74–5, 129
  and rhythm/motion 71, 73, 75, 76, 93
dancehall 51
Danielsen, Anne 72–3, 121, 139, 145
"Darkest Light" (The Lafayette Afro Rock Band) 78–80
David Lee Roth Band 127, 135, 137
Davies, Dil 118
"Dazed and Confused" (Led Zeppelin) 89–93
Decemberists
  "Make You Better" 82
  What a Terrible World, What a Beautiful World 82
decentralized analytical approaches to musical works 12, 21, 39
De La Soul 78
democratization of rhythmic values 70–1
Dibango, Mani 78
"Digital Pulsing Visual Metronome" (Gary Duke) 112–14
digital recording technology 111, 123
disco 3, 109–10, 129
displacement consonance 72
Dixieland 13
DJs 67, 110
Donwood, Stanley (b. Dan Rickwood) 13, 14, 17, 18, 147
Doobie Brothers, The 135
Dowd, Tom 83
Dunworth, Charles 101
Dyck, Ralph 108
Dylan, Bob 131, 140

Eagles, The 124
Earth, Wind & Fire 78, 134
"Edge of Seventeen" (Stevie Nicks) 49–50
EDM (electronic dance music) 10, 80, 110
Eidsheim, Nina Sun

The Race of Sound 78
8-bit processor 135
Electric Lady Studios 131
electronic drum machines 97, 122, 129, 134, 145
  and loss of gigs for live drummers 131
electronic music 13, 47
Ellis, Shirley 18
Elvis 9, 74
embodiment 5, 93, 116, 118
Eno, Brian 110
entrainment
  definition/nature of 1–4, 74
  and development of modern human brain 41
  historical and technological considerations 97–120
  and the human-technology interface 97–146
  and metric understanding 9, 11, 38, 42, 73, 93
  sociological and aesthetic considerations 121–46
ethnographic
  fieldwork 11
  research 11, 38
ethnomusicology/ethnomusicologists
  author's identity 1, 4, 8
  programs 57
  research in/by 6, 11, 71, 123
Everclear 132
Everett, Walter 72
expectation 3, 4, 10, 11, 33, 42
experiencing time together 6
exploratory competence 40, 41
expressive power of music 93
Ezrin, Bob 126, 127, 136, 146

Factory Studios 96
Fairbairn, Bruce 126, 127
Fairlight keyboard 140
Fall Out Boy 132
fan culture 12, 14, 57
fans' interpretive insights 11, 12, 57, 66, 93
Fast, Susan 90
feel

drum machine 133–5
  human 25, 120, 121, 136, 145
  machine 145
  straight 143
  swing 28, 31, 33, 143
female artists 6, 123
Fleetwood Mac 49, 130, 135
  Fleetwood Mac 109
  "Rhiannon" 109
Flicker, Mike 115, 127, 129, 141
Fongheiser, Denny 127, 141
  burying the click 138–9
  on drum machines 133, 134
  playing around the click 139
  on recording in studios 144
  on rhythmic feel 143
Foraker, Brian 127, 132, 139
Foreigner 135
Forsey, Keith 110
frames per beat/second 100, 107
Fraser, Mike 107, 126, 127, 137
Freed, Alan 74, 75
Frenette, Matt 83–4, 140
Fricke, David 61
From the Basement 61
Frondelli, Mike 82, 83, 127, 131–2
funk 3, 72, 73, 78, 87

Gabriel, Peter 136, 143
  "In Your Eyes" 82
  So 82
"garden path" phenomenon to music 24, 52
Garity, William 100, 102
Genesis 123
Gen X 131
Glass Tiger 115
Godrich, Nigel 13, 14, 61, 63, 68
Gong 123
Goodwin, Andrew 122
Gordon, Jim 141
Gordy, Berry 78
Grammy Awards
  for Best Album Package 16, 56
  for Best Alternative Music Album 13, 16, 56
  for Best Hard Rock Performance 87
  for Best Rock Instrumental Performance 47
Greenwood, Colin 12, 19, 54, 63
Greenwood, Jonny 12, 19, 54, 62–3
  Bodysong 56
  There Will Be Blood 56
Griffiths, Dai 8, 24, 29
Griffiths, Gibson, and Ramsay Productions 108, 126
groove
  and compositional technique 9, 10, 42, 43, 80, 134
  as feel 3, 135, 138, 143
  in popular music 73, 93, 121–2
  and racialization 77
Group Humanizer 120

Haley, Bill
  "Crazy Man, Crazy" 74
  "Rock Around the Clock" 74
Hall and Oates 140
Hamel, Keith 118, 127
Hammersmith Apollo (London) 61
"Han-Mi Karak" (Rhythms from Korea and the United States) (Nathan Hesselink) 96
Hanson, Michael 115
Harrison, Gavin 80
Hartman, Kent 109
Heart
  Dreamboat Annie 129
Hein, Ethan 76–7
Hennemann, Rolf 127, 129, 130
hi-hat
  as a click track 138, 140
  as creating swing 132
  and off-beat syncopations 46, 47, 51, 61
hip-hop 3, 77, 78, 111, 143
Hogarth, Ross 110, 115, 127, 135, 142
Holden, James 120
Holland, Jools 46
Hoskyns, Barney 124
Human Clock 120
Human League, The 108
Huron, David 2, 9, 10, 24, 52, 72
hypermetric convergence/level 88, 89

Idol, Billy   132, 146
   "Eyes Without a Face"   132
   Rebel Yell   131
"Ilgop Mach'i" (Seven Strokes)
   (Nathan Hesselink)   96
Indiana Jones and the Last
   Crusade   148
Indian traditional percussion music   3
interactive and collaborative music
   analysis   11
internet
   communities   11, 38, 39, 128
   fieldwork   5
   research   11, 56
intros (rock/pop music)   9, 42, 43, 52, 55, 87
Iwerks, Ubbe "Ub"   100, 101

Jackson, Janet   78
Jackson, Michael   9
Jackson, Wilfred   100, 102
Jacksons, The   138
Jagger, Mick   87
Jaubert, Pierre   78
Jay-Z
   "Show Me What You Got"   78
jazz   13, 36, 44, 77
   big-band   3, 74
   drumming   70, 75, 77, 82, 143
   improvisational practice   87
   and swing feel   28, 30
Jeanius Electronics   108
jingles   126, 130
Joel, Billy
   "Piano Man"   93
   Piano Man   93
John, Elton   138
Jones, John Paul   92, 133
Jones, Rickie Lee   131
jump bands   107
"Just What I Needed" (The Cars)   80–2

Kaluli   42
"Kashmir" (Led Zeppelin)   88–9
Keane
   "Broken Toy"   94
   Under the Iron Sea   94

Keltner, Jim   130–1
Kendun Recorders   125
Kennedy, John F.   88
Kimsey, Chris   130
King, B.B.   124
King, Sharman   126, 127
King Crimson   123, 140
   "Three of a Perfect Pair"   94, 95
   Three of a Perfect Pair   94
KISS   132, 136
Kraftwerk   108
Kwasniewski, Peter   76

Lafayette Afro Rock Band, The
   "Darkest Light"   78–80
   "Hihache"   78
   Malik   78
   Nino and Radiah   78
Lain, Warren   57, 64
Leaf, David   125, 127
Leckie, John   13, 14
Led Zeppelin
   "Dazed and Confused"   89–93
   "Kashmir"   88–9
   Led Zeppelin   90
   Physical Graffiti   88
Lennon, John   131
Lerdahl, Fred and Ray Jackendoff
   A Generative Theory of Tonal Music   48, 71, 90–1
Levitin, Daniel   7, 10, 52, 92
Levy, Marcy   129
Ligeti, György
   Symphonic Poem for 100 metronomes   106
Linett, Mark   127, 137
Linkin Park   132
Linn
   LinnDrum   129–33
   LM-1   129
   9000   129, 135, 140
Linn, Roger   129, 130
listener
   interpretations   9, 17, 21, 39, 47, 65, 88, 90, 92, 96
   participation   5, 10, 24, 67, 68, 93
listening
   as creative act   5, 41–2

and expectation 11, 33, 43
and extended communities 5, 8, 12, 43
Little Mountain Sound Studios 96, 107, 126, 127
Living Colour 86–7
"Cult of Personality" 84, 87–9
Vivid 87
LL Cool J 78
Locke, David 71
Loggins, Kenny 138
London, Justin 10, 20, 24, 26, 43, 72
Lord, Gord 108, 127
Los Angeles 85, 124, 127
Loverboy 83, 140
Loverboy 126, 127
"Strike Zone" 140
Lynch, Stan 109, 127–9, 144–5
Lynyrd Skynyrd 132

Mabel and Fatty Viewing the World's Fair at San Francisco, Cal. 101
Macdonald, Jim 102
MacDonald, Ralph 138
Madonna 138
Mahon, Maureen 78, 87
Right to Rock 87
Malcolm X 87
manuscript music paper 145
Mark of the Unicorn Performer 118
Marley, Bob and the Wailers
Burnin' 46
Marotta, Jerry 143
Martin, George 124
Mason, Konda 86
mass collaboration 39
math metal 67
Mendes, Sergio 134
Messiaen, Olivier
"Fête des belles eaux" 19
Metallica 127
meter
accentless 71
binary expectation 33, 71
compound 23, 28–31
mixed 36–8
non-isochronous 26–8
quadruple 69, 93

in 7/4 or 7/8 94–6
simple 33–6
and strong and weak beats 70, 73
and syncopation 72
triple 85, 93–4
and Western historical and musicological norms or assumptions 70–4
"Method and Apparatus for Synchronizing Photoplays" (Disney patent) 102
metrical
ambiguity 10, 12, 67, 86, 149
complexity 3, 8, 50
prediction 42, 93
metrically ambiguous pre-chorus 87
metric fakeout 24, 50
metronome 5, 97, 98, 101
in compositions 106
digital 107, 118, 137, 139, 140
Maelzel 100
in the studio 97, 102, 141, 146
tactile 99, 115–18
visual 99, 106, 112–15
Meyer, Leonard 41, 64–5
Michael, George
"Cowboys and Angels" 94
Listen Without Prejudice Vol. 1 94
microtemporal deviations 121, 139, 145
microtiming variations 70, 122, 132
MIDI (Musical Instrument Digital Interface)
and click tracks 118–20
and electronic metronome 114–15, 117
and electronic musical instruments 110–11
intergration with time code 106
military band music 72, 77
Mingus, Charles 148
"Freedom" 18, 19, 28
Mitchell, Joni 133
Mitchell, Mitch 84
Modern Drummer 46, 53, 118, 128, 137, 142
Moffett, Jonathan 138
Moog modular 110

Moon, Keith 84, 109
Moroder, Giorgio 108, 110
Mötley Crüe 127, 135
Motown 78
Mulholland, Garry 15
multitracking 111, 122, 123, 143
Muse
 Absolution 93
 "Blackout" 93
Mushroom Studios 107, 127
music hall 44
musicology/musicologists 4, 6, 70
music theory/music theorists 4–6, 10, 38, 93
 and aesthetics 12
 and individual analytical engagements 11

Newman, Alfred 101
Newmark, Andy 138
new timing technologies and sociological and aesthetic transformations 106, 128
new wave 6, 44, 80, 81, 85
New York City 86, 87, 124, 131, 141
Nicks, Stevie 50, 132, 140
 Bella Donna 49
 "Edge of Seventeen" 49–50
1975, The
 The 1975 82
 "Talk!" 82
Nirvana
 Nevermind 54, 142, 143
"Northshore" (Tegan and Sara) 85–6, 88, 89
numerical ratios 25, 32
numerology 38

Oberheim DMX 129
O'Brien, Ed 12, 54, 66, 147
Olsen, Keith 108–9, 127, 135, 136, 141
Ommen, Ann 72
ondes Martenot 19
one drop/one-drop rhythm 46
"Optical Metronome" (Juan del Castillo) 112–13
Osborn, Brad 39, 82

Osbourne, Ozzy 135
Oxford 147–8
 Balliol College 147
 St John's College 8, 147

Parlophone/EMI 12, 13, 56
Patel, Aniruddh 2, 98
Payolas
 "Eyes of a Stranger" 126
pay-what-you-want download 56
Peart, Neil 140
perfect rhythm 122, 140, 141, 145
perfect time 113, 122, 138, 140
performance in the studio 144
Perron, Marius 108
Peterson Body Beat Sync™ 116–17
Petty, Tom and the Heartbreakers 109, 129, 133
Phillips, Sam 74
Pink Floyd 131, 136
 Dark Side of the Moon 95, 109
 A Momentary Lapse of Reason 126
 "Money" 95
Plant, Robert 92, 93
play
 creative 40, 41, 55
 musical 82
 rhythmic-formal 3–5, 40–2, 53, 55, 67, 68, 80, 86, 87, 147
 structural-compositional 5, 41, 43, 45, 46, 53–4, 68
playing
 with the beat 6
 in time 6, 97, 110, 113, 143, 145–6
Poison 82, 127
Police, The 42, 44–7, 53–4
 "Bring On the Night" 43, 45, 47–53, 65, 67
 "Contact" 46
 "Deathwish" 46
 "Don't Stand So Close to Me" 45
 Ghost in the Machine 44, 45
 "Message in a Bottle" 46
 Outlandos d'Amour 44–6
 Reggatta de Blanc 44–6
 "Roxanne" 46

"So Lonely"   45, 46
"Spirits in the Material World"   45
Synchronicity   44
"Walking on the Moon"   46
Zenyatta Mondatta   44, 45
pop(ular) music
   post-1950s   5, 69
   studies   4, 5
Price, Thommy   131
Prince   9
   "Diamonds and Pearls"   91
   Diamonds and Pearls   91
Prism
   "Spaceship Superstar"   126
Pritchard, Bob   118, 127
psychology   4
Public Enemy
   "Show 'Em Whatcha Got"   78
"Pulsating Metronome" (Manuel Diaz)   116
Putnam, Bill   124
"Pyramid Song" (Radiohead)   1, 7–39, 61, 147–9

quantization   134
quantized rhythmic musics   112, 122, 134
queer artists   6, 84

R&B (rhythm and blues)   3, 76–8, 86
radio and TV advertisements   106
Radiohead   5, 7–39, 54, 147–9
   "2+2=5"   55
   Amnesiac   8, 13, 15–18
   The Bends   13, 14, 55
   "Creep"   7, 54
   "Egyptian Song" (earlier title of "Pyramid Song")   18
   Hail to the Thief   13
   "I Might Be Wrong"   16
   I Might Be Wrong: Live Recordings   12
   In Rainbows   13, 15, 56, 63, 66
   "Jigsaw Falling Into Place"   61
   Kid A   13, 15
   Kid A Mnesia   16
   Kid Amnesiae   16, 19
   The King of Limbs   13, 67
   "Knives Out"   16
   A Moon Shaped Pool   13
   "Nothing to Fear" (earlier title of "Pyramid Song")   18
   OK Computer   13
   OK Computer OKNOTOK 1997 2017   13
   Pablo Honey   13, 54
   "Packt like sardines in a crushd tin box"   55
   "Paranoid Android"   55
   "Pop is Dead"   55
   "Pyramid Song"   1, 7–39, 61, 147–9
   "Pyramid Strings"   19
   Radiohead TKOL RMX 1234567   13, 67
   "Scotch Mist" (*In Rainbows*)   63
   "There There"   64
   "Videotape"   43, 54–67
   "You"   54
Radiohead and Philosophy (Michael Thompson)   21–2
ragtime   77
Raine-Reusch, Randy   109, 115, 127, 139
rap   78, 86, 87, 106, 111
RCA   124
recording
   as live performance   144–5
   multitrack   123, 128
   non-linear   111, 118, 123, 144
recording studios
   LA-based   85, 124–5
   London-based   126
   New York-based   87, 124, 131
   Seattle-based   107
   Vancouver-based   96, 107, 115, 125–7, 129, 141
Record Plant Recording Studios   124, 125, 132
Red Hot Chili Peppers   137
reggae   44–7, 49–52
Reid, Vernon   86, 87
REM   135
rhythm and imagination   4, 149
rhythmic
   ambiguity   4, 8, 10, 58, 67

cueing technology 98, 104, 112, 120
deception 4
displacement 47, 57
expectations 3
holy grail 147–9
illusion 57, 80
rhythmic fakeout
  complete 43, 54–67
  temporary 43–54
rhythmic play
  in composition 41
  and deception 5
  and development of the modern brain 41
  and emotional bonding 40
  and human development 41
  through metrical-structural manipulation 46, 55, 67
  and pleasure 1, 3, 6, 46
  and trust in and respect for audiences 53, 55
Rhythm in the Age of Digital Reproduction (RADR) 121
Richardson, Jack 136
Richmond, Charlie 107, 127
riff 83, 87, 88, 90–2
rock (music)
  alternative 12
  and authenticity 53
  Black 79, 86–8
  blues- 82
  British 4, 43
  classic 88–93
  grunge 54, 143, 146
  hard 87, 96
  jazz- 67
  pop- 44, 48, 94
  post-punk 13, 85
  progressive 13, 36, 44
  psychedelic 80, 90
  punk 44, 45, 84, 85, 131, 142
  reggae- 44–7
Rock, Bob 126, 127
Rock and Roll Hall of Fame 74
rock 'n' roll 3, 87, 107, 124
  and its distinctive beat 74–5, 77, 97, 143

and racism 70, 75
Roland
  808 129
  MC-8 Microcomposer 108
  Rhythm Ace 129, 134
Rolling Stones 130, 133
  Steel Wheels 130
Roosevelt, Franklin D. 88
Ross, Alex 14–15, 23
Roth, David Lee 127, 135, 137
Rush
  "Limelight" 89
  Moving Pictures 89
Russian Dragon 108, 109
Rythmikon 105

"St. Augustine in Hell" (Sting) 95–6
samplers 122
Santana 135
Schaeffer, Steve 118
Schuller, Gunther 71
  Early Jazz: Its Roots and Musical Development 70
Scorpions 127
Scott, Jim 127, 133, 145
Seal 133
  Batman Forever: Music from the Motion Picture 93
  "Kiss From a Rose" 93
Selway, Phil 12, 15, 23, 28, 54, 147
  and "Videotape" 61, 63, 64
sequencers 110, 111, 120, 129, 144
  as click track 6, 97, 98, 108
Shapiro, Mike 107, 119, 127, 134
shuffle 29–31
Shure SM57 132
Simon, Carly 131, 138
Simon, Paul 137
sixteen note one drop 51–2
ska 46
Sly and the Family Stone 138
  "It's a Family Affair" 111
SMPTE (Society of Motion Picture and Television Engineers) time code 106
sociology 8
solenoids 104–5, 116
soul (music) 78, 111

INDEX

Soundbrenner Pulse 116–17
Sound City 85, 125
sound-on-film synchronization 99
Spears, Britney
   "Mad Love" 78
Spicer, Mark 44, 47, 48
   accumulative form 43, 55, 67, 80
Springfield, Rick 135
Stalling, Carl 100–2
Starr, Ringo 109, 135
Steely Dan 131
Stewart, Rod
   Every Beat of My Heart 126
Sting/Gordon Sumner 44, 45, 50, 53, 54, 133
   bass lines 47, 48, 50
   "St. Augustine in Hell" 95–6
   Ten Summoner's Tales 95
Stone, Chris 124
streamers and punches 101
subtactus 2, 26
Summer, Donna
   "I Feel Love" 110
   "Love to Love You Baby" 110
   Remember Yesterday 110
Summers, Andy 44–6, 50, 53
Sundance Film Festival 2001 19
Sunset Sound 124, 125
"Sunshine of Your Love" (Cream) 82–3
"swung" eighth notes 30–2, 34
syncopation 71, 74
   in "Pyramid Song" 24, 31, 32, 36
   in rock music 67, 71–2, 75–7
   in "Videotape" 57, 64, 65
synthesizers 110, 131
   analog modular 108
synth pop 44
Szymczyk, Bill 124

"Tactile Tempo Indicating Device" (Scott Fulford) 116
tactus-preserving polymeter 87
Taj Mahal (musician) 76–7
TAMA Rhythm Watch 137
Tamlyn, Gary 77
Tangerine Dream 108
tape 110, 124

degradation 111
   loops 109, 135, 136
   splicing 128
Tate, Greg 86
tbd (record label) 12, 13
Tchock/Dr. Tchock/Tchocky (Thom Yorke) 13, 14
technological mediation of time 4, 5
Tegan and Sara (Quin) 84
   High School 84
   and LGBTQ equality and gender justice 84–5
   "Night Watch" 95
   "Northshore" 85–6, 88, 89
   Plunk 84
   and queer and feminist activism 84
   Sainthood 85, 95
Temperley, David 67, 72
tempo map 117–19
Thornton, Willie Mae "Big Mama" 78
"Three of a Perfect Pair" (King Crimson) 94, 95
Throne Thumper, The 117, 118
Thunderbird Arena (University of British Columbia) 7
Thursday (band)
   "Cross Out the Eyes" 82
   Full Collapse 82
Tibetan Freedom Concert 1999 18
"Time-Measuring Device" (William Duncan) 112
Tomlinson, Gary 3
Toto 108, 131, 135
Tower of Power 78
"Tribulation" (Tappa Zukie) 51–2
Turner, Geoff 126
turning the beat around 80, 83–4
Twentieth Century-Fox 101

UA 960 (digital metronome) 107
UCLA (University of California-Los Angeles) 57, 119
underdetermination 10, 20, 38
United Western Recorders 124, 125
Universal Audio Company 107
Universal console 124

"Universe of Style" (the Police) 44, 48
University of British Columbia (UBC) 7, 96, 108
UREI 964 Digital Metronome 107, 108

Vancouver, British Columbia 96, 107, 115, 125–7, 129, 141
  popular and avant-garde scenes 109, 126
Van Halen 127, 135
Veloso, Caetano 134
Vermeulen, Ron "Obvious" 107, 109, 115, 127, 141
vibrotactile feedback and/or stimulation 99
"Videotape" (Radiohead) 43, 54–67
Village Recorder 124, 125
Visual Conductor, The 115
"Visual Metronome" (Burrell George) 115
"Visual Music Conducting Device" (Kestner-Clifton and Vogel) 114, 115
Viziklik 114

Wachtel, Waddy 49
Waits, Tom
  "Clap Hands" 18
Wallace, Ian 140
Walsh, Joe 124
Walt Disney Studios 100, 102–5, 116
  Mickey Mouse 100
  The Skeleton Dance 101
  Steamboat Willie 100
waltz rhythm 93–4
Warner Brothers 124
Waterman, Richard 24
Waters, Keith 87
Waters, Roger 135
Watson, Andi 14

Watts, Charlie 130
weeping Minotaur 17, 18
Weezer 132
Western Broadcasting 126
Western metrical hierarchies 70–4
Westlake Recording Studios 125
White Chocolate Farm, The (Thom Yorke) 13, 14
White Citizens Council 75
Whitesnake 127
Who, The
  Who's Next 109
  "Won't Get Fooled Again" 109
Wilco 133
Wired 62
wisdom of the crowds 39
Wood, Art 130
Wood, Ronnie 138
Wu-Tang Clan 78–9

XL (record label) 12, 13

Yamaha RX11 129, 133
Yellow Magic Orchestra 108
Yes 123, 132
Yorke, Thom 12, 14, 28, 54, 55, 66
  on *Amnesiac/Kid A* 15, 17–19
  The Eraser 56
  "The Mother Lode" 63
  on "Pyramid Song" 18, 19, 22, 23, 147–8
  Tomorrow's Modern Boxes 14, 63
  on "Videotape" 57, 60–3
YouTube
  fan-created content 21, 35, 57, 59

Zagorski-Thomas, Simon 110, 123
Zappa, Frank 133, 137
Zuckerkandl, Victor 73
Zukie, Tappa
  "Tribulation" 51

www.ingramcontent.com/pod-product-compliance
Lightning Source LLC
Chambersburg PA
CBHW061833300426
44115CB00013B/2368